THE
DEPARTURE

THE
DEPARTURE

GOD'S NEXT CATASTROPHIC INTERVENTION INTO EARTH'S HISTORY

TERRY JAMES
General Editor

DEFENDER

CRANE, MISSOURI

The Departure: God's Next Catastrophic Intervention into Earth's History
Defender
Crane, Missouri 65633
©2010 by Terry James

ISBN 10: 0984061169
ISBN 13: 9780984061167

A CIP catalog record of this book is available from the Library of Congress.

Cover illustration and design by Daniel Wright.

Scripture quoted is taken from the Authorized King James Version, with quotation marks added by the editor for clarity of reading and with deity pronouns capitalized.

This book is dedicated, with the deepest love possible,
to my mother, Kathleen McDuffie-James-Basse,
whose nurturing love and consistent demonstration
of her devotion to Jesus in her daily walk
so profoundly and eternally affects my life.

ACKNOWLEDGMENTS

So many are deserving of acknowledgment for the production of this book. The first and foremost is to our Lord, to whom this book is devoted.

I believe each and every contributing author—to whom I also am deeply grateful—will agree that the Lord Jesus Christ should receive all honor and glory.

As always, I give my love and thanks to my family, as follows, for their love and support during the researching and writing of this book:

To Margaret, Terry Jr., Nathan, Jeanie, Kit, and Todd, for being there for me, even when I might have been a bit cranky and hermit-like on occasion.

Most especially to my "daughters," research assistant Dana—for always quickly finding just the right item for use in the writing process; and Angie—in my view, the premiere editor in the book-writing world—my love and deepest gratitude.

My thanks to my great friend, Tom Horn, for seeing the worth in this volume and for bringing it to publication.

Finally, to the reader of this book, my profound thanks, with the prayerful hope that it will bless your life with special insight from on high.

CONTENTS

ONE GIANT LEAP!

By Terry James

Man's dealing with the evil of this world has failed miserably at every level. Therefore, God's next catastrophic intervention into earth's history is imminent. Bible prophecy overlays the issues and events of this troubling day in an astonishing presentation that provides the forewarning.

Something stupendous is about to happen!

An unidentifiable, pent-up energy pervades the atmospherics of these ominous times. Every indicator that exposes the human condition points to a coming moment of truth—an impending transformation—that will alter the way things are forever.

Evil permeating the current generation of earth's inhabitants, one can sense, creates demand that things be set right and calls for change that judges the bad and liberates the good.

Man's Failure

Winston Churchill, one of history's greatest leaders and thinkers in the quest for world peace, framed humanism's core hope for mankind following World War II:

> A world organization has already been erected for the prime purpose of preventing war. [The] UNO [United Nations Organization], the successor of the League of Nations, with the decisive addition of the United States and all that means, is already at work. We must make sure that its work is fruitful, that it is a reality and not a sham, that it is a force for action and not merely a frothing of words, that it is a true temple of peace in which the shields of many nations can someday be hung up, and not merely a cockpit in a Tower of Babel. Before we cast away the solid assurances of national armaments for self-preservation, we must be certain that our temple is built not upon shifting sands or quagmires, but upon the rock.[1]

Churchill didn't realize how prescient his final words of this excerpt were. The British prime minister was wrong in the first part of his statement about how to assure peace on earth, but was on the mark—even if unwittingly—in the last part. The only way a truly peaceful world will ever be built is not on human government, not upon military might, but "upon the rock." True, lasting peace will in fact be built upon the "stone" of Daniel 2:34 and 45—the "stone" cut without hands that will smash to pieces the anti-God, man-made governmental system of this fallen world. That "rock" is none other than Jesus the Christ. He told His disciples this unalterable truth as recorded in Matthew 16:13–18.

Planet earth's humanistic roadmap for achieving mankind's loftiest goals isn't working out. Human government, as a matter of fact, is observably taking the world on the fast track to destruction.

"Change" is the mantra of every political candidate and political party looking to wrest power from incumbents in the American political process today. Each politician strives to point out the faults and failings of those who have governed. "Throw the rascals out" is theatrically comedic phraseology, but it accurately encapsulates the fervor each person seeking office hopes to generate as campaign seasons get underway in earnest. "Change" isn't working out either. Each political implementation that supersedes the previous speeds the descent toward doomsday.

Lest we submerge totally into the gloom of cynicism—even fatalism—in the beginning of this book (we who present our biblically centered worldviews in this volume intend to be optimistic, not pessimistic), let me assure readers that the future is glorious beyond all mankind could ever produce or even imagine.

True change is coming. Indeed, the reconstitution of how business is conducted on earth will assure a thousand years of goodwill and true peace on earth.

First the Storm

Those who are God's spiritual meteorologists know that before the glorious, golden day of ultimate prophetic fulfillment, there will first come a storm of epic fury. Jesus wrapped the forecast of that coming end-times tempest in the following prophecy:

> And there shall be signs in the sun, and in the moon, and in the stars; and upon the earth distress of nations, with perplexity; the sea and the waves roaring; Men's hearts failing them for fear, and for looking after those things which are coming on the earth: for the powers of heaven shall be shaken. (Luke 21:25–26)

So, who are the spiritual meteorologists to whom I refer? Are they those who are born with the supernatural powers to foresee things to come? Are they like Nostradamus, Edgar Cayce, or some other sup-posed soothsayer foolishly aggrandized by many today for having had some occult gift of prophecy? No, not at all. Rather, these are the ones who are supernaturally born again (see John 3:3) and imbued by God the Holy Spirit with the power, if the person chooses to utilize the gift, of discernment to understand the prophetic times—the signals of things to come. These are the children of God, people who have been redeemed from the sin-fallen state through belief in Jesus Christ, having accepted His death on the cross of two millennia ago as the once-and-for-all sacrifice for their sin.

There are those, even among Christians, who will disagree with me here. I believe that there is the gift of prophecy among God's children in the sense that some can, through Holy Spirit revelation, "forth-tell" what certain contemporary occurrences mean in terms of their future effects. This is not to say I believe they can foretell specific events yet future, in the sense of an Old or New Testament prophet proclaiming things to come. But, I believe that regardless of whether one has the specific gift of prophecy, all who are born again into the family of God and who are of physiological mental maturity can be spiritual meteorologists. They have the capability of discerning the times and seasons, in the prophetic sense.

Conversely, those who are not born again cannot discern the pro-phetic times in which this generation lives. Jesus spoke to people of this sort during His time of interacting with mankind upon earth. He dressed down the ecclesiastical and legal Jewish hierarchy for not rec-ognizing the time of the prophesied Messiah's coming among God's chosen people, Israel.

> The Pharisees also with the Sadducees came, and tempting desired Him that He would shew them a sign from heaven. He answered and said unto them, "When it is evening, ye say, 'It will be fair weather: for the sky is red.' And in the morning,

'It will be foul weather today: for the sky is red and lowering.' O ye hypocrites, ye can discern the face of the sky; but can ye not discern the signs of the times?" (Matt. 16:1–3)

Asleep on the Job

Jesus questioned the Sadducees and Pharisees, implying that they couldn't discern the prophetic times in which they were living. The Messiah walked among them, yet they couldn't and wouldn't discern the critical fact of their circumstance. These were in need of salvation the Messiah could give them. He alone could regenerate their fallen minds and give them spiritual sight that would let them appropriate discernment.

It is just as sad—maybe even more troubling—that those who do have the capability of achieving discernment for these present prophetic times choose not to concern themselves with their commission as spiritual meteorologists.

Jesus, while He sat on the Mount of Olives giving what has come to be called the Olivet Discourse, said the following to God's people who would live throughout the balance of history, regarding the many signs of the end of days He had just foretold: "And what I say unto you I say unto all, 'Watch'" (Mark 13:37). He further gave the end-times generation of Christians comfort and encouragement following the Olivet Discourse on things to come: "And when these things begin to come to pass, then look up, and lift up your heads; for your redemption draweth nigh" (Luke 21:28).

The things Jesus prophesied have long since "begun" to come to pass. Yet those who should have discernment for the signs of the times—Christians—are for the most part slumbering rather than keeping watch. The spiritual meteorologists who are awake and laboring to alert a world directly in the path of the horrific end-times storm are few.

The frequency and intensity of the squalls bursting ahead of the storm itself are often astonishing to behold, to those who are truly watching as Jesus commanded. Yet, the church (all born-again believers), including the preachers and teachers of God's Word, the Bible, are for the most part oblivious to the approaching Tribulation thunder and lightning.

Signals of Coming Storm

Jesus prophesied a great future apocalyptic tempest for the time just before His Second Advent. It will, He said, be of unprecedented virulence: "For then shall be great tribulation, such as was not since the beginning of the world to this time, no, nor ever shall be. And except those days should be shortened, there should no flesh be saved" (Matt. 24:21–22a).

A furious maelstrom is currently churning within the cauldron that engulfs the human condition. While gale-force winds aren't yet at the full-blown strength Jesus forecast, the waves those winds are creating are sending out signals of the approaching time of Tribulation that cannot be missed.

Violence Fills the Whole Earth

Perhaps the major manifestation of the coming end-times storm, the Tribulation, is one specific indicator that marks the present generation. Jesus, the greatest of all of the prophets, foretold that the generation alive at the time of His Second Coming will be filled with this indicator on a worldwide scale: "And as it was in the days of Noe, so shall it be also in the days of the Son of man" (Luke 17:26).

We look, then, to discover what the times were like in the "days of Noah." One particular characteristic of that time leaps from the Scriptures:

The earth also was corrupt before God, and the earth was filled with violence…. And God said unto Noah, "The end of all flesh is come before Me; for the earth is filled with violence through them; and, behold, I will destroy them with the earth." (Gen. 6:11, 13)

Economic chaos rampant today causes violence to explode. The following excerpt tells of violence escalating on a worldwide scale:

The ongoing slaughter in Mexico may be monopolizing overseas crime headlines, but other parts of the world have also seen sharp rises in criminal violence in 2008 and the early months of 2009 as the global economic crisis has deepened. With legal jobs disappearing, growing numbers of unemployed youth are unsurprisingly drawn to what's still available—illicit professions or jobs in the military and police that, in many countries, are ill-paid but allow access to bribes. Just such a process appears to be under way in impoverished parts of Africa, Asia and Latin America…. In fact, it's an irony that, as global trading and other aspects of economic globalization are breaking down, crime may be globalizing.[2]

Growing pirate activity threatens shipping in parts of the high seas, and hostage-taking is an ever-present threat. But, it is another fact of life in today's world that makes it impossible to escape the truth that this is a generation filled with violence. The "War on Terror" that has been front and center since September 11, 2001, continues to require that governments warn their citizenry at varying levels of alert that terrorists might strike at any moment. At the same time, dictators such as Iran's Mahmoud Ahmadinejad threaten to wipe Israel from the Middle East and are developing nuclear weaponry to try to accomplish that goal.

Vile Behavior Degrades Humanity

Another key manifestation of these being the end of days is the debauched activities rampant within this generation. Behavior that would have been totally unacceptable just a few decades ago today is not only tolerated, but pounds at us in staccato pulsations during our every waking hour through entertainment venues—even through hourly news. Jesus said it would be so at the time of His return to earth:

> Likewise also as it was in the days of Lot; they did eat, they drank, they bought, they sold, they planted, they builded; But the same day that Lot went out of Sodom it rained fire and brimstone from heaven, and destroyed them all. Even thus shall it be in the day when the Son of man is revealed. (Luke 17:28–30)

Again, we look at the book of Genesis to find what so disturbed the Creator of all things that He brought His judgment and wrath upon the peoples of Sodom and Gomorrah:

> And the LORD said, "Because the cry of Sodom and Gomorrah is great, and because their sin is very grievous; I will go down now, and see whether they have done altogether according to the cry of it, which is come unto me; and if not, I will know." (Gen. 18:20–21)

Chapter 19 of Genesis then records that the Lord destroyed the cities because of their grievous sins against Him. The chief sin for which He brought wrath upon them was homosexuality. One who reads Genesis 19 with any degree of rationality whatever will see clearly that this heinous debauchery was key in God's decision to bring judgment.

Today, the phrase "gay rights" is the hue and cry from a minority that is set to overrule the majority within the United States and the world. Hate crimes are being legislated and implemented against anyone who speaks against this sin God calls "abomination" (Lev. 20:13). The ongoing movement into total depravity is a major indicator of how near the God of heaven might be to again intervening into mankind's rebellion with judgment and wrath.

Deception Deludes a Generation

Deception and deceivers will be part of the end-times generation, according to Jesus, who foretold conditions leading up to His Second Advent. As a matter of fact, deception and deceivers comprised His very first forewarning indicator as He gave His Olivet Discourse.

> And as He sat upon the Mount of Olives, the disciples came unto Him privately, saying, "Tell us, when shall these things be? and what shall be the sign of Thy coming, and of the end of the world?" And Jesus answered and said unto them, "Take heed that no man deceive you. For many shall come in My name, saying, I am Christ; and shall deceive many." (Matt. 24:3–5)

Deception has always been part of the human circumstance. Today, deceivers and deception are elements of the reality of sinfulness to a greater degree than any other time in history.

Adolf Hitler's propaganda minister, Joseph Goebbels, was perhaps the most infamous deceiver of the twentieth century. He took American psychologist and philosopher William James' apothegm, "Tell a lie long enough and loudly enough, and soon it will be believed as truth," and used it as damnable philosophy to mesmerize the German people into worshiping the Führer and bringing destruction upon the German nation.

Deception has grown exponentially from that past century. Now, American public schools preach a lie under a totally unproved, pseudo-scientific theory called evolution. The deception is picked up and shouted loudly and with longevity by the mainstream media. "The Bible is wrong; evolution is truth" is the message we've been force-fed for decades. Joseph Goebbels' philosophy lives!

A growing number of television documentaries go to great lengths to explain away "scientifically" the supernatural acts described in the Bible. For example, one program claims that the Red Sea parting was the result of a strong wind that even today—in a certain area and during a certain season—can blow back water that is six inches deep, creating a clear pathway for anyone wanting to cross the area. The producers of the program make no effort to explain how the entire Egyptian army that pursued the children of Israel happened to drown in that six inches of water when it closed in on them.

However, Jesus' words of forewarning about deception and deceivers were most referring to the great *religious* deception that will come upon the end-times generation. This egregious activity—so rampant today—will be dealt with in-depth within this volume.

Perilous Times of Treachery

No deception is more destructive than that used as a device to keep sinners from God's truth about redemption from sin. Paul the apostle forewarned of the "perilous times" to come just before the return of Jesus Christ at the end of the age of grace (church age). Paul's prophecies, recorded in 2 Timothy 3, give a comprehensive list of specific characteristics of end-times mankind. Among these is the warning of false forms of religious activity: "This know also, that in the last days perilous times shall come. For men shall be…lovers of pleasures more than lovers of God; Having a form of godliness, but denying the power thereof" (2 Tim. 3:1–2a, 4d–5a).

Jude the apostle forewarned of religious wolves in sheep's clothing who would lead people into false belief systems:

> For there are certain men crept in unawares, who were before of old ordained to this condemnation, ungodly men, turning the grace of our God into lasciviousness, and denying the only Lord God, and our Lord Jesus Christ.... Even as Sodom and Gomorrah, and the cities about them in like manner, giving themselves over to fornication, and going after strange flesh, are set forth for an example, suffering the vengeance of eternal fire. Likewise also these filthy dreamers defile the flesh, despise dominion, and speak evil of dignities.... But these speak evil of those things which they know not: but what they know naturally, as brute beasts, in those things they corrupt themselves. Woe unto them! For they have gone in the way of Cain, and ran greedily after the error of Balaam for reward, and perished in the gainsaying of Core. These are spots in your feasts of charity, when they feast with you, feeding themselves without fear: clouds they are without water, carried about of winds; trees whose fruit withereth, without fruit, twice dead, plucked up by the roots; Raging waves of the sea, foaming out their own shame; wandering stars, to whom is reserved the blackness of darkness forever. (Jude 1:4, 7–8, 10–13)

Today, the apostle Paul's words echo into the ears of this generation. The forewarning is clear: "But evil men and seducers shall wax worse and worse, deceiving, and being deceived" (2 Tim. 3:13). Abortion, same-sex marriage—these are readily accepted by a growing number of leadership within what passes for Christianity. To these religionists, God's Word is no more absolute truth than the words of Salinger, Mailer, Hemingway, and all other writers of fiction. The shed blood of God's Son on the cross at Calvary—in the view of these false teachers—has no place in this age of doing what is right in one's own eyes. To the deceivers, the wolves in sheep's clothing, salvation is wrapped up in such things as saving the planet by following the Mother Earth religion that is represented by the color green. They put forth a feel-good, do-good pabulum that requires no repentance of sin or accountability to the Living God of heaven.

This is a clear apocalyptic weather warning flag for where this generation stands on God's prophetic timeline. But there are few spiritual meteorologists to see the coming storm and issue warnings.

Babel-like Rebellion Rules

Mankind exhibits the hubris of Lucifer, the fallen one. Pridefulness grows in geometric progression while humanity proceeds deeper into history. Pride and rebellion in this sin-immersed world are synonymous. The world of rebels has made full circle and stands again where the tower builders of Babel stood in the Genesis account of God's intervention into the evil affairs of man following the Flood. Heaven's judgment thus cannot be far in the future.

The Genesis record frames the problem God confronted:

> And they said, "Come, let us build us a city and a tower, whose top may reach unto heaven; and let us make us a name, lest we be scattered abroad upon the face of the whole earth." And the LORD came down to see the city and the tower, which the children of men builded. And the LORD said, "Behold, the people is one, and they have all one language; and this they begin to do: and now nothing will be restrained from them, which they have imagined to do. Go to, let Us go down, and there confound their language, that they may not understand one another's speech." So the LORD scattered them abroad from thence upon the face of all the earth: and they left off to build the city. Therefore is the name of it called Babel;

because the LORD did there confound the language of all the earth: and from thence did the LORD scatter them abroad upon the face of all the earth. (Gen. 11:4–9)

Modern-day one-world-order builders have been able to circumvent the language barriers the Lord set in place to prevent the construction of the Tower of Babel. Technology makes possible instant communication from any place on earth to most any other place around the globe, no matter the language spoken.

The neo-one-worlders are every bit as set on trying to usurp God's control over mankind as Nimrod and his cronies of that ancient time. The globalists-elite today are observed at work within the United Nations, the Non-Governmental Organizations (NGOs), and the G-8 and G-20 nations' constant efforts to formulate a new world configuration. Their grasp for power is joined by the many social engineers and scientists who seek to foist the "global warming" hoax upon the rest of humanity. Their climate-change conferences—which thus far have not reaped the economic windfalls they hoped for—have failed miserably. Their pseudo-science, which was proved to be based upon fraudulent and contrived climate data, exposed their hubristic grab for power.

Warped Worldview Pervades

This generation, represented by the globalists-elite's drive for one world order, fits well the description of rebellious earth-dwellers given in the final book of God's recorded Word—Revelation. The neo-Babel builders exhibit hatred for those who want governance from the God of heaven, not from humanistic, reprobate thinking. Saints of the Tribulation era will appeal to the Lord against such heathen "kings of the earth" and "rulers" who "imagine a vain thing" as outlined in Psalms 2:1–4.

Those who will have been martyred for the cause of Christ will ask the Lord a heart-wrenching question in that future time of horror: "How long, O Lord, holy and true, dost thou not judge and avenge our blood on them that dwell on the earth?" (Rev. 6:10). These who "dwell on the earth" today mock God and embrace anti-Christ concepts. The anti-Christ spirit is alive and well, and growing stronger in its influence.

The generations that have grown with the fantastic scientific breakthroughs seem to have a visceral pride that makes them pull from the traces God has designed for the moral governance of humankind. Humanity, in cultures and civilizations, always seems to go through the same cycle of deportment toward total rebellion and judgment.

This is the case of the current generation in America, for example. Founded on Judeo-Christian principles, the next stage was falling away from godly moorings in the Gay Nineties (1890s). World War I followed. Then came the end of that Great War to end all wars, followed by wild times in the Roaring Twenties, which led to correction (the Great Depression, the Dust Bowl, and World War II).

There followed a more godly time, with a return to church attendance and to sane family values. America burst forth as the leader of the world in every category that constitutes modernity.

But, that era of the late 1940s and 1950s was followed by Supreme Court decisions that attempted to remove God from classrooms and made murder of babies by abortion legal. The drug-and-unbridled-sex generation burst upon a nation that witnessed violence of a lost war and assassinations of leaders.

Unnatural Is Normal

Abortion is the sacrifice to the gods of convenience—doing what is right in humankind's own mind. Nothing more aptly exhibits the trait "without natural affection" than for a baby to be so unwanted by a mother that the mother will allow that child to be murdered in her womb.

The 2 Timothy 3 "perilous times" characteristic, "without natural affection," is manifest in this closing time of the church age through the horrors of murdering babies in their mothers' wombs.

When the departure—the Rapture—takes place, I believe God is going to make a profound statement about when life begins. I'm of the conviction that every child below the age of ability to make a personal decision about whether to accept Christ for salvation—including those in the womb at the time of the Rapture—will be taken to be with Jesus.

But today babies are killed by abortionists at the rate of more than four thousand per day in the United States. As many as fifty-two million human beings have thus been murdered since *Roe v. Wade* in 1973. It is the law of the land that this infanticide stands, making "unnatural affection" the norm and protection of the lives of innocents the abnormal.

Demonic Invasion

Paul the apostle told of what makes the insanity of these end-of-the-age days like they are—why babies are slaughtered at the altars of convenience of those who want to do what is right in their own eyes (i.e., birth control—after the fact, in most cases); why men desire to have sex with men, and women with women; and why the whole world is reprobate—upside down—in these troublous times: "For we wrestle not against flesh and blood, but against principalities, against powers, against the rulers of the darkness of this world, against spiritual wickedness in high places" (Eph. 6:12).

We have entered a dark, spiritual warfare time of history. Mankind's thinking—flawed since the time of the Fall from God's way for His creation called man to conduct business on earth—now has descended and continues to descend to deeper regions of rebellion. The founding fathers of America recognized the "depravity of man" in their formulation of the founding documents. That depravity is reaching new lows each day.

The Christian who is spiritually attuned to things developing senses that we are bumping up against the end of the age. It is indeed becoming, like Jesus prophesied, "as it was in the days of Noah."

Technologies and scientific experimentation in the areas of human genetics validate, I believe, that Satan is once again attempting to reintroduce, as he first did as recorded in Genesis 6, corruption to the human race in a genetic as well as in a spiritual way.

The increase in UFOs and other anomalous phenomena foreshadows the Tribulation era, when Satan will be cast to earth for the final time. For example, I believe that the Revelation prophecy of the False Prophet calling down fire in the sight of the first Beast (Antichrist) will be a deception that extraterrestrial landings are taking place—maybe when Satan and his forces are cast down to earth (Rev. 12:7–9). "And he doeth great wonders, so that he maketh fire come down from heaven on the earth in the sight of men" (Rev. 13:13).

The dark spiritual invasion seems almost at the point of becoming part of the visible reality of our world today. This is a major signal of the Tribulation storm about to break upon an undiscerning world.

Media and Reprobate Minds

The modern media has prepared the fallen minds of mankind for the delusion that is already underway. That delusion—the lie of 2 Thessalonians 2—will be fully presented the great masses of humanity and will be accepted as truth once the departure takes place. The world's final führer, Antichrist, will be chief perpetrator of the great satanic lie, as described here.

> Even him, whose coming is after the working of Satan with all power and signs and lying wonders, And with all deceivableness of unrighteousness in them that perish; because they received not the love of the truth, that they might be saved. And for

this cause God shall send them strong delusion, that they should believe a lie: That they all might be damned who believed not the truth, but had pleasure in unrighteousness. (2 Thess. 9–12)

Hollywood has long been "entertaining" the masses with every kind of spiritual lie imaginable. Remember, as I pointed out earlier, what social philosopher and psychologist William James said—and which Hitler's propaganda minister proved by the constant Nazi diatribe against the Jews and for the claimed superiority of the Aryan race: "Tell a lie long enough and loudly enough, and it will one day be accepted as truth."

Satan has been hard at work with books that tell the deluded, gullible audiences that there are many ways to God and many ways to achieve entrance to heaven. These books, movies, and television programs—along with the Internet venues—lead souls down the broad way to destruction.

God's Word, through Paul, foretells that a moment is coming when God the Holy Spirit will withdraw from restraining the evil within the minds of people left behind when believers are gone from planet earth. With the church going to heaven, the Holy Spirit as restrainer of evil and the consciences of mankind will remove in that office. Satanic delusion and the Antichrist regime will have sway on earth for the most part. Those who have rejected Christ as God's only way to salvation (John 14:6) will believe that system's deluding lie.

Religionists and Itching Ears

Tragically, not only the entertainment and news media are paving the way for Antichrist to deceive the masses in the post-Rapture world. Television and church ministries with the largest audiences/congregations/contributors preach and teach "another gospel," as Paul put it.

But though we, or an angel from heaven, preach any other
gospel unto you than that which we have preached unto you,
let him be accursed. As we said before, so say I now again, If
any man preach any other gospel unto you than that ye have
received, let him be accursed. (Gal. 1:8–9)

With only a quick click through the channels that have "Christian"
programming today, one quickly comes upon the "prosperity gospel"
encouraging viewers to give in order to receive blessings from God.
The gospel Paul preached and the gospel about which he wrote in the
above warning is, if ever mentioned, relegated to an obscure portion
of the program and given only a few seconds.

When the "other" gospel Paul warned about isn't overt, it is in the
guise of the feel-good, do-good message that there is no condemnation
for sin; only the love of God should be considered. The "other gospel"
of today is one of total inward-turning for self-centered reasons. It in
complete opposition to Christ's gospel of reaching out to others with
the truth that there must be repentance of sin and that Jesus alone is
the sacrificial Lamb that takes away the sins of the world. Meanwhile,
people perish and, like the rich man in Jesus' account of the rich man
and Lazarus, lift up their eyes in hell, forever separated from the God
of heaven who sent His Son Jesus to shed His blood on the cross so all
might be reconciled to Him.

Preachers and teachers of "another gospel," whether by omission
or commission, tickle and scratch the itching ears of the lost souls who
hear them and feed those who are truly Christians sugar-sweet syrup
that has no spiritual nutritional value.

Today seems almost certainly the time of Paul's prophecy. This is
a key signal that the departure—the Rapture of true believers—must
be very near indeed.

For the time will come when they will not endure sound
doctrine; but after their own lusts shall they heap to themselves

teachers, having itching ears; And they shall turn away their ears from the truth, and shall be turned unto fables. (2 Tim. 4:3–4)

Arming for Armageddon

The prince of Persia (Dan. 10:13, 20) himself seems to be directing Iran's leadership in its hatred for Israel in its modern incarnation. The Gog-Magog forces are on the front pages and in broadcast and Internet news headlines today. Reports from Iran, ancient Persia, and Russia—almost certainly Rosh, from which Gog, the leader of the Ezekiel 38–39 forces, will come—leap at the student who believes in literal prophetic fulfillment.

Many hostility-filled forces around the world—including militant Islam—are shaping to be the armies that will invade the Middle East and will ultimately be slain in the Gog-Magog battle, then at Armageddon as Christ returns with the armies of heaven (Rev. 19:11).

Discerning observers of eschatology (the study of end-times things), by overlaying prophetic Scriptures upon headlines of today and looking a bit into the future in a prayerfully discerned way, recognize that the intensive preparation means that Christ's shout—"Come up hither!"—of Revelation 4:1–2 cannot be far distant.

Isolating Israel

No real estate on earth is more important than Mt. Moriah, the Temple Mount. This is God's touchstone to His creation called man. This is where the past and future temples have sat and will sit.

It is the focus of the battle between good and evil—between God and Lucifer, the fallen one who still wants to establish his throne above God's throne. Satan couldn't accomplish this in heaven, so was cast out—lost forever. He is still attempting to usurp Christ's future throne—the millennial throne that will sit atop a supernaturally elevated Mt. Zion.

The Temple Mount is where the veil between God and man was torn from top to bottom, giving mankind direct access to God the Father through the shed blood of His Son.

Past history and recent conflicts are constant reminders of the volatility of this Jerusalem promontory. The Temple Mount is coveted by Jews, Christians, and Muslims and continues to be, it is feared by the world's diplomatic community, the prime trigger point for nuclear Armageddon.

The nerve jangling on a global scale is evident while the major players on the geopolitical scene today strive to force a peace in this region that has been the focus of hatred by many for millennia. The peace covenant—called by God "the covenant made with death and hell" (Isa. 28:15, 18)—seems in process today with the "Roadmap to Peace." Whatever peace document ultimately eventuates from dealing treacherously with God's chosen people will, the prophet Zechariah foretold, inflict destruction upon the whole world:

> "The burden of the word of the LORD for Israel," saith the LORD, which stretcheth forth the heavens, and layeth the foundation of the earth, and formeth the spirit of man within him. "Behold, I will make Jerusalem a cup of trembling unto all the people round about, when they shall be in the siege both against Judah and against Jerusalem. And in that day will I make Jerusalem a burdensome stone for all people: all that burden themselves with it shall be cut in pieces, though all the people of the earth be gathered together against it." (Zech 12:1–3)

Israel at the center of the developing Tribulation storm front is the number-one signal forewarning of God's wrath and judgment to come.

One Giant Leap!

As surely as the apocalyptic lightning can be seen flashing and the thunder heard crashing violently upon the not-too-distant horizon of world history, the Lord of heaven is at the very gates of glory about to make His presence known to this generation. We know this is true because Jesus alerted His spiritual meteorologists who will be living at the time of His break-in upon an unsuspecting world of unbelievers. The Lord said that when those who are watching for His coming again to earth see all the things He forewarned begin to come to pass, they can know He is very near, even at the doors of heaven (Luke 21:28; Matt. 24:33).

Jesus said the spiritual weather observers will know, then, that the time of their "redemption" is drawing very near. "Redemption" in this instance is tied up with salvation, both spiritual and physical. The redeemed—believers of the church age, or age of grace—will be removed before the Tribulation, the time of testing that will come upon the whole world of unbelievers.

The ascended Jesus, through John the prophet, speaking to the true church (the believers who will be alive at the time of His coming for them; see John 14:1–3), said the following: "Because thou hast kept the word of my patience, I also will keep thee from the hour of temptation, which shall come upon all the world, to try them that dwell upon the earth" (Rev. 3:10).

Paul prophesied the following about this very same time of God's future "testing" the world of rebellious earth-dwellers—the time of God's wrath. He was writing to believers—the church:

> For God hath not appointed us to wrath, but to obtain salvation by our Lord Jesus Christ, who died for us, that, whether we wake or sleep, we should live together with him. Wherefore comfort yourselves together, and edify one another, even as also ye do. (1 Thess. 5:9–11)

The "departure" is the meaning of the Greek noun *apostasia*, which Paul used in his second letter to the Thessalonians:

Now we beseech you, brethren, by the coming of our Lord Jesus Christ, and by our gathering together unto Him, That ye be not soon shaken in mind, or be troubled, neither by spirit, nor by word, nor by letter as from us, as that the day of Christ is at hand. Let no man deceive you by any means: for that day shall not come, except there come a falling away first, and that man of sin be revealed, the son of perdition; Who opposeth and exalteth himself above all that is called God, or that is worshipped; so that he as God sitteth in the temple of God, shewing himself that he is God. (2 Thess. 2:1–4)

The "falling away" term of this passage in the King James Version (KJV) is taken from the Greek noun *apostasia.* Extensive studies in the Scriptures confirm for the authors of this book that this word in almost every case means a "departure from"—a *physical* departure.

The Thessalonians were worried that the Day of Christ had already come, as some were telling them, and that they and their dead loved ones who had been believers had missed Paul's prophesied departure—the *harpazo* (the Greek term) or the "snatching away" that Paul had prophesied in an earlier letter to them (read 1 Thess. 4:13–18).

Paul was assuring them—and, by prophecy, all believers of the church age—that the Day of Christ had *not* come. They would, Paul assured, be gathered unto the Lord before the Tribulation and the revealing of the son of perdition—Antichrist—took place. There would first be the "departure."

Every spiritual weather indicator points to the Tribulation storm that is about to break upon a judgment-deserving world. Millions of believers in Jesus Christ as the one and only Savior will vanish in the twinkling of an eye—an *atomos* of time that can't be divided.

Each author of this book believes the "departure" is about to take place. Consider carefully their words herein given. These are true spiritual meteorologists and in my opinion—yours truly excepted—are true prophets of God in this latter-day sense. Look up. Lift up your head. Your redemption is drawing near. If you belong to Him, you are about to make one giant leap!

CHAPTER ONE

WORLDWIDE VIOLENCE

As It Was in Noah's Day

By Chuck Missler

The Bible has maintained that God has intervened in the history of planet earth numerous times. The plagues in Egypt, the judgments upon the Northern Kingdom, and the captivity of the Southern Kingdom are well-known examples. Furthermore, several events were far more catastrophic—probably beyond human comprehension. For instance, the fall of man in Genesis 3 altered creation so much that we are unable to determine its previous state.

There are also acts of God described in the Bible that are *yet to happen*. One example is a time of judgment referred to as the "Day of the Lord"—an outpouring of the wrath of God. This will be preceded by a mysterious "snatching-up" of some people in what is undoubtedly the most bizarre event in the entire Bible, hinted at in the Old Testament as well as described expressly in the New Testament.[3] (More discussion of this "departure" will follow.)

Perhaps among the most misunderstood and underestimated of the more catastrophic biblical events was the Flood of Noah. God chose eight people to save and eliminated all the others on the entire planet! And this did not come as a complete surprise: It had been preached about for four generations. (In fact, the Bible records the first "astronaut" who left the earth in advance of this catastrophe: Enoch, in Genesis 5:24.)

The reality of the worldwide Flood is not the focus of this chapter. However, one of the issues that does affect our inquiry is this: *Why* did God send such a drastic judgment upon planet earth?

The circumstances that led to the Flood are not simply of historical interest; they are important to us for very practical reasons as well. Jesus left us an ominous warning: "As the days of Noah were, so shall also the coming of the Son of man be" (Luke 17:26). Apparently, the conditions during the days of Noah *will be repeated.* Yet what were the "days of Noah" like? What made them so unique? We must try to understand what was really going on in order to appropriate His warning.

A Principal Cause: Violence

According to the Genesis record (Gen. 6:5, 6), violence and wickedness were principal causes for the judgment of the Flood. With that in mind, it is disturbing to realize that the twentieth century was the most violent period of recorded post-biblical history. Furthermore, a form of a highly organized commitment to violence has also emerged as one of the most rapidly growing characteristics of our times: Islam. Falsely described as a peaceful religion, Islam is neither peaceful nor even a religion: It is a complete system of life. Islam has religious, legal, political, economic, social, and military components.

The Islamic Threat[4]

Islamization begins when there are sufficient Muslims in a country to agitate for their religious privileges. When politically correct, tolerant, and culturally diverse societies agree to Muslim demands, some of the other components tend to creep in as well. As long as the Muslim population remains around or under 2 percent in any given country, it will for the most part be regarded as a "peace-loving" minority and not as a threat to other citizens. This is the case in United States (0.6 percent Muslim), Australia (1.5 percent Muslim), Canada (1.9 percent Muslim), China (1.8 percent Muslim), Italy (1.5 percent Muslim), and Norway (1.8 percent Muslim).

When the Muslim population in a country reaches 2 percent to 5 percent, it begins to proselytize from other ethnic minorities and disaffected groups, often with major recruiting from the jails and among street gangs. (This is happening in Denmark, Germany, the United Kingdom, Spain, and Thailand.) From the 5 percent mark and upward, Muslims exercise an inordinate influence in proportion to their percentage of the population. For example, they will push for the introduction of *halal* food (clean by Islamic standards), thereby securing food preparation jobs for Muslims. This is occurring in France, the Philippines, Sweden, Switzerland, the Netherlands, and Trinidad and Tobago.

When the number of Muslims in a country approaches 10 percent of the population, the Muslims tend to increase lawlessness as a means of complaint about their conditions. In Paris, we are already seeing car burnings, etc. Any non-Muslim action offends Islam and results in uprisings and threats, such as in Amsterdam, with opposition to Mohammed cartoons and films about Islam. Such tensions are seen daily, particularly in Muslim sections, in Guyana, India, Israel, Kenya, and Russia.

After the population of a country reaches 20 to 30 percent Muslim, nations can expect hair-trigger rioting, jihad militia formations, sporadic killings, and the burnings of Christian churches and Jewish synagogues, such as has happened in Ethiopia. At 40 percent, nations experience widespread massacres, chronic terror attacks, and ongoing militia warfare, such as in Bosnia, Chad, and Lebanon.

At 60 percent Muslim population and above, nations experience unfettered persecution of non-believers of all other religions (including non-conforming Muslims), sporadic ethnic cleansing (genocide), use of *sharia* law (Islamic law governing religious and daily affairs) as a weapon, and *jizya*, the tax placed on infidels, such as in Albania, Malaysia, Qatar, and Sudan.

After 80 percent and above, expect daily intimidation and violent jihad, some state-run ethnic cleansing, and even some genocide as these nations drive out the infidels and move toward reaching a population of 100 percent Muslim, such as has been experienced and in some ways is ongoing in Bangladesh, Egypt, Gaza, Indonesia, Iran, Iraq, and Jordan.

It is important to understand that in some countries with well under 100 percent Muslim populations (such as France), the minority Muslim populations live in ghettos, within which they are 100 percent Muslims living by sharia law. The national police do not even enter these ghettos. There are no national courts, schools, or non-Muslim religious facilities. In such situations, Muslims do not integrate into the community at large. The children attend Muslim schools called *madrassas*. They learn only the Koran. To even associate with an infidel is a crime punishable with death. Therefore, in some areas of certain nations, Muslim imams and extremists exercise more power than the national average would indicate.

Another Cause: Wickedness

Where is the most dangerous place for an American to be?

In the mother's womb! That's where a person has one chance in four of being murdered. In fact, there have been almost 50 million such murders since *Roe v. Wade* in 1973.

We murder babies who are socially inconvenient. We change marriage partners like they're a fashion statement. We seem to have abandoned the sanctity of commitment in all of our relationships: our marriages, our business associations, etc. And homosexuality is just an "alternative lifestyle."

In the Bible, God rebuked Israel for its brutality, murder, and warfare. But we have had brutality in Waco, Texas; at Columbine High School in Littleton, Colorado; and in numerous other incidents. New York City has recorded more crimes than England, Scotland, Wales, Ireland, Switzerland, Spain, Sweden, the Netherlands, Norway, and Denmark *combined.*

Immorality and deceit have come to characterize the highest offices of our nation as well. Our politics have condoned and covered up more murders than we dare list. Our public enterprises have been prostituted to the convenience of the elite. Our entertainment industry celebrates adultery, fornication, violence, aberrant sexual practices, and every imaginable form of evil. We have become the primary exporters of all that God abhors.

There was widespread wickedness in the days of Noah. Yet, there apparently may have been more going on than most people are aware of. Just as God has intervened in the events on planet earth, other beings—hostile ones—apparently had also entered the arena, and apparently will do so again.

A Gene Pool Problem

Most people, including serious students of the Bible, are unaware of the peculiar circumstances that led to the Flood of Noah. This has been widely misunderstood (and mis-taught) for centuries. The strange but critical goings-on are among the most controversial issues considered by serious scholars, and we should maintain open minds as we proceed through the murky mists of the deep past. To understand this astonishing period of prehistory, we need to examine the precedent events as recorded in Genesis 6:

And it came to pass, when men began to multiply on the face
of the earth, and daughters were born unto them, that the
sons of God saw the daughters of men that they were fair; and
they took them wives of all which they chose.... There were
giants in the earth in those days; and also after that, when the
sons of God came in unto the daughters of men, and they
bare children to them, the same became mighty men which
were of old, men of renown. (Gen. 6: 1, 2, 4)

This strange passage describes the bizarre circumstances that led
to the cataclysmic disaster of the famous Flood of Noah. The Hebrew
term translated "sons of God" is *b'nai ha Elohim,* a term consistently
used in the Old Testament for "angels."[5] When the Hebrew Torah,
which of course includes the book of Genesis, was translated into
Greek in the third century before Christ (giving us what is known as
the Septuagint translation), this expression was translated "angels."[6]
With the benefit of the best experts at that time behind it, this translation carries great weight and was the one most widely quoted by
the writers of the New Testament. The book of Enoch also clearly
treats these strange events as involving angels.[7] Although this book
was not considered a part of the inspired canon, it was venerated by
both rabbinical and early Christian authorities from about 200 BC
through about AD 200 and is useful to authenticate the lexicological
usage and confirm the accepted beliefs of the period. The biblical
passage refers to "supernatural beings" intruding upon planet earth.
(There are alternative interpretations of this, which we will examine
shortly.)

"The daughters of men" (*benoth Adam;* literally, "the daughters of
Adam") refers to the natural female descendants of mankind. (Notice
that no particular genealogical strain is specified.) The errant, supernatural, "alien" beings apparently mated with human women and produced unnatural, *superhuman* offspring! The term translated "giants"

is from the Hebrew *nephilim,* and literally means "the fallen ones" (from the verb *nephal,* "to fall"). In the Greek Septuagint translation, the term used was *gigantes,* or "earth-born."

Apparently these unnatural offspring, the Nephilim, were monstrous—and they have been memorialized in the legends and myths of every ancient culture in the world. The Nephilim also seem to be echoed in the legendary Greek demigods.[8]

Why was the presence of the Nephilim so great a threat that God would resort to such an extreme measure as the worldwide Flood? In Genesis 6 we encounter another strange reference: "These are the generations of Noah: Noah was a just man and perfect in his generations, and Noah walked with God" (Gen. 6:9).

The word for "generations" is well understood since it is frequently used to refer to genealogies. But what does "perfect in his generations" mean? The word translated "perfect" is *tamiym,* which means "without blemish, sound, healthful, without spot, unimpaired." This term is used of *physical* blemishes,[9] suggesting that Noah's genealogy was not tarnished by this intrusion of the fallen angels. It seems that this adulteration of the human gene pool was a major problem on the planet, and apparently Noah was among the few left who were not thus contaminated.

The "angel" view of this classic Genesis text is well documented in both ancient Jewish rabbinical literature and early church writings. In accordance with the ancient interpretation, the early church fathers understood the expression "sons of God" as designating angels. These included Justin Martyr,[10] Irenaeus,[11] Athenagoras,[12] Pseudo-Clementine,[13] Clement of Alexandria,[14] Tertullian,[15] Commodianus,[16] and Lactantius,[17] to list a few. This interpretation was also espoused by Martin Luther and many more modern exegetes including Klaus-Peter Koppen, Detlev Christian Twesten, D. Moritz Dreschler, Johannes von Hofmann, Siegmund Jakob Baumgarten, Franz Delitzsch, W. Kelly, A. C. Gaebelein, and others.

The "Lines of Seth" View

Yet, many scholars hold a different view. Many students of the Bible have been taught that Genesis 6 refers to a failure to keep the "faithful" line of Seth separate from the "worldly" line of Cain. The idea is advanced that after Cain killed Abel, the line of Seth remained faithful while the line of Cain became ungodly and rebellious. The "sons of God" are deemed to be referring to the line of Seth, the "daughters of men" to the line of Cain, and the resulting marriages blurred the separation between them. (Why the resulting offspring are called the "Nephilim" is, within this view, still without any clear purpose.)

The "sons of Seth and daughters of Cain" interpretation obscures the intended grammatical antithesis between the sons of God and the daughters of Adam.[18] Attempting to impute this view to the text flies in the face of the earlier centuries of understanding of the Hebrew text among both rabbinical and early church scholars. Substantial liberties must be taken with the literal text to propose this view. Furthermore, the term "daughters of Adam" does not denote a restriction to the line of Cain, but indicates that many of Adam's descendants seem to have been involved. In fact, these "daughters" are the same as those referred earlier *in the same sentence!*

And what about the "sons of Adam?" Were they innocent? Why were they not spared in the judgment? Perhaps even more to the point, procreation by parents of differing religious views does not produce unnatural offspring. Believers marrying unbelievers may produce "monsters," but hardly superhuman, unnatural, children! The lexicological antithesis clearly intends to establish a contrast between the "angels" and the women of earth.

It should be pointed out that most conservative Bible scholars reject the "Sethite" view.[19] Among those supporting the "angel" view are G. H. Pember, M. R. DeHaan, C. H. McIntosh, F. Delitzsch, A. C. Gaebelein, Arthur W. Pink, Donald Grey Barnhouse, Henry Morris, Merrill F. Unger, Arnold Fruchtenbaum, Hal Lindsey, and Chuck Smith.

New Testament Confirmations

In biblical matters, it is always essential to compare Scripture with Scripture. The New Testament appears to confirm the "angel" view in its comments concerning the judgment of these fallen angels. Both the apostle Peter and Jude comment on these issues in their letters.

> For if God spared not the angels that sinned, but cast them down to hell *[Tartarus]*, and delivered them into chains of darkness, to be reserved unto judgment; and spared not the old world, but saved Noah the eighth person, a preacher of righteousness, bringing in the flood upon the world of the ungodly. (2 Pet. 2:4–5)

Even Peter's vocabulary is provocative. Peter uses the term *Tartarus,* here translated "hell." This is the only place that this Greek term appears in the Bible. *Tartarus* is a Greek term for "dark abode of woe," "the pit of darkness in the unseen world." As used in Homer's *Iliad,* it is "as far beneath Hades as the earth is below heaven."[20]

In Greek mythology, some of the demigods, Chronos and the rebel Titans, were said to have rebelled against their father Uranus and after a prolonged contest were defeated by Zeus and condemned to Tartarus. Here and in his earlier epistle, Peter's comments even pinpoint the time of the fall of these angels as during the days of Noah:

> By which also [Christ] went and proclaimed[21] unto the spirits in prison; which sometime were disobedient, when once the longsuffering of God waited in the days of Noah, while the ark was a preparing, wherein few, that is, eight souls were saved by water. (1 Pet. 3:19–20)

Jude's epistle[22] also alludes to the strange episodes when these "alien" creatures intruded upon the human reproductive process:

And the angels which kept not their first estate, but left their
own habitation, he hath reserved in everlasting chains under
darkness unto the judgment of the great day. Even as Sodom
and Gomorrah, and the cities about them in like manner,
giving themselves over to fornication, and going after strange
flesh, are set forth for an example, suffering the vengeance of
eternal fire. (Jude 6–7)

The allusions to "going after strange flesh," keeping "not their
first estate," having "left their own habitation," and "giving themselves over to fornication" seem to fit the alien intrusions of Genesis
6. It is interesting that the word translated "habitation," *oiketerion,*
refers to the heavenly bodies from which they had disrobed. This term
appears only twice in the New Testament, each time referring to the
body as a dwelling place for the spirit.[23] The "giving themselves over to
fornication and going after strange flesh" seems to have involved their
leaving their earlier "first estate," that is, the body they were initially
"clothed with."

The Capabilities of Angels

We know relatively little about the nature, essence, powers, or capabilities of angels. We know that they seem to have no problem materializ-
ing into our space-time. They spoke as men, ate meals (Gen. 18:1–8;
19:3), took people by the hand (Gen. 19:10, 16), and were capable of
direct combat. One was responsible for the death of the firstborn in
Egypt (Exod. 12). Another killed 185,000 Syrians (2 Kings 19:35; Isa.
37:36). You don't mess around with angels!

They always seem to appear as men (John 20:12; Acts 1:10).
The New Testament indicates that many of us may have encountered
angels without discerning any uniqueness: "Be not forgetful to entertain strangers: for thereby some have entertained angels unawares"
(Heb. 13:2).

Some regard Christ's comments regarding marriage in heaven as disqualifying the "angel" view of Genesis 6:

> But they which shall be accounted worthy to obtain that world, and the resurrection from the dead, neither marry, nor are given in marriage: Neither can they die any more: for they are equal unto the angels; and are the children of God, being the children of the resurrection. (Luke 20:35–36; see also Matt. 22:30; Mark 12:25)

In heaven, there is no need for procreation. Marriage is a human institution to prevent the extinction of the race by death. This statement by Jesus Christ makes no comment on the capability for sex or other mischief of the *fallen* angels. They can fall; they can aspire to degeneracy. What limits their technologies? Some ancient traditions attribute the various arts and sciences of the ancient world to the disclosures of angels.[24] Angels are always rendered in the masculine. Remember, they were attractive targets for the homosexuals of Sodom (Gen. 19:5).

Post-Flood Appearances

Regarding the Nephilim, Genesis 6:4 also includes the haunting phrase "and also after that." Apparently these strange events were not confined just to the period before the Flood. We find that there seems to be some recurrence of these things that resulted in unusual giants appearing in subsequent periods in the Old Testament narrative, specifically the giant-races of Canaan. A number of tribes were giants, among them the Rephaims Emims, Horims, and Zamsummims (Gen. 14:5; 15:20; Deut. 2:10–12, 22). The kingdom of Og, the King of Bashan, was the "land of the giants" (Deut. 3:11, 13; Josh. 12:4; 13:12).

When Moses sent his twelve spies to reconnoitre the land of Canaan, they came back with the report of giants (Num. 13:33). The term used was "Nephilim." Their fear of those terrifying creatures resulted in their being relegated to wandering in the wilderness for thirty-eight years.

When Joshua and the nation Israel later entered the land of Canaan, they were instructed to wipe out every man, woman, and child of certain tribes (Josh. 6:21, et al.; also see 1 Sam. 15:3). That strikes us as disturbingly severe. It would seem that in the land of Canaan there again was a "gene pool problem." These Rephaim, Nephilim, and others seem to have been established as an advance guard to obstruct Israel's possession of the Promised Land. Was this also a stratagem of Satan? Later, we find more giants: Arba (Josh. 14:15; 15:13; and 21:11), Anak and his seven sons (the "Anakim"), and the famed Goliath (1 Sam. 17:4 ff.) and his four brothers (2 Sam. 21:16–22).

The Destiny of the Nephilim

Most students of the Bible tend to assume that the demons of the New Testament are equivalent to the fallen angels. Angels, however, seem to have the ability to materialize, etc. (that is, except those which are presently bound in Tartarus). In contrast, demons seem desperate to seek embodiment (see Matt. 8:28–34, Mark 5:1–20, and Luke 8:26–39). Angels and demons seem to be quite different creatures. The Nephilim, the unnatural hybrid offspring, are not eligible for resurrection.[25] The bodies of the Nephilim, of course, were drowned in the Flood. What happened to their spirits? Could they be the demons of the New Testament?

These may well have continued through the *dæmones incubi* of the Middle Ages and may be recurring through the UFOs of today. Are the increasing number of "abduction" reports a recurrence of this kind of intrusion?

The Return of the Nephilim

Even our common expression, "the idol has feet of clay," apparently comes to us from the classic passage in Daniel 2, with its vision of the metallic image with its feet of clay—in fact, miry clay. In its apparent timeline of the series of world empires, it is this final one that arrests our attention. But what is represented by the "miry clay?" It seems to be strangely mixed—but not completely—with the iron in Nebuchadnezzar's dream.

The term "miry clay" refers to clay made from dust,[26] a biblical idiom that suggests death. (The *Rephaim,* a tribal term for some of the giants, is also a term often translated "death."[27]) What makes this famous prophecy especially suggestive for our exploration here is the strange allusion in verse 43: "And whereas thou sawest iron mixed with miry clay, *they* shall mingle themselves with the seed of men: but they shall not cleave one to another, even as iron is not mixed with clay" (Dan. 2:43, emphasis added).

Switching to a personal pronoun, *they* "shall mingle themselves with the seed of men." This is extremely suggestive when viewed in the light of the warning of our Lord regarding "the days of Noah" returning. Just what (or who) are "mingling with the seed of men?" Who are these "non-seed"?

It staggers the mind to contemplate the potential significance of Daniel's passage and its implications for the future of global governance. Could this also be a hint of a return to the mischief of fallen angels as in Genesis 6? Are "aliens" and their hybrid offspring part of the political makeup of an emergent world empire? Are the UFO incidents part of a carefully orchestrated program to lead us toward a global political agenda?

What about America?

Any serious student of eschatology recognizes that virtually all of the end-time players are well identified in the biblical text except one. The most frequently asked question is, "Where is America in prophecy?" It seems conspicuously absent of any identifiable mention.

One frequent observation is that America is clearly overdue for judgment. Billy Graham cleverly quipped several decades ago, "If God doesn't judge America, He will have to apologize to Sodom and Gomorrah!" Thomas Jefferson offered a similar warning in 1781: "I tremble for my country when I recall that God is just; and that His justice will not sleep forever."

Most of us now recognize that the United States is in serious trouble. Our debts are gigantic—and are growing faster than most people realize. The debt tally is no longer in the millions or billions; it is in the trillions. Most people have no grasp of what trillions are. Think of simply seconds of time. A million seconds are about twelve days. A billion seconds are thirty-two years. A trillion seconds amount to thirty-two thousand years! Those are not just increased quantities; they are qualitatively quite distinctive.

The debts of the United States may well prove fatal. If increased taxation and lavish spending could save an empire, Rome would still be ruling the world.

But America's problem isn't just financial; we are in a moral free fall. We are victims of *spiritual* warfare: We have a media masking truth, arrogantly shaping opinion rather than informing the electorate. We have courts perverting justice. We have schools deliberately dumbing down our youth as part of a planned agenda. We have replaced our traditional heritage with multiculturalism, revisionism, and values relativism. Instead of seeking truth, we deny its existence. Then we wonder why our youth have no sense of destiny. We have replaced our previous God-fearing values with humanism and other forms of paganism. Our traditional patriotism has now been relegated into a form of obsolete idol worship.

But there is yet another factor: the Abrahamic Covenant.

A Notable Date in History

March 23 has been a notable date in human history: On March 23, 1775, Patrick Henry delivered his famous address to the Virginia

Provincial Convention, in which he declared, "Give me liberty, or give me death!" On March 23, 1919, Benito Mussolini founded his fascist political movement in Milan, Italy. On March 23, 1933, the German Reichstag adopted the Enabling Act, which effectively granted Adolf Hitler dictatorial powers. On March 23, 2000, Pope John Paul II paid his respects at Yad Vashem, Israel's Holocaust Memorial.

These moments in history—reminders of the cost of American liberty, the rise of fascism, and the Holocaust—set the tone for March 23, 2010, when Barack Obama signed the momentous trillion-dollar health-care overhaul that represents the largest shift in U.S. domestic policy since the 1960s and the giant leap toward a socialized America. In what was hailed by the press as a great "victory" speech, Obama's words hearkened to this same day in history—when Mussolini and Hitler were riding a similar wave of arrogance. In front of the press and his White House entourage, Obama declared:

> With all the punditry, all the lobbying, all the game-playing that passes for governing here in Washington, it's been easy at times to doubt our ability to do such a thing, such a complicated thing, to wonder if there are limits to what we as a people can still achieve.

Apparently for Obama there are no limits. While still riding high on his health-care legislation "victory," *he also chose to shake his fist in the face of God.*

On that afternoon of March 23, Obama met with Israeli Prime Minister Benjamin Netanyahu. The ninety-minute meeting was the culmination of two weeks of anti-Israel rhetoric from the Obama administration. The meeting ended uncharacteristically without a joint statement, without a meeting with reporters, and without pictures.

Israel's perceived offense against the U.S. was the decision of the Jerusalem District Planning and Building Board to approve the future construction of sixteen hundred housing units in northern Jerusalem. The nature of the personal attacks against Netanyahu raised many questions because he has no jurisdiction in the decisions of the Planning and Building Board. Some Israeli analysts see the purpose of this attack by the Obama administration as twofold: 1) The U.S. seeks to undermine the legitimacy of Israel's control over Jerusalem in order to weaken Israel's standing among the American public; and 2) The U.S. seeks to topple Netanyahu's government in hopes of replacing it with a leftist government led by Tzipi Livni and the Kadima party.

Indeed, the Obama administration sees Netanyahu's unwillingness to ban the building of the apartments as a roadblock to an Israeli-Palestinian peace agreement—an agreement Obama ostensibly believes will decrease anti-American sentiment in Iraq and Afghanistan, where fighting is raging. Netanyahu responded to the Obama administration's rejection of the building project with the statement, "Jerusalem is *not* a settlement; *but* Israel's capital!"

While sparring between Obama and Netanyahu is not uncommon, this personal confrontation appears to be a manifestation of Obama's political manipulation that appears to demonstrate a *major geopolitical rift.*

The Jewish Institute for National Security Affairs (JINSA) released a report in January detailing a change in the status of U.S. support for maintaining Israel's military qualitative edge in the region. The Institute reported that over the last year, the Obama administration has refused to approve any major Israeli weapons requests. Additionally, the report asserts that the refusal of weapons represents a new White House policy to link arms sales to Israel with the Netanyahu government's willingness to surrender Judea, Samaria, and most of Jerusalem to the American-backed Palestinian Authority. While refusing the sale of AH-64D Apache Longbow helicopters to Israel, the Obama administration has approved the sale of advanced F-16 multi-role fighters to Egypt. Additionally, the sale to Egypt of Harpoon Block II anti-ship missiles, Hellfire air-to-ground missiles, fast-attack craft, and helicopters has been approved. Other Arab League states, including Kuwait, Jordan, Morocco, Saudi Arabia, and the United Arab Emirates have been approved for $10 billion in U.S. arms sales.

At stealth speed, Obama is proving his intent upon dividing Jerusalem, arming Israel's enemies, and establishing a socialized American welfare state. As we watch the status of U.S.-Israel relations, we may well remember March 23, 2010, as the day Obama placed America squarely in the middle of Zechariah 12:2–3, in which the Lord tells us:

> Behold, I will make Jerusalem a cup of trembling unto all the peoples round about.... And in that day will I make Jerusalem a burdensome stone for all peoples: all that burden themselves with it shall be cut in pieces, though all the people of the earth be gathered together against it.

Thus, there are many biblically sensitive observers who see Ezekiel 38 emerging on our near horizon. However, we often overlook several problems. The major players in the Ezekiel account are a distant ring of attempted invaders motivated by greed for spoil: gold, silver, cattle and goods. Also, where are Israel's immediate neighbors: Lebanon? Syria? Iraq? Egypt? And the Palestinians? Furthermore, Israel is portrayed as living securely, in peace and "without walls." (There is a wall twenty-five feet high extending for four hundred and thirty miles there today!)

A Forthcoming Surprise?

Psalm 83 deserves closer attention. The protagonists there are those immediate neighbors not mentioned in Ezekiel 38. And their motivation isn't conventional greed: They are confederated to "wipe Israel off the map"!

Is it possible that an isolated Israel finally says "enough!" and simply takes charge of its security, becomes "an exceedingly great army,"[28] estab-lishes its own security, enforces and enlarges its borders, and enjoys the resulting peace and prosperity that thus become the lure for the outer ring of would-be protagonists of Ezekiel 38?

Some of us suspect that *both* of these events are *preceded by* the *harpazo* (commonly referred to as the Rapture of the church).[29] But the "departure"—call it what you will—may be much closer at hand than most of us would dare to admit. We may watch the fulfillment of Psalm 83 from the mezzanine!

Stay tuned: Film at eleven.

CHAPTER TWO

TWENTY-FIRST CENTURY SODOM

As It Was in Lot's Day

By Larry Spargimino

God leaves clues—wake-up calls—that alert us that the time of our Lord's return is coming closer. Like a dash of cold water in the face, they are intended to awaken the carnally complacent. The Lord Jesus Christ places the judgment of Noah's Flood and the doom of Sodom alongside each other to warn those in the end times that He will indeed come in judgment. One of these warnings is found in Luke 17:28–30:

> Likewise also as it was in the days of Lot; they did eat, they drank, they bought, they sold, they planted, they builded; But the same day that Lot went out of Sodom it rained fire and brimstone from heaven, and destroyed them all. Even thus shall it be in the day when the Son of Man is revealed.

What happened in Sodom and the attendant circumstances are recorded in Genesis 19. There we are told that two angels came to

Sodom and were greeted by Lot (v. 1). Lot insisted that the visitors stay with him in his home and not on the street. Lot—whom the Scripture says was "vexed with the filthy conversation of the wicked" (2 Pet. 2:7)—knew what Sodom was like and couldn't bear the thought that his guests would be subject to abuse.

> But before they lay down, the men of the city, even the men of Sodom, compassed the house round, both old and young, all the people from every quarter: And they called unto Lot, and said unto him, "Where are the men which came in to thee this night? Bring them out unto us, that we may know them." And Lot went out at the door unto them, and shut the door after him. And said, "I pray you, brethren, do not so wickedly. Behold now, I have two daughters which have not known man; let me, I pray you, bring them out unto you, and do ye to them as is good in your eyes: only unto these men do nothing; for therefore came they under the shadow of my roof." (Gen. 19:4–8)

Though these visitors were angels (Gen. 19:1), they were perceived as men (v. 5) by the gay men, who were not aware of their angelic identity (See Heb. 13:2). Jude 7 describes the situation: "Even as Sodom and Gomorrha, and the cities about them, in like manner giving themselves over to fornication, and going after strange flesh, are set forth for an example, suffering the vengeance of eternal fire."

They gave themselves over to "fornication"—sexual immorality. But it involved sex with "strange flesh" *(sarkos heteras)*. *Heteras* refers to something that is qualitatively different, another of a different kind. The "strange flesh" at Sodom "refers to the perception of the [homosexual] men of Sodom who thought that they were going after a same-gender relationship when in fact they were pursuing after a different flesh—angelic rather than human."[30] These angels were in the appearance of men. "Where are *the men* which came in unto thee this night?" was the demand (Gen. 19:5, emphasis added). They wanted to engage in same-sex relations.

The Scripture is clear. Conditions on earth will be like they were in the days of Lot. This is what it will be like in that day when the Son of Man is "revealed." What about conditions today? Can we align Scripture and society and learn that the return of Lord is very near?

In the Shadow of the Great Coming Out

In September of 1990, two gay activists, Marshall Kirk and Hunter Madsen, published a 432-page book titled *After the Ball: How America Will Conquer Its Fear and Hatred of Gays in the 90s.* Various strategies were suggested—strategies that are being used with telling effect in 2010: Talk about gays and gayness as loudly and as often as possible; portray gays as victims and not as troublemakers; make gays look good; make the "other side" look bad and dominated by hate and ignorance; get into the media; solicit funds.

This plan is being followed with unswerving faithfulness. Gay activists are vilifying those who oppose their lifestyle. Their strategy is working with troubling success. Bible-believing Christians are at the center of the fray. Portrayed as radically dangerous right-wingers motivated by hate, those who hold a biblical worldview are painted as homophobes clinging to their Bibles and guns. Radical homosexuals are not looking for passive tolerance but public repentance. Activists demand that all must champion gay rights because it is a mode of sexual expression just as valid as heterosexuality. Under the persuasive cloak of stamping out discrimination, those who hold to traditional values are subject to everything from crude jokes to expensive litigation.[31] On occasion, the opposition is so vehement that their attempt to fight oppression morphs into terrorism. In his book, *The New Absolutes,* William Watkins writes:

While homosexuals promote the message that they are victims of an oppressive, heterosexist, homophobic society, nearly a hundred of them terrorized Christians on a Sunday evening while they were attending church services. Homosexual activists "vandalized church property, replaced the church's Christian flag with a homosexual flag, harassed and scared children, pounded on doors during the service, and hurled eggs and rocks at churchgoers." Activist couples were arrayed in "bondage attire," and many men and women displayed their "bare breasts, bare genitals, and buttocks." Some male couples were "totally naked." At another church they shouted, "Bring back the lions. Bring back the lions," and they disrupted the guest speaker's talk.[32]

While multitudes of Americans have been preoccupied with their busy schedules, homosexual activists have been quietly infiltrating the government, media, and even theological seminaries. No one is immune to a flood of insidious propaganda that is changing our nation into a veritable Sodom. Starting in the elementary school, and by means of every mode of public communication, people are being told a number of tall tales: Traditional Christianity has misunderstood the Bible; the Bible never gives a blanket condemnation of homosexual practices; those who oppose same-sex "marriage" are violating the Constitution; the gay rights movement is just as necessary as the civil rights movement.

The radical gay agenda finds its earliest and most complete expression in a piece by Michael Swift, first published in *Gay Community News*, February 15–21, 1987. This piece is billed as "an eruption of inner rage, on how the oppressed desperately dream of being the oppressor," as indicated in the original preface.

We shall sodomize your sons, emblems of your feeble masculinity, of your shallow dreams and vulgar lies. We shall seduce them in your schools, in your dormitories, in your gymnasiums, in your locker rooms, in your sports arenas, in your seminaries, in your youth groups.... Your sons shall become our minions and do our bidding. They will be recast in our image. They will come to crave and adore us.... All laws banning homosexual activity will be revoked. Instead, legislation shall be passed which engenders love between men.... All churches who condemn us will be closed.[33]

The radical gay agenda has made wide advances because of its new and influential devotees who are committed to advancing its goals. Gays are now found in every walk of life and in every profession. Many gays are highly educated, have training in law, science, and finance, and have risen to the highest positions in business, industry, and government. They are receiving backing even from U.S. President Barack Obama, who issued a proclamation making June 2009 LGBT [Lesbian, Gay, Bisexual, Transgender] Pride Month. Though too long to quote in its entirety, portions of the proclamation follow:

LGBT Americans have made, and continue to make, great and lasting contributions that contribute to strengthen the fabric of American society.... I am proud to be the first President to appoint openly LGBT candidates to Senate-confirmed positions in the first one hundred days of an Administration.... My Administration has partnered with the LGBT community to advance a whole range of initiatives....

Now, THEREFORE, I, BARACK OBAMA, President of the United States of America, by virtue of the authority vested in me by the Constitution and laws of the United States, do hereby proclaim June 2009 as Lesbian, Gay, Bisexual, and Transgender Pride Month....

IN WITNESS WHEREOF, I have hereunto set my hand this first day of June, in the year of our Lord two thousand nine,

and of the independence of the United States of America the
two hundred and thirty-third.[34]

How did a nation founded on Christian principles only few hun-
dred years ago come to this deplorable condition? The answer: The
American people, many of whom are professing Christians, voted
Barack Obama into office.

John Kerry received 16 percent of his vote from the 18–29
year-old, self-styled evangelicals. The figure was almost double that
for Barack Obama.[35] Here we have professing Christians voting like
pagans. Neither John Kerry nor Barack Obama supports evangelical
causes, yet evangelicals have voted for them. This puts 1 Peter 4:17 in
a new and brighter light: "For the time is come that judgment must
begin at the house of God." Is this national death by suicide?

On January 27, 1838, Abraham Lincoln gave an address before
the Young Men's Lyceum of Springfield, Illinois. His subject: "The
perpetuation of our political institutions." The following quotation
may answer the above question.

> At what point shall we expect the approach of danger? By
> what means shall we fortify against it? Shall we expect some
> transatlantic military giant to step the ocean and crush us
> at a blow? Never! All the armies of Europe, Asia and Africa
> combined, with all the treasure of the earth (our own excepted)
> in their military chest, with a Bonaparte for a commander,
> could not by force take a drink from the Ohio, or make a
> track on the Blue Ridge in a trial of a thousand years. At
> what point, then, is the approach of danger to be expected? I
> answer, if it ever reach[es] us it must spring up amongst us; it
> cannot come from abroad. If destruction be our lot we must
> ourselves be its author and finisher. As a nation of free men
> we must live through all time, or die by suicide.[36]

We must put the blame where it belongs: on the churches. God's people are to be salt and light preserving the society and exposing sin and proclaiming the whole counsel of God (see Acts 20:26–27). In many of the upbeat Christian fellowships, leaders are expressing uncertainty as to whether the gay lifestyle is really contrary to the perfect will of God. Included in the list of those who have waffled on this issue are Chuck Smith Jr., son of pastor Chuck Smith; Grammy Award-winning gospel singer Cynthia Clawson, who has been rightly criticized for being a singer at pro-gay events but who stubbornly defends her actions; popular gospel artist Ken Medema; and emerging church leader Brian McClaren.[37] In the culture wars of the present hour, the church—the *ekklesia* of God—has been infiltrated. Truth has become a casualty.

The current culture war has positioned men and women to believe a lie. An all-too-common scenario is as follows: A young man writes to his pastor or sits down with his parents and says: "I'm coming out. I am tired of struggling. I am being true to myself—I'm gay. Please don't preach to me. Please don't tell me to repent. I now have peace." Those who are "coming out" seem to follow a well-rehearsed script. They all claim they are being true to themselves and that they now have "peace." Four observations are in order:

First, they are wrong. Any peace they have is the calm before the storm. The Bible says, "There is a way which seemeth right unto a man, but the end thereof are the ways of death" (Prov. 14:12). Those who have given in to sin have set themselves up for a lifestyle that has serious emotional and physical consequences, not to mention eternal consequences.

Second, they have fallen victim to some very bad theology. Somewhere along the road of their spiritual pilgrimage, they have picked up the idea that struggle is wrong and not true to the Christian life. But struggling is not sinning. We may struggle to get out of bed in the morning, we may struggle to stick to a diet, we may struggle to do right, but struggling is not sinning. "If sinners entice thee, consent thou not" (Prov. 1:10) is the biblical admonition.

Third, they have fallen victim to media bias. The airwaves and printed media are flooded with "I'm gay and I'm okay." This message is attractively prepared in the devil's kitchen. Sitcoms, news reports, and supposedly scientific studies all send the message that this lifestyle is perfectly all right.

Fourth, people who "come out" and argue that they are now being true to themselves are irrational. Who would apply that kind of thinking to other areas of life? "I was born a bank robber. I can't resist the thrill of seeing the teller tremble when I pull out my snub-nosed .357. Therefore, I will be true to myself and rob banks."

The Changing Moral Climate in America

The devastating erosion of a biblical worldview has had a ripple effect throughout our society and culture. Sex-education classes in public schools are exposing children at younger and younger ages to information they are not ready to process. Rather than viewing human sexuality as a gift from God, it is presented more as a lesson in "mechanics for mating." With such objectives currently in view, we shouldn't be surprised that a leading condom manufacturer has created extra-small-sized condoms for twelve-year-old boys.[38] Even well-known and formerly traditional youth organizations have gone over the edge. A Planned Parenthood brochure, *Healthy, Happy and Hot,* was handed out at a "no-adults welcome" Girl Scout event at which girls ages ten to fourteen were counseled on how to be "hot."[39]

The goal: destroy the innocence of childhood. Judith Levine's *Harmful to Minors: The Perils of Protecting Children From Sex* [40] has sparked a storm of controversy. Robert Knight, executive director of the Culture and Family Institute, calls the book "every child molester's dream—and every parent's nightmare," while Joycelyn Elders, former U.S. surgeon general, says it is "a vitally important book." Levine claims that the Christian standard of sexuality is unfair to children and "sabotages their right to healthy, pleasurable sexual expression."[41]

Shockingly, new trends in new thinking have even led to "gay theology," a term used to defend the belief that Christianity and homosexuality are perfectly compatible. The strategy is to show that the traditional arguments gleaned from the Bible grow out of fear, ignorance of Scripture, and an unbiblical view of God. The foundation for a gay theology was laid by John Boswell in his *Christianity, Social Tolerance, and Homosexuality.* This volume "is to the gay Christian movement what *Uncle Tom's Cabin* was to the abolitionist movement—a reference point and inspiration."[42]

Activists even have their own edition of the Bible. A new edition of the New Revised Standard Version (NRSV) gives notes that reinterpret key passages of Scripture that have been traditionally understood to condemn homosexual practices. It also waters down the deity of Christ and the sanctity of human life. This edition claims that the sin of Sodom and Gomorrah was inhospitality. The text note on Genesis 19:5–8 states:

> Though disapproval of male homosexuality is assumed here, the primary point of this text is how this threat by the townspeople violates the value of hospitality.... As a result of his protection of his guests, he (Lot), like Noah, "finds favor" with God and he and his household are rescued out of destruction.[43]

The Metropolitan Community Churches are an important avenue for the expression of gay theology. Their Web site claims that the organization is "the world's first church group with a primary, positive ministry to gays, lesbians, bisexual, and transgender persons. The first worship service in 1968 launched an international movement which has grown to forty-three thousand members in almost three hundred congregations in twenty-two countries."[44]

The apostle Paul bears the most attention from revisionist gay theologians. Romans 1, they allege, has been misunderstood because it in fact condemns *heterosexuals* who commit sex acts with other men. This, they say, is what is "against nature." But, say the revisionists, homosexuals having sex with homosexuals and living in committed homosexual "marriages" are not included in Paul's condemnation. Of course, the apostle is not making a distinction between true homosexual acts (those committed by true homosexuals) and false homosexual acts (homosexual acts committed by heterosexuals). The condemnation is against the *practice* of homosexuality, whoever engages in it.

Gay Death

The Centers for Disease Control has a data analysis showing that homosexuals have an HIV infection rate that is more than forty-four times higher than that of sexually normal men. One observer states that homosexual activists "are handing out death sentences like candy by celebrating behavior that kills. Where is the compassion in that? Pro-family groups are promoting life while homosexual groups are promoting death."[45]

It is no surprise that the homosexual lifestyle is so harmful to physical health. Multiple partners, bathhouse encounters with strangers, and the very nature of male-with-male sex is an invitation to ill health and even death.

Attorney J. Matt Barber wrote a very frank article entitled "'Intolerance' Will Not Be Tolerated! The Gay Agenda vs. Family Values." The article may offend some readers—it got Barber fired from Allstate—but Barber's tongue-in-cheek style powerfully communicates to those who think that homosexuals do little more than walk through the tulips hand in hand.

At the risk of being arrested, charged with a "hate crime," and dragged away to a "progressive" re-education camp, I'll put aside for a moment the flawed, emotion-based, irrational silliness that is "political correctness" (in the event I've been overly PC thus far). Rather than approaching our analysis of homosexual behavior from the traditional, liberal, PC perspective, let's look at it from the rarely visited, "Biologically Correct" (BC) vantage point. For one to believe that homosexual behavior, the act of sodomy in particular, follows the biological order of things, one must ignore the fact that sodomy violates natural law—you know, wrong plumbing, square hole/round peg. The whole thing really is a testament to man's creativity. Give us something good, and we'll bend over backwards to twist it into something else.

Without delving into overly descriptive mechanics, suffice it to say that, scientifically speaking, the sexual act was designed for procreation—nothing more, nothing less. I know, not very romantic, but we're talking science here. Further, the design behind the human digestive system was solely and entirely intended for digestion, not for makeshift sexual activity—there's not a sex organ in the mix. The notion that the act of sodomy is a natural, biological event simply does not square with biological reality. It may be PC but it sure ain't BC.[46]

While the attempts to warn people about the dangers of smoking and heart-stopping foods are widespread, there are no widespread warnings about gay sex. There are a multitude of "don't-drink-and-drive" ads on TV, but not a single one about a sin that has widespread ramifications for the health of the general population. The American public has been deliberately left in the dark about the massive medical risks involved in homosexual activity because of the influence of pro-homosexual political agendas. "All the news that's fit to print" means "all the news that the news media thinks is fit to print." While we must treat all who give themselves the self-identification of "gay and lesbian" with compassion, respect, and sensitivity, the desire to protect the health and welfare of millions must not be trampled.

The risks are high. In fact, *CNN Health* reports:

> Young black gay men, black women, and white gay men in their thirties and forties are much more likely to be newly infected with HIV than other groups in the United States, according to a new analysis from the Centers for Disease Control and Prevention.[47]

As early as June 2001, even pro-gay publications were reporting that "young gay men in U.S. cities are contracting the AIDS virus at rates rivaling the early days of the epidemic, the federal Centers for Disease Control and Prevention warned yesterday."[48]

Prophetic Unfolding and Our Present Responsibility

Before the Antichrist can have an effective "ministry," the seeds of corruption must first be sown. Gay rights activism has all the marks of the end-time scenario: the corruption of the Word of God, the destruction of society, and the undermining of the Christian home. In gay rights activism, Satan has found a committed ally. What does all of this mean for us?

First, remember what Scripture says about Satan's work and destiny. His work is evil, but his end is sure. Satan is a defeated foe. While it will get worse, it is going to get better. We shouldn't be trembling at Satan's New World Order, but rather rejoicing at the Messiah's New World Kingdom—the millennial reign of Jesus Christ on this earth.

Second, remember that God has not changed His mind about the lost. His heart is still open to those who are trapped in sin. He continues to love sinners, though He hates sin. The mandate is still to go into all the world and preach the gospel. Paul concluded from the vision of the man from Macedonia who said "Come over into

Macedonia, and help us" that "the Lord had called us for to preach the gospel unto them" (Acts 16:9–10).

Consequently, we must resolutely reject all unscriptural attempts to date-set. Such is not warranted by Scripture and has the unfortunate effect of chilling our attempts at winning the lost and reaching out with the glorious gospel of the Lord Jesus Christ. Though "scholars" have recently been setting dates—2012 by the Mayan calendar, 2015 by the Jewish feasts, and other elaborate schemes—such feeds defeatist hysteria. As a pretribulationist, I believe the Rapture is imminent. Nothing needs to be fulfilled before the trumpet sounds. To look for signs, to set dates, and to conclude that "this is the FINAL warning because the feast days and the stars are lining up" is ludicrous.

The Rapture is imminent, but it has been imminent for two thousand years. The inspired authors of the New Testament never tell us to look for signs, but for the Lord (Tit. 2:13; 1 Thess. 1:10). Church history is strewn with the disgraced prognostications of those who have set dates and discredited the Word of God by their repeated errors. Will we ever learn to avoid such foolishness? The preterists are at least right in criticizing some of the prophetic doomsayers who always end up with mud in their faces and yet never seem to learn their lesson.

Third, we must stand strong in the Christian virtue of unconditional love. Just as Jesus prayed to His Heavenly Father for divine forgiveness to be poured upon those who put Him on the cross (Luke 23:34), we too must pray and live in the same manner. We must never hate homosexuals, and we must disavow violence of any sort. "The weapons of our warfare are not carnal, but mighty through God" (2 Cor. 10:4). Threats of violence and intimidation are not the ways of Christ. People need a heart change, not a face change.

Unfortunately, some Christians are not demonstrating unconditional love, especially when it comes to this important issue. Supposedly cute quips that we often hear—such as "God made Adam and Eve, not Adam and Steve"—serve no useful purpose. We must avoid crass words and phrases that cause the other side to bristle like porcupines.

Our goal should not be to insult, anger, and vilify (they do that to us and we don't like it), but to speak the truth in love (Eph. 4:15).

When it comes to answering the question "What are the origins of homosexuality?" various answers have been given, some of which breed a malevolent attitude toward gays. Without doubt, homosexual acts are sinful and contrary to the will of God. There is no proof that it is genetic or that there is a "gay gene" any more than liars lie because of a "lying gene." But what about the frequently heard argument voiced in some conservative circles that gays *choose* to be gay? James Dobson brings the issue into focus when he writes:

> Homosexuals deeply resent being told that they selected this same-sex inclination in pursuit of sexual excitement or some other motive. It is unfair, and I don't blame them for being irritated by that assumption. Who among us would knowingly choose a path that would result in alienation from family, rejection by friends, disdain from the heterosexual world, exposure to sexually transmitted diseases such as AIDS and tuberculosis, and even a short lifespan? No, homosexuality is not "chosen" except in rare circumstances. Instead, bewildered children and adolescents…find themselves dealing with something they don't even understand.[49]

Fourth, remember that this is a battle between right thoughts and wrong thoughts, truth and error. The Scripture gives our mandate: "Casting down imaginations, and every high thing that exalteth itself against the knowledge of God, and bringing into captivity every *thought* to the obedience of Christ" (2 Cor. 10:5, emphasis added). The radical gay agenda involves terror by error. We must, therefore, in our attempts to reach homosexuals for Christ, be able to deal with some common arguments:

- **Argument:** "Jesus never directly condemned homosexuality."
Response: While this is true, it is not the whole truth. Jesus

spoke many times about marriage and sexuality, but it was *always* in terms of a husband-and-wife-relationship, never in terms of two men or two women. Jesus never directly condemned beating one's wife, molesting little children, or breaking the speed limit, but His silence on these issues must not be understood as an endorsement.

- **Argument:** "Ten percent of the population is gay. Therefore, since gays are a sizable minority, they should be allowed to marry and adopt children."

    Response: Two points must be made here. First, the justification of a behavior must never be made to reside in the percentage of individuals engaged in that behavior. The next time you are audited by the IRS, try telling them that ten percent of the population cheats on their income tax and see if that will keep you from having to pay a fine or even suffering something worse. Second, it is simply not true that ten percent of the population is gay. This figure is from Alfred Kinsey's studies. Kinsey, an aberrant personality in many ways, took his sampling from men in prison. Of course, such a sampling is not an accurate reflection of American society.[50]

- **Argument:** "Homosexuality is genetic and innate. How can you criminalize such behavior?"

    Response: Though this has been claimed, it has never been scientifically proven. But even if such a "gay gene" were found, it proves nothing. Supposing one was to claim discovery of a "murder gene" or a "bank-robber gene." Would that be grounds to decriminalize such acts?

- **Argument:** "Opposition to the homosexual lifestyle is nothing but prejudice."

    Response: "Prejudice" is an irrational bias against something. However, nothing is "irrational" about a refusal to accept the gay lifestyle as normal. Such a lifestyle has been condemned by almost every society in human history, has many harmful effects on the health of the population, and involves the redefinition of major societal conventions and values. We have to ask, "Where will it all end? What grotesque novelty will now be offered as acceptable?" A small, special-interest group wanting to legitimize a certain behavior is not sufficient grounds to make it legitimate. We are on the brink of complete social chaos. People will claim that they have the right to marry little children, household pets, and their golf clubs.

- **Argument:** "David and Jonathan had a homosexual relationship."

  Response: Some find the words of 1 Samuel 18:1—"and Jonathan loved him [David] as his own soul"—to be proof of this. Other passages are used to support such a conclusion, including "and they kissed one another, and wept one with another" (1 Sam. 20:41) and 2 Samuel 1:26: "Thy love to me was wonderful, passing the love of women."

  However, nothing in these passages suggests erotic activity. There is some rather explicit material in Scripture, such as in the Song of Solomon, Proverbs 5:18, Genesis 39:7, and Ruth 4:13, to mention but a few. The conclusion: When the Bible wants to speak about sex, it does. The absence of such statements in the relationship between David and Jonathan suggests that their relationship was not erotic. How sad that revisionists equate love between men with sex between men. The Scripture says that the souls of David and Jonathan were "knit together" (1 Sam. 18:1). It does not say that they became "one flesh." They were "soul mates," not "bed mates."

The rampant proliferation and normalization of the gay lifestyle is a sobering wake-up call regarding the soon return of the Lord for His church, and the near unfolding of the apocalyptic events detailed in Scripture. This should be a challenge to all Christians to compassionately share the gospel of Christ in the power of the Holy Spirit.

1 Peter 3:15 states: "Be ready always to give an answer to every man that asketh you a reason of the hope that is in you *with meekness and fear*" (emphasis added). Practicing homosexuals are sinners. But being a heterosexual does not immediately put a person in a state of grace.

CHAPTER THREE

NOSTRADAMUS, 2012,
AND OTHER DECEPTION

By Terry James

W e wanted to inquire about the possibility of your being a part of a documentary we are filming for the History Channel" were the words the young woman on the other end of the line was saying in my ear. "*The Nostradamus Effect* is the name of the series."

I agreed to participate in the project, and the filming of my part in the production was done in June 2009 at a television studio in Minneapolis, Minnesota. Twelve hour-long episodes were aired, I believe. Each examined prophecies from many sources, both religious and secular.

The official description of the series, in part, read:

Michel de Nostradamus was a sixteenth-century French physician and astrologer whose very name is synonymous with apocalyptic visions of the near and distant future. His ominous writings appear to have accurately anticipated numerous natural disasters, plagues, and wars. *The Nostradamus Effect* examines these and other end-of-time predictions from cultures across the globe, from centuries ago, and connects the dots with current global events to separate the prophecies that appear to be inspired visions from those that are merely crackpot conspiracy theory.[51]

This series and many other programs dedicated to looking into the future have been the nightly TV fare in America for several years. It seems the public's appetite for programming involving supposed supernaturalism is nothing short of voracious. Although the level of fascination of late has exploded within the viewing public, such has been the interest of people throughout history.

Soothsayers and Doomsdayers

The list of those credited with the ability to prophesy is long. Here are a few of the more notable.

Michel de Nostradamus (1503–1566)

This French seer is perhaps the single most analyzed of the "prophets" by today's entertainment media. He is credited with everything from predicting the rise of Adolf Hitler and the assassination of John F. Kennedy to the rise of Antichrist and the end of the world. As just mentioned, the most recent current events and issues, as they might pertain to an apocalyptic future for the earth, were cocooned in the *Nostradamus Effect* series. There is scarcely a documentary on the subject of prophecy that doesn't include his quatrains (his prophecies are couched in poetic language).

Nostradamus mentioned in his work entitled *Centuries* that a "threat from the East" will cause the apocalypse. His frequent fore-telling of fire falling continues to have the analysts delving into what he might have meant. Some interpreters believe he might have been predicting an asteroid slamming into the earth. Others speculate he might be talking about a third world war or some other catastrophe that will cause great havoc upon the planet.

Despite the fact that Nostradamus' foretellings are so nebulous as to be non-interpretable by—apparently—anyone but a chosen few, his are the most highly sought and valued of the prophecies of things to come by most who seek to know the future.

Edgar Cayce (1877–1945)

This American psychic was known as "the sleeping prophet." He is still considered among the most sought-after for knowing the future, despite a relatively recent failure.

Cayce, during some of his sleeping sessions, dreamed that great cat-aclysmic changes would take place in the topography of America and other places. He said cracks would develop within the American con-tinent that would portend disaster. He predicted shifting of the poles that would cause volcanic eruptions in the tropics. And he prophesied that the island of Japan would submerge into the Pacific Ocean.

These and other apocalyptic events were to take place during and around 1998. Further, he predicted that the year 2001 would bring global catastrophe of the geophysical sort.

Many who study Edgar Cayce's ruminations today believe the prophecies are still on track and that the psychic simply made a mis-take in the years they were to happen.

Jeane Dixon (1918–1997)

This columnist and frequent seer of more recent vintage presented annual predictions of future events. She was held as an icon of the foretelling business by the entertainment world, and even by the public. While many astrologers and psychics were considered charlatans and/or "nut cases," Ms. Dixon could command the ears of presidents, movie stars, and leaders of business with her supposed psychic capability.

She received greatest notoriety upon the assassination of President John F. Kennedy. She had predicted that in 1956, based upon a dream in 1952, a young man with thick, brown hair—a Democrat—would become president, but would die in office.

She is said to have been enlisted by First Lady Nancy Reagan to help President Ronald Reagan negotiate his presidential schedule from an astrological standpoint. She fell from Mrs. Reagan's favor, however, and was replaced by Dixon's rival astrologer, Joan Quigley, when the first lady apparently surmised Dixon had lost her prophetic powers.

Dixon's wrong predictions—such as her assertion that World War III would begin in 1958—were often overlooked by media.

Seraphim Sarovsky (1759-1833)

This man, considered a Russian saint, prophesied about the Antichrist and the horrors the advent of this tyrant would bring to the world. He predicted that when Antichrist came on the scene, the earth would be incinerated to nothing more than ashes. He foretold several times that the Kazan Cathedral in St. Petersburg, Russia, would be lifted into the air. This, of course, hasn't happened. His prophecy is still defended as being an allegory, and his followers believe that perhaps it will yet eventuate.

Matrona Moskovskaya (1881-1952)

This woman is also held as a Russian saint with great predictive powers. She is said to have foretold the 1917 Russian Revolution, World War II, and many other world-shaking events.

She also supposedly prophesied that the whole world would basically implode, and is credited with foretelling such obscure things to come in frightening language, such as follows: "There will be no war, you will all die without a war, there will be many victims, you all will be lying on the ground dead.... In the evening, everything will be on the ground and in the morning you will rise—everything will fall through the ground."[52]

Some say this will come to pass in the form of natural calamity.

Padre Pio (1887-1968)

This Capuchin priest from Italy was among the most famous prophets of the twentieth century. He gave the "Three Days of Darkness" and the "Era of Light" prophecies.

He said that in the beginning of the twenty-first century, an earthquake would destroy "one of the most powerful cities in the world." He said that on the last night of the "three days of darkness," Satan himself, "spreading fear and grief around the world," would "appear. Then, the Blessed Virgin" would "come, bringing the era of light."[53]

I could find no excuse from any source as to why his prophecy might have failed.

Vanga (1911-1996)

This famous blind Bulgarian prophet predicted apocalypse of the most destructive sort. She said: "Everything will melt like ice." But first, she said, mankind will suffer horrific hunger, thirst, and diseases. Natural disasters involving the earth being denuded of plant life of various kinds will, according to this prophet, plague the human race.

2012: The End?

Enter the Mayan prophecy that has the entertainment world—and many others—on the edge of panic. At 11:11 PM universal time,

December 21, 2012, planet earth will experience such traumatic stress that the poles will reverse, tectonic plates will slide upon one another, and the world as it is now known will likely end. This is the gist of the prophecies given by Mayan shamans who have long since disappeared with the dissolution of their civilization.

An entire book/movie/documentary industry has leaped forth from this prophesied cataclysm. The entertainment tsunami is likely to grow until the critical time and date are reached.

John Major Jenkins, the author of *2012 Story* and one who is considered an authority on the matter, offers a synopsis of the astro-physical configuration involved:

> The galactic alignment is the alignment of the December solstice sun as viewed from earth with the galactic equator. The galactic equator is basically the Milky Way, as it's perceived in the sky. This is an alignment that is caused by the procession of the equinoxes, and it happens only once every twenty-six thousand years.[54]

To repeat, the dynamic stresses put on the planet will, it is feared by many, tear the earth apart. It seems that the soothsayers of an extinct civilization command more attention by far than does the Word of God. This is evident by the multi-millions of dollars being gener-ated and the news interest being stirred up concerning the Mayan Calendar predictions. Sour grapes by a writer of books dealing with Bible prophecy? Well, okay…honestly, yes—just a little, maybe…

Regardless, the tremendous interest in the 2012 date and its end-of-the-world inferences by many speak to the accuracy of God's prophetic Word, which says there will be great deception in the end of days.

Deception is the very first forewarning signal of the wind-up of human history given by the greatest of all prophets. Jesus Christ, while He sat on the Mount of Olives, began prophesying things that will signal the time leading up to His Second Coming:

And as He sat upon the Mount of Olives, the disciples came unto Him privately, saying, "Tell us, when shall these things be? and what shall be the sign of thy coming, and of the end of the world?" And Jesus answered and said unto them, "Take heed that no man deceive you. For many shall come in my name, saying, I am Christ; and shall deceive many.... And many false prophets shall rise, and shall deceive many." (Matt. 24: 3–5, 11)

Counterfeit Christs

False prophets and false prophecies have been previously touched upon in a relatively light way in this chapter. Such deception could fill several volumes, so prolific have these deceivers been down through the ages. Let us turn now to the very first forewarning the Lord Jesus Christ gave as the signal of the time very near His Second Advent.

Christ's prophecy of this type of deceiver is even more manifest today than those in the "false prophet" and "false prophecy" categories. Jesus said, "Take heed that no man deceive you. For many shall come in my name, saying, I am Christ; and shall deceive many" (Matt. 24:4–5).

Practically all people claiming to be deity have in recent decades invoked the name of "Jesus," "Christ," or "Messiah" in promoting themselves before the world. There have been more renowned and less recognized false Christs. The following is a brief overview of some of the more prominent—and the less notable—of the counterfeit Christs.

Sun Myung Moon

In 2004, a South Korean, self-proclaimed reverend—Sun Myung Moon, a wealthy businessman with a sizeable cult following—proclaimed before a dozen U.S. lawmakers in Washington DC that he had attained new heights. Moon declared himself "Messiah" during a congressional reception, according to a report excerpted here:

> At the March 23 ceremony in the Dirksen Senate Office Building, Rep. Danny K. Davis (D-Ill.) wore white gloves and carried a pillow holding an ornate crown that was placed on Moon's head. The Korean-born businessman and religious leader then delivered a long speech saying he was "sent to earth...to save the world's six billion people.... Emperors, kings, and presidents...have declared to all heaven and earth that Reverend Sun Myung Moon is none other than humanity's savior, messiah, returning lord, and true parent."[55]

Moon said his teachings have helped Adolf Hitler and Joseph Stalin be "reborn as new persons." He still holds considerable sway over millions of followers. While his reign seems to evoke a relatively placid type of emotional slavishness, other self-proclaimed messiahs have wreaked deadly havoc among their flocks.

Jim Jones

This self-appointed religious leader from America's Midwest formed the People's Temple, perhaps what would become the most infamous of the messianic cults. Jim Jones led a cadre of around a hundred people—mostly African-Americans—to California, where the cult's members would soon have many more join their ranks.

The temple swelled with new members—up to twenty thousand, Jones claimed. But his services became stranger and stranger. He would "heal" parishioners by pretending to draw forth "cancers" that actually were bloody chicken gizzards.

And his megalomania soared.

One of his associates said, "Jim stopped calling himself the reincarnation of Jesus and started calling himself God. He said he was the actual God who made the heavens and earth."[56]

Jones and the People's Temple left a demonic mark on American history when on November 18, 1978, Congressman Leo Ryan and a small contingent that accompanied him on a fact-finding mission about the cult in Guyana were ambushed by Jones' Temple militia. Following the killing of Ryan and others, Jones ordered more than nine hundred of the cult members to commit suicide by drinking poison-laced Kool-Aid.

David Koresh

This man's Branch Davidian cult experienced one of the most tragic of endings, in which many men, women, and children died in a fiery holocaust. Clinton administration attorney general, Janet Reno, ordered forces under her control to raid the Branch Davidian compound outside Waco, Texas, on April 19, 1993. Whether the invading forces caused the fire or the Davidians themselves set the blaze, the Waco "messiah" had accomplished the apocalypse about which he incessantly warned his sequestered followers.

> It sounds like crazy talk now. Who could have believed it? But there they were, dozens of devotees, lured to a lonesome place on the Texas prairie by the promise of salvation. They had traveled from all over the country and beyond—Hawaii, Britain, Australia. Koresh had recruited many on his forays around the globe in search of new blood. Some turned all their worldly goods over to him. In several cases, that amounted to hundreds of thousands of dollars. They were holed up in the fortress with the man who claimed to be both a prophet king and a warrior angel with the keys to heaven. Maybe even the Messiah.[57]

Maitreya

This false Christ has been on the periphery of emerging from the shadows seemingly forever. The title "Maitreya" has long been proclaimed by a self-anointed forerunner for the New Age messiah. Now there is a human name put to the title: Raj Patel, a native of London who now lives on Potrero Hill in San Francisco, California.

He is a reluctant "Lord Maitreya," apparently saying he is just an "ordinary bloke."

> People began to believe otherwise on January 14 [2010] in London when Benjamin Creme, the leader of Share International, who is also known as the Master, proclaimed the arrival of Maitreya. The name of the deity has Buddhist roots, but in 1972, Mr. Creme prophesied the coming Maitreya as a messiah for all faiths called the World Teacher.
>
> Mr. Creme did not name the messiah, but he revealed clues that led his devotees to fire up their search engines on a digital scavenger hunt that would lead them to the one....
>
> Mr. Patel has emphatically and publicly denied being Maitreya. Bad move. According to the predictions, "Maitreya will neither confirm, or will fail to confirm, he is Maitreya," said Cher Gilmore, a spokeswoman for Share International.[58]

Lesser Imitators of Immortals

Listing all who have claimed to be Christ, Messiah, and/or other titles of their supposed immortality could constitute an entire book, not just a chapter. A few lesser known who come in the name of Christ, or Messiah, follow:

David Shayler

This former MI5 spy, disgraced after breaching the Official Secrets Act by giving information about British and American clandestine service agencies, proclaimed himself to be God:

> Last night, in an interview with *More4 News*, Mr. Shayler made the astonishing claim that he had seen a psychic who[m] he believes channeled the spirit of Mary Magdalene and anointed him as the Messiah.
>
> He told the program: "Suddenly my whole life made sense. I felt a sense of peace. I suddenly realized why it had been how it had—why I seem to get such a strange deal from the universe, when I seem to be trying to tell the truth about everything."[59]

Wayne Bent

Bent, who goes by the name of Michael Travesser and claims to be the Messiah, is accused of touching three underage female followers, one of whom was twelve, when they lay naked with him in 2006 and 2007....

Wayne Bent, whose adopted name Travesser is the name of a creek in the area, is a former Seventh-day Adventist minister who separated from that church in 1987 and formed The Lord Our Righteousness movement. He announced in 2000 that he is the Messiah.[60]

And One Who Contacted Me, Personally...

As partner in www.raptureready.com with Todd Strandberg, I, like Todd, get email of every description. None fascinates me more than those who claim special revelation from God. Even more interesting are those—and there are more than one might think—who claim to actually be commissioned by Deity as last-days prophets and more.

I share a few words from one such…gentleman…who recently emailed both Todd and me.

> Jesus Christ has raised me from the dead to the office of "Peter the Roman"…Jesus Christ's resurrecting me is in His fulfillment of an agreement of contract law (Matt. 3:15) into which both He and I entered prior to my baptising Him.… I normally use my Christian surname…but I remain: the resurrected John, Prophet of the Most High, whom Jesus Christ called the "Elias who was to come," St. John the Baptist, enjoying the Rapture in the call of duty as Peter the Roman.[61]

The email's subject line read: "Jesus Christ has raised me from the dead!"

Modern-Day Demonic Deception

Just as Jesus foretold in His Olivet Discourse, false prophecies abound in the news today, given by false prophets who are quite recognizable as the end of the age nears.

While in exile in Babylon, Daniel the prophet reported that an angel sent to give him a message from the Lord had been detained in battle by an evil one called "the prince of Persia." Michael, the archangel, then assisted the messenger, and he was freed to finally get to Daniel with the prophecy.

Today it seems that the "prince of Persia" is active in that ancient region of the world and continues to bedevil Daniel's people, Israel.

Iranian President Mahmoud Ahmadinejad consistently threatens to wipe the nation Israel and all Jews from the face of the earth. He believes that earth's final war—Armageddon—must begin so that the twelfth imam, the Mahti (one version of Islam's messiah), can emerge from some ancient well to rule over the earth. This will make Islam, for Allah, the only belief system in existence.

It is as if Ahmadinejad were personally indwelt by that ancient vile minion of Satan, the prince of Persia. The Iranian leader's hate-filled prophecy is undoubtedly manifestation of the deluding spirit about which the Lord made His first forewarnings of things that will come to pass just before His return.

But Mahmoud Ahmadinejad's dire prediction and all deception that has gone before will pale in comparison to the great delusion that will one day assault all who live upon the planet.

The Lie

There is coming, according to God's Word and the apostle Paul, a particular deception that will ensnare the world of people who oppose the Creator of all things. When thinking on 2 Thessalonians chapter 2 about "the lie" Paul mentions, it seems to me there can be but one sort of lie that Satan would be so determined to foist upon humanity left behind after the Rapture of the church. Here is the prophecy:

> Even him, whose coming is after the working of Satan with all power and signs and lying wonders, and with all deceivableness of unrighteousness in them that perish; because they received not the love of the truth, that they might be saved. And for this cause God shall send them strong delusion, that they should believe a lie: That they all might be damned who believed not the truth, but had pleasure in unrighteousness. (2 Thess. 2:9–12)

Lucifer, the fallen one, has always sought to separate man from the Lord and His governance. Satan was successful in accomplishing his goal when, in the Garden of Eden, Eve fell victim to the serpent's seduction and then Adam willfully joined her, thus believing Satan rather than the Lord.

God then promised the supernatural seed through mankind that would eventually produce a Savior who would ultimately destroy the serpent and overcome his great lie that separated God and man. Jesus is that seed, the Redeemer of mankind. He said: "I am the way, the truth, and the life: no man cometh unto the Father, but by Me" (John 14:6).

Jesus is the only way to forgiveness of sin, which separates man from God. This is what is meant by the first Scripture I and many other young children learned in Sunday school: "For God so loved the world that He gave his only begotten Son, that whosoever believeth in Him should not perish, but have everlasting life" (John 3:16).

Spirit of Antichrist

Paul foretold in the 2 Thessalonians 2 account that the lie the Antichrist regime will impose upon those left behind on earth after the church is taken to be with Christ forever will involve the refusal to believe the truth. They will reject God's way to redemption. They will deny that Jesus Christ—the Truth—is the way to salvation.

The lie, then, will be wrapped up in a grand deception that Christ didn't truly come—in Jewish flesh—to die for the sin of man. This, after all, is the spirit of Antichrist about which John warned:

> Beloved, believe not every spirit, but try the spirits whether they are of God: because many false prophets are gone out into the world. Hereby know ye the Spirit of God: Every spirit that confesseth that Jesus Christ is come in the flesh is of God: And every spirit that confesseth not that Jesus Christ is come in the flesh is not of God: and this is that spirit of antichrist, whereof ye have heard that it should come; and even now already is it in the world. (1 John 4:1–3)

That spirit-of-Antichrist lie was intrinsic within Hitler's Nazi regime. The Jews were painted as "Christ-killers and the scourge of mankind," not as the chosen people through whom God brought His Only Begotten Son into the world to seek and save lost mankind. That future führer—the satanically empowered son of perdition— will likely mesmerize the post-Rapture world with a lie that denies Jesus Christ ever came to be the sacrifice for mankind. As a matter of fact, Bible prophecy paints him as the one who comes in place of the real Christ. He will claim to be the Savior. He will sit in the temple of God on Moriah in Jerusalem, declaring himself to be God! (See 2 Thess. 2:4; Matt. 24:15.)

The Departure to Cause Crisis

I believe the groundwork is being laid today for the lie that will doom much of the world's population after the Rapture. The lie will have to be part of a fearful crisis of some sort. The disappearance of millions will certainly provide a crisis that will have the attention of the peoples of the world. Any leader who can answer the question of what on earth has happened will get the instant attention and the adulation of a panicked world.

As mentioned above, the earth is being prepared, I'm convinced, for just such an answer as the Antichrist will concoct. A recent news story gives more than an inkling of the groundwork being laid for that lie.

It has been the subject of movies for decades—but what would REALLY happen if aliens visited earth? This may sound like a topic for conspiracy theorists or mad UFO obsessives, yet this week, science's finest minds gathered in London to debate that very question.... The conference, the Detection of Extraterrestrial Life and the Consequences for Science and Society, was held at the high-brow Royal Society HQ in central London....

It is often said the discovery of other civilizations would shatter world religions. Delegates were not so sure. Professor Ted Peters, a theologian, briefed the meeting on some survey results that suggested that rather than undermine religious beliefs—whatever the faith—it would strengthen them, by making God's creation seem even bigger and more wonderful.

Not everyone agreed. British physicist Paul Davies thought Christians would have a problem, given the central belief that Jesus died to save us. If we discover other civilizations, it would raise the awkward question: Why just us?[62]

The lie of 2 Thessalonians 2 could well bring into its orbit and make totally believable: 1) Universalism—the deception that all people are God's children and that there are many ways to salvation; and 2) The notion that Jesus Christ couldn't have been the Savior, or else He would have to die on other worlds for those inhabitants and for others in other universes.

With the way psychologically and demonically paved for there to be a massive UFO invasion during the Tribulation, millions looking for explanation of why their world is upside-down will undoubtedly readily believe such a lie—the lie telling them that the extraterrestrials who have just removed millions of rebels from earth have now come to rescue the world from oblivion.

The prophecy that tells of this very event might well be found in the following description given in God's Word:

And he doeth great wonders, so that he maketh fire come down from heaven on the earth in the sight of men, and deceiveth them that dwell on the earth by the means of those miracles which he had power to do in the sight of the beast; saying to them that dwell on the earth, that they should make an image to the beast, which had the wound by a sword, and did live. (Rev. 13:13–14)

The calling down of fire the False Prophet will perform will, I'm convinced, involve Satan and the fallen angelic hordes being cast out of heaven for the final time. The following prophecy tells of that future invasion of earth:

> And there was war in heaven: Michael and his angels fought against the dragon; and the dragon fought and his angels, and prevailed not; neither was their place found any more in heaven. And the great dragon was cast out, that old serpent, called the devil, and Satan, which deceiveth the whole world: He was cast out into the earth, and his angels were cast out with him.... Woe to the inhabiters of the earth and of the sea! For the devil is come down unto you, having great wrath, because he knoweth that he hath but a short time. (Rev. 12: 7–9, 12b)

Our world is filled today with great deception. Lies come from many governmental leaders, media sources, and even from many people in the pulpits of America. It is incumbent upon each who names the name of Christ to be discerning in these closing days of the church age. Lost souls hang in the eternal balance.

CHAPTER FOUR

PERILOUS-TIMES TREMORS

An Apostle's Departure

By Dix Winston III

A s the grains of sand slowly drain from the top of the hourglass, a solitary saint writes. He is imprisoned but not without pen. The man, a father named Paul, writes his last letter to his dearly beloved son, Timothy. The Spirit binds Paul to Timothy not by blood, but by faith. There will be no more missionary journeys for the older man. He will never again feel the wind of the Spirit blow against his spirit. Sacred script will never again flow from his fingers.

Paul uses two metaphors to describe his impending death at the hands of Caesar. He says that he is "ready to be offered" and that "the time of [his] departure is at hand" (2 Tim. 4:6). The Greek word for "offered" used here—*spendo*—indicates the pouring out of a libation, and the idea is rooted in the Old Testament (see Lev. 23:37). Paul sees himself as a drink offering *being poured out completely to the Lord* as he writes. And, like the libation, the last drops of his life are now being drained from the chalice.

The second metaphor, "the time of my departure is at hand," also speaks of Paul's looming death. The word for "departure" is used in reference to striking a tent, releasing shackles, or freeing a boat from its moorings and dock. This last image gloriously portrays Paul as shoving off from this earthly shore and journeying to the celestial bay.

Having pulled in the anchor, untied the moorings, and pushed off, he looks back on thirty years of sacrificial ministry. He tells Timothy how he would like to be remembered and how he sums up his ministry. His brevity of words is beautiful. Not boasting, but feeling blessed, he says, "I have fought a good fight, I have finished my course, I have kept the faith" (2 Tim. 4:7).

For Paul, the Christian life has not been easy; it has been agonizing. We get our English word "agony" from the word *agon,* translated "fought the good fight." Paul has lived the Christian life like an athlete training for the Olympics. His effort has involved sacrificial focus, great mental discipline, and a will to excel.

More than thirty years earlier, God had recruited Paul to compete in the spiritual arena. As the apostle told the Ephesian elders: "Neither count I my life dear unto myself, so that I might finish my course with joy, and the ministry, which I have received of the Lord Jesus, to testify the gospel of the grace of God" (Acts 20:24). His earthly comforts, day-to-day concerns, and even his own life had been subordinate to finishing the race.

Paul does not just want to finish; he wants to finish well. And to finish well, he has to finish in faith. In 2 Timothy 4:7, he says he "kept the faith." The Greek word for "kept," *tereo,* means "to watch over or guard a treasure." Paul had done this by faithfully proclaiming the gospel the Lord had given to him during his dramatic conversion as he had approached the city of Damascus (Acts 9) many years earlier. Paul knew that Jesus had "committed unto [him] the word of reconciliation" (2 Cor. 5:20), and from that time onward he had not added or subtracted from it.

But one task remains for the aged apostle: making sure Timothy continues to fight the good fight, run his course, and guard the faith.

That is why Paul is writing to his beloved son in the faith. This epistle—his second letter to Timothy—will be the last one he writes and the final one Timothy receives, so for Paul it carries extra weight.

In 2 Timothy 1, Paul recounts Timothy's faithfulness (vv. 3–7); encourages the younger man to keep on keeping on (vv. 8–14), and warns him of the consequences of unfaithfulness and the profits that come from faithfulness (vv. 15–18). He charges Timothy with enduring hardship and remaining faithful to the "unfeigned faith" (2 Tim. 1:5). He uses seven pictures to encourage Timothy (and us as well) to remain faithful: a son (v. 1), a soldier (v. 3), an athlete (v. 5), a farmer (v. 6), a laborer (v. 15), a vessel (v. 21), and a servant-slave (v. 24).

The Warning: Hard Times Ahead

While chapters 1 and 2 of Paul's second letter are largely encouraging for Timothy, chapters 3 and 4 serve as a warning. An old nautical adage says, "Red sky in the morning, sailors take warning. Red sky at night, sailors delight." This warning was even known during the time of Jesus (see Matt. 16:2–3). The gist of it is that if you see a red sky in the morning, things could get a little dicey midday. You should therefore act prudently before you set sail. If you don't, you could meet with unpleasant consequences. That, perhaps, is what Paul was attempting to do in the third and fourth chapters of his second letter: Give Timothy adequate warning so he could "act prudently."

In chapter 3, Paul reveals to Timothy what societal and spiritual conditions will exist in the last days. In verses 1–7, he *defines, describes,* and *depicts* the conditions that will exist in the last days. He closes the letter with a *directive.*

Last Days Defined

Dr. Dwight D. Pentecost is helpful in pointing out that the term "last days" can refer to either God's program with Israel or His program with the church. Failing to distinguish the two leads to an imprecise definition of the term "last (or latter) days."

Within this present age between the two advents of Christ, God is bringing to fulfillment two distinct agendas: 1) That with the church, which will be completed at the Rapture of the church, and 2) That with Israel, which will be completed after the Rapture at the Second Advent of Christ. Scripture includes descriptive passages concerning the end times for each of these events and their respective programs. There is a reference to the "last times" for the church (1 Pet.1:20 and Jude 18) and to the "last time" for the church (1 Pet. 1:5 and 1 John 2:18). There is also reference to the "latter days" for Israel (Dan. 10:14; Deut. 4:30) and for the church (1 Tim. 4:1). Further, Scripture refers to the "last days" for Israel (Isa. 2:2; Mic. 4:1; Acts 2:17) and also for the church (2 Tim. 3:1; Heb 1:2), as well as to the "last day" for Israel (John 6:39–40, 44, 54)—although this usage of "day" may refer to a program rather than to a time period. It is important to remember that the reference to any given period must be related to the program of which it is a part. When used in reference to Israel's programs, it cannot refer to the program for the church.[63]

Dr. Lewis Sperry Chafer, co-founder of Dallas Theological Seminary and author of many books, details the more narrow definition of the last days as it applies to the church:

A very extensive body of Scripture bears on the last days for the church. Reference is to a restricted time at the very end of, and yet wholly within, the present age. Though this brief period immediately precedes the Great Tribulation and in some measure is a preparation for it, these two times of apostasy and confusion—though incomparable in history— are wholly separate the one from the other."[64]

Paul is obviously writing to Timothy, who is a pastor, and the older man is talking about the last days in reference to the church. So the last days in this context is that time immediately preceding the Rapture of the church.

Last Days Described

In 2 Timothy 3:1, Paul says the days preceding the Rapture will be "perilous." The word he used in that verse, *chalepos,* is used only one other time in the New Testament—in Matthew 8:28, where it is translated as "exceeding fierce" in describing the Gergesenes demoniac's ferocity: "And when he was come to the other side into the country of the Gergesenes, there met him two possessed with devils, coming out of the tombs, exceeding fierce, so that no man might pass by that way." People feared for their lives if confronted by this demoniac. It was "pass at your own peril."

This is the word Paul chooses to describe the times leading up to the Rapture. They will be dangerous and difficult. People will be concerned for their own personal well-being, and they will be anxious and uncertain about the future. People will be hardened and untrusting. It will not be a pleasant time to be alive.

The *Bible Speaks Today Commentary* says this:

These seasons Paul denotes as "times of stress." The Greek adjective *chalepos* means basically "hard" or "difficult," and implies either "hard to bear" (for example, in the case of physical or mental pain) or "hard to deal with, violent, dangerous" [William F. Arndt and F. Wilbur Gingrich, *A Greek-English Lexicon of the New Testament and Other Early Christian Literature* (University of Chicago and Cambridge University, 1957)], "menacing." The word was used in classical Greek both of dangerous wild animals and of the raging sea. Its only other New Testament occurrence is in the story of the two Gadarene demoniacs who were as savage and untamed as wild beasts and whom Matthew describes as "so *fierce (chalepos)* that no one could pass that way" (Matt. 8:28). This gives us an idea of the kind of seasons which the church must expect in the last days. They will be both painful and perilous, hard to endure and hard to cope with.[65]

Perhaps Paul wants to remind Timothy that if he is to be alive during this period, he will need to be watchful and prayerful. Unlike the young Thessalonian believers, he must not be "shaken in mind or be troubled…as that the day of the Lord is at hand" (2 Thess. 2:2) or has already come. This period, although perilous and difficult, is not the Tribulation; rather, it is a portentous precursor to it.

How do things get so bad? Paul tells us as he depicts this time frame in the next verses.

Later Times Depicted

This is not the first time Paul has written to the young pastor concerning the last days. He briefly addresses this scenario in 1 Timothy 4:1: "Now the Spirit speaketh expressly, that in the latter times some shall depart from the faith, giving heed to seducing spirits, and doctrines of devils." In this passage, Paul pulls back the curtain and lets us see the inner workings of Satan. His first tactic is to deceive ("giving heed to seducing spirits"). The Greek word for deceive is *planos*, which means "to wander" or "lead astray." Satan is subtle. He diverts by deception. He has many minions assisting him in this global deception, from members of the mass media and the movers and shakers in Hollywood to politicians and environmentalists, to name a few. He does not want those alive before the Rapture to be occupied with the state of their souls. Anything that keeps mankind from giving thought to their eternal destination causes them to drift farther from the heavenly harbor.

But God did not create the mind for the mundane. And like nature, the mind abhors a vacuum. So Satan fills it—not with the mundane, but with the profane: "the doctrine of demons." In other words, those whom he wishes to indoctrinate he first deceives. The Greek word for doctrine is *didaskalia*. It is the same word used in Acts 2:42: "They were continually devoting themselves to the apostles' teaching [*didaskalia*] and to fellowship, to the breaking of bread and to prayer." The apostles' teaching kept the early church from drifting.

Sadly, some churches today—instead of being "the pillar and ground of truth"—assist Satan with "seeker-sensitive," "touchy-feely," "felt-needs" sermons versus "real-needs" sermons. Instead of a full, faithful, and overflowing exposition of doctrine, we have sermonettes for Christianettes.

The stream of truth has run too shallow for too long within many modern churches. What little water is left is only a trickle. There is nowhere to genuinely slake one's spiritual thirst. Only the counterfeit fountain of the "father of lies" invites all to come—and most do. Noted American educator Horace Mann was spot-on when he said, "Keep one thing forever in view—the truth; and if you do this, though it may seem to lead you away from the opinion of men, it will assuredly conduct you to the throne of God."[66] Satan's deception and indoctrination leads to the cultural corruption found in 2 Timothy 3:2–5, where Paul lists specific characteristics depicting these last days. Is there an order to it? Dr. Thomas Constable believes there is a chiastic structure—one that places concepts or ideas in an order or symmetry:

Paul wrote this list…in a somewhat chiastic arrangement. His list begins and ends with two groups of two words expressing a misdirection of love. Then come two groups with three terms each that focus on pride and hostility toward others. Then come two groups, five words followed by three words, all of which begin with *a* in the Greek text that negate some good quality that God's common grace affords. These eight words—the first one is in a two-word phrase—depict people who are devoid of the most basic characteristics of human life. The center of the chiasm is the word *diaboloi,* meaning slanderers, devilish people (cf. [2 Tim.] 2:26; 1 Tim. 3:11; Titus 2:3).[67]

Bible commentator Donald Guthrie sees a resemblance between 2 Timothy 3:2–5 and Paul's "ethical list" in Romans 1:

> The list itself seems to lack any premeditated order as was usually the case in the ethical lists used by the Greek moralists. On the other hand, the pastoral catalogues of vices, and especially this one, show many affinities with Jewish descriptions, and are particularly akin to Philo's lists. There is also the suggestion that this list may have been based on some previous apocalyptic. There are many similarities between this catalogue and the vices mentioned in Romans 1, the main difference being that in the latter Paul is describing the contemporary Gentile world, whereas here a future condition is being envisaged.[68]

Perhaps the best way to understand the structure in the 2 Timothy passage is to see the "bookends," as Guthrie points out. The list begins with loving self and money and ends with loving pleasure more than God.

The first two characteristics Paul lists, "lovers of themselves" *(phil-autoi)* and "lovers of money" *(philargyroi),* supply the key to the rest of the list. Moral corruption follows love that is falsely directed. Self-centeredness and material advantages, when they become the chief objects of affection, destroy all moral values and the subsequent list of vices is their natural fruit. It is significant that the list ends with a similar pair of words compounded with *philo:* loving pleasure rather than loving God (verse 4). It has been suggested that this passage is based on the Hellenistic writer Philo because of a striking parallel of expression. The implication here is that pleasure is regarded as a substitute for God. Basically, materialism is opposed to piety and is bound to end in irreligion.[69]

John Stott, evangelical Anglican preacher, teacher, and author of many commentaries on the Bible, concurs by pointing out that "four of the nineteen expressions are compounded with 'love' (*phil-*), suggesting that what is fundamentally wrong with these people is that their love is misdirected. Instead of being first and foremost 'lovers of God,' they are 'lovers of self,' 'lovers of money'…and 'lovers of pleasure.'"[70]

Between these four characteristics come fifteen other expressions, which are almost entirely descriptive of the breakdown of our relationships with one another. The following list from 2 Timothy 3 describes the characteristics of people in Satan's ideal society:

1) They love themselves (v. 2).

Once a civilization has been deceived and then indoctrinated, it is easily debased. Whether or not this list has a specific structure, it certainly begins with the greatest sin of all: loving one's self and not God. Our Lord said that the greatest commandment of all is to love Him (Mark 12:28–31):

> And one of the scribes came, and having heard them reasoning together, and perceiving that He had answered them well, asked Him, "Which is the first commandment of all?" And Jesus answered him, "The first of all the commandments is, 'Hear, O Israel; The Lord our God is one Lord: And thou shalt love the Lord thy God with all thy heart, and with all thy soul, and with all thy mind, and with all thy strength:' this *is* the first commandment. And the second is like, namely this: 'Thou shalt love thy neighbour as thyself.' There is none other commandment greater than these."

Paul used the Greek word *agapao* for love in this passage. It means unconditional love, and is the love vowed at many a nuptial—the "forsaking-all-others" type of love. God calls men and women to love Him first and foremost. But men and women in the last days will not love God supremely. They will love themselves. Their minds will have been so deceived and indoctrinated that their hearts will have become fixated on themselves.

In the latter days, men and women will have hearts that love neither God nor His commandments. King Solomon instructs his son to use his heart to keep God's commandments (Prov. 3:1). He tells him why he must do so a chapter later: "Keep your heart with all diligence; for out of it are the issues of life" (Prov. 4:23). Latter-day hearts have become polluted and therefore spew out the rest of Paul's cultural corrupters.

2) They are covetous (v. 2).

Those who love themselves must find something outside of themselves to love. In this case, it is money. The word for "covetous"— *philarguros*—means a "lover of silver." The fact that those in the last days do not love God and His commandments—instead, they love themselves along with money—makes perfect sense. In the Sermon on the Mount, Jesus pointed out, "No man can serve two masters: for either he will hate the one, and love the other; or else he will hold to the one, and despise the other. Ye cannot serve God and mammon" (Matt. 6:24).

Those who will not bow before the one "in whom are hid all the treasures of wisdom and knowledge" (Col. 2:3) bow before the altar of avarice. One needs only to look into America's recent past "irrational exuberance" that caused the stock market to run up the hill and roll quickly down it, or at the boom and bust of the housing market, to see greed unchecked.

Gordon Gekko, the character played by Michael Douglas in the 1987 film *Wall Street,* typified unrestrained greed and covetousness when he said, "Greed, for lack of a better word, is good." I wonder if those who lost life savings or homes would think "greed...is good"? When it comes to the treasures of this world, "more and more" is not.

The next three characteristics on the 2 Timothy 3 list expand on the implications of self love. Those who think too highly of themselves invariably look down with contempt on all others. They are boasters, they are prideful, and they speak evil against others.

3 & 4) They are boasters and prideful (v. 2).

These two traits go hand in hand. The first refers to what a person *does* and the second describes what a person *is*. People boast because they are proud.

The Greek word *alazon,* translated as "boasting," is also used in Paul's list in Romans 1:30. Commentator C. E. B. Cranfield says it refers to "the frantic boast and foolish word of the heathen heart, the sort of thing which is reflected in Isaiah 10:7–11; in fact all the presumptuous claims and ostentatious behaviour of men by which they seek to impress one another, and very often delude themselves."[71]

Pride, which means thinking more highly of one's self than one should, is simply heart disease (see 2 Chron. 39:26); it is symptomatic of not fearing the Lord (see Prov. 8:13), and is destructive to the soul (see Prov. 16:18; 29:23). It is dangerous because it sets up an adversarial relationship with God, who "resisteth the proud, and giveth grace to the humble" (1 Pet. 5:5).

God wants us to glory in and boast about Him (see 1 Cor. 1:31). But in the latter days, men and women will not boast about their Lord; they will boast about what they have done. This is seen in the young athlete who is "trash talking" (something learned from the professional athlete) and in the Wall Street baron who is bragging on a big bonus check.

5) They are blasphemous (v. 2).

Most commentators think the blasphemy spoken of here is not directed toward God but toward other human beings. It is used in this sense in Acts 6:11 and 2 Peter 2:11. This would logically follow the previous two cultural corrupters, boastfulness and pride. These are not humble men and women. These are not compassionate men and women. These are not encouragers of their fellow men and women. They are destroyers.

The Bible commands believers not to destroy but to encourage, "and let us consider one another to provoke unto love and to good works" (Heb. 10:24). Hebrews 3:13 says the reason we should encourage one another is due to the hardening effect of sin. But men and women who have rejected God to love money care little about their fellow human beings. The only thing they care about is themselves and making themselves look good. In order to do this, they must make others look bad.

How tragic it is when Christians are not encouragers, but destroyers. It bears mentioning that believers are not immune from these cultural corrupters. Unless we are walking *by* the Spirit (see Gal. 5) we are walking *against* the Spirit!

6) They disobey their parents (v. 2).

God ordained three institutions to preserve and promote goodness in culture: the government, the church, and the family. The government "is the minister of God to thee for good. But if thou do that which is evil, be afraid; for he beareth not the sword in vain: for he is the minister of God, a revenger to execute wrath upon him that doeth evil" (Rom. 13:4). The church is to be "salt" and "light" (see Matt. 5). And God designed the family, among other things, to impart spiritual truth and values (see Deut. 6:7 and Eph. 6:4).

Disobedience destroys a family's spiritual effectiveness. In the latter days, children will not just be disrespectful; they will also be disobedient to their parents. This lack of respect for authority will eventually grow into a lack of respect for any authority.

Today, this disobedience is being taken to the courtroom as even children are suing their parents—for a number of reasons. One of the more extreme reports is of a young man who sued his parents for his circumcision, claiming it had violated his human rights. Imagine this trend extending to include lawsuits over diet ("You fed me too many trans fats"), playtime ("I was shorted the customary play time for a six-year-old"), or even feeding ("You bottle fed and did not breast feed, depriving me of the warmth and nurturing a small child must have").

7) They are not thankful (v. 2).

Some think this trait, along with the next three, deals with the family unit. But this one and the others could also apply to society as a whole. Children by nature are unthankful, but unthankfulness seems to be a societal trait as well.

This is the negation of the trait of thankfulness, *eucharistia*, found in 1 Corinthians 14:16, 2 Corinthians 4:15, and Ephesians 5:4. Unthankfulness means not being grateful for what one has and manifests itself in the "entitlement" mentality present today. Rather than being thankful for what one has, far too many expect and demand more.

8) They are unholy (v. 2).

This, of course, is the opposite of holiness and it "describes the person who has no fellowship with God and so is living a merely 'secular' life."[72] Nothing more accurately describes the mentality of those who are living in the latter days. Sadly, it is the mindset that is most abundantly growing and thriving in the world today. Men and women today are not even as spiritually advanced as the ancient Athenians, who at least did not want to ignore any of their gods, so had a statue to the unknown god (see Acts 17).

Today, the American Civil Liberties Union (ACLU)—an organization solidly secular in its orientation—wants to remove any acknowledgement of God within society. It is against nativity displays, crosses on public buildings, or any other recognition of God. The people of the ACLU and others who follow that philosophy are known as "secular progressives," a term coined by Fox News commentator Bill O'Reilly. It is the attitude that supports death (abortion and euthanasia) and perversion (same-sex marriage and open affirmation of homosexuality).

Unless God intervenes, unholiness will continue to metastasize in our culture until in the latter days it becomes the dominant thought.

9) They do not feel or demonstrate "natural affection" (v. 3).

The Greek word translated to "natural affection," *astorgos*, is only found in Romans 1:31 in the New Testament. It means without family affections—in other words, members of the family lack the natural love and affection that are common to the familial unit. In the latter times, blood will not be thicker than water.

One of the indicators of this lack of natural affection in America is the high divorce rate. America has one of the highest divorce rates, climbing close to 50 percent, according to a number of sources, including the National Center for Health. Adults, for the most part, seem to give little thought to how the dissolution of marriage will affect their children, extended family, friends, or even society. The high percentage of "deadbeat dads" is a sad indicator of the number of men who lack natural affection for their children. But perhaps one of the most disturbing and alarming indicators of a lack in natural affection is the number of mothers who abandon their children and walk out of marriages without informing anyone as to where they are. A woman named Lorraine Colombo did just, according to an online news source. Following her husband's discovery of her extramarital affair, she disappeared, leaving her husband to raise their two children by himself.[73]

Look for this trend to continue as "lovers of selves" demonstrate that this type of love leaves little for someone else.

10) They do not keep their word (v. 3).

The Greek word *aspondos*, translated as "trucebreakers," means "one without a treaty or covenant." Therefore, trucebreakers are irreconcilable and implacable. It means there is so much animosity that there cannot be any reconciliation.

Our litigious society displays this ugly trait often. Think of how many television shows are geared to this topic: *Judge Judy, Judge Hatchett, Judge Alex,* and *Judge Mathis,* plus *Criminal Court* and *Divorce Court.* What a pathetic commentary on a society where, in their free time, people find it fun to watch people sue each other and to witness their pain and suffering!

As we move toward the departure, look for people to find dark and morbid fun from others' misfortunes.

11) They are false accusers (v. 3).

This phrase comes from two Greek words that mean to "throw over or across." It means to slander or insult someone. This could certainly be a companion culture corrupter with a trucebreaker, and is yet another indicator of a sick society. Instead of getting along and helping their fellow man, people are heaping insults and false accusations upon others.

It is in the political environment that this trait finds the most fertile soil in which to root and produce noxious weeds. Every day, politicians maliciously throw accusations at one another. Washington has become a toxic atmosphere for the flower of civility.

12. They are incontinent (v. 3).

The Greek word translated "incontinent" is *kratos*, which is the word for "strength"—but it is accompanied in the original language by a negation particle alpha, which transforms the word into its opposite. Therefore, this term means "without strength, without self-control, or without the ability for self-restraint." Today in our society, most people demonstrate little, if any, self-control. Examples of people choosing not to self-moderate abound everywhere we look—from the entertainment industry to the financial bulwarks of Wall Street.

To people who are behaviorally incontinent, there is no such thing as a sin; transgressions are called "addictions" (that makes no one responsible for curbing them or reining them in). One shining—or better said, tarnished—example of late is professional golfer Tiger Woods, who seems to have forgotten the "forsaking all others" aspect of marriage.

A recent study reported by *Science Daily* says that self-control or the lack of self-control is contagious. Researchers found that "watching or even thinking about someone with good self-control makes others more likely to exert self-control. The researchers found that the opposite holds, too, so that people with bad self-control influence others negatively. The effect is so powerful that seeing the name of someone with good or bad self-control flashing on a screen for just ten milliseconds changed the behavior of volunteers."[74] In the latter days, there will be far more examples of people demonstrating a lack of self-control than of those who regularly use self-control.

13) They are fierce (v. 3).

The word "fierce" in Greek—*anemeros*—means "savage" or "brutal." It is the antithesis of civilized. My wife and I recently visited a large metropolis. We were warned that some areas were safe to visit during the day but dangerous at night because after dark, local gangs were vying for turf. One's safety and well-being could not be assured once the sun went down. In Mexico, just south of the U.S. border, gun-toting and gun-firing drug wars erupt. Civilians risk life and limb if caught in the crossfire. "Man's inhumanity to man" will continue to increase and violence will abound in the latter days.

14) They despise those who are good (v. 3).

The psalmist says that God is good to Israel (Psa. 73:1). Jesus told the rich young ruler that only God is good (Mark 10:18). Paul said that everything created by this good God is therefore good (1 Tim. 4:4). In the last days, people will not love good; they will despise it. Could it be that they know their conduct is not good? Could it be that they know they do not measure up to the goodness of God? Could it be that they love the darkness rather than the light?

In the last days, men and women will not struggle to be better. They will not work on themselves. They will not strive to improve society. Instead, they will hate the good within society.

The almost reverent and sacrosanct devotion to the murder of innocent children hates good. The pathological tolerance of homosexuality hates good. The irrational fear of anything seen as infringing on the so-called separation of church and state hates good. Yet, this hatred of good is largely tolerated and celebrated in our society. It is merely a precursor to the hatred of all that is good, noble, and pure in the latter days.

15) They are traitors (v. 4).

The Greek word for "traitors"—*prodotes*—is used to describe Judas (Luke 6:16), the betrayer also referred to as the "son of perdition" (John 17:12). The act of being traitorous can only take place among good friends or simpatico people. How devastating betrayal is! Whether found in a marriage, business partnership, or national alliance, it is difficult to recover from a betrayal. It undermines and destabilizes interpersonal relationships. It inflicts a deep wound that is resistant to healing. It births a selfishness and self-centeredness in those who think they can only depend upon themselves.

16) They are heady (v. 4).

Heady people are rash and reckless. The Greek word *propetes* means "to fall forward or headlong," indicating that in the latter days, people will not think through their actions. They will act rashly without considering the consequences.

A familiar adage says, "You can choose your action or choose your consequences, but you cannot choose both." However, today, many individuals are trying to choose both. The boomer generation (of which I am a member) does not like this. But aging boomers are not experiencing the consequences of a rash and reckless life. The concomitant consequences of an unrighteous life are unavoidable.

Sadly, in the latter days, people will think they can avoid the consequences of rushing recklessly into sin.

17) They are high-minded (v. 4).

This phrase means having an unwarranted sense of self-importance. It is the "it's-all-about-me" mindset that focuses only on what will satisfy and gratify one's self. People who are high-minded are the sun within the solar system of relationships. If not for them, they believe, the relational universe would spin out of control.

18) They love pleasure more than they love God (v. 4).

It is fitting that people with even a few of the aforementioned traits would not love God, but rather would love only pleasure. The tragedy is that true pleasure is found along the path of God, after coming into His presence and receiving blessings from His hand (Psa. 16:11).

Seeking pleasure outside the restraints of righteousness is a fool's errand. It follows the path of the law of diminishing return. It is like a drug: In the beginning, a small amount will satisfy; however, the more it's used, the more is needed.

In the latter days, people will be crazed for what only God can give, and they will seek it in ever more outrageous and unrighteous ways.

19) They have a form of godliness, but deny its power (v. 5).

As bad as those living in the latter days will be, the "faith" of most of those alive at that time will be even worse. God says He has "set the world in" the human heart (Eccles. 3:11). The word "world" is translated from the Hebrew *olam*, which means "eternity for forever." We were created to not only live forever, but to worship forever as well. So one thing sin cannot strip out of most of the hearts of the latter-days lost is a desire to live forever and worship. Paul is clear that if one does not worship the Creator, he or she will worship the creation (Rom 1:22–23). The desire to live forever and worship something greater is fertile soil for the coming one-world religion described in Revelation 17.

It is worth noting that the type of religion described here is impotent. In the phrase, "having a form of godliness but denying its power," the Greek word for "form"—*morphosis*—means "outward appearance" or "shape." In other words, it looks good on the outside but is empty on the inside. The shape, so to speak, is "godliness." This means piety or reverence. People will take seriously *their* (as opposed to God-revelation) religion, but nothing is there. Donald Guthrie sums up the essence of this religion as follows: "Indeed, it is not simply a matter of an organized religion which has ceased to function, but a religion which is not intended to function."[75] This religion is truly the opiate of the "perditioned."

Paul has no idea of a newspaper, magazine, or a news broadcast. But he does know what the latter times will look like. He looks around and identifies these cultural corrupters that will be observable to those who have eyes to see and ears to hear. They were observable in his day, but today they are almost immeasurable. As we peruse the daily news, we find it riddled with evidence of Paul's cultural corrupters. This list represents the passions, pursuits, and people that populate a dead and dying world. These are the ones who will witness the greatest exodus of mankind, the Rapture. It saddens the heart to see so many people literally hell-bent. But it gladdens the heart of those who will be heaven-sent, escaping and departing the wrath to come.

Latter-Day Directives

In 2 Timothy 3:1–5, Paul gives a warning concerning the latter days. Next, he begins his latter-day directives. The first thing he mentions is that there will be evangelists of evil. These are identified in 2 Timothy 3:6–7; they prey upon the susceptible. He specifies two examples in verses 8–9: James and Jambres, the Egyptians who opposed Moses (Exod. 7:11, 9:11).

Paul goes on to explain that the closer we get to the great departure, the Rapture, the worse things will become. Satan will continue his grand deception (2 Tim. 3:13). Paul therefore directs Timothy to the only thing that can "deception-proof" him and his congregation: the Scriptures. Timothy must first *pursue* the truth (2 Tim. 3:14–17) and second *proclaim* the truth (2 Tim. 4:1–5).

Surely the time of departure is much closer today than it was in Paul's day. He departed this world with peace of mind, fully expecting Timothy to "watch ["be sober," New American Standard Version (NASV)] in all things, endure afflictions, do the work of an evangelist, [and] make full proof ["fulfill," NASV] of thy ministry."

The question for you and me today is this: If Paul were writing to us today, would he be as confident in us as he was in Timothy?

May God encourage and strengthen us to faithfully minister until the day of our departure.

CHAPTER FIVE

HUMANISM'S HUBRIS AND THE COMING COLLAPSE

By Jack Kinsella

According to my word processor's dictionary, "hubris" means "excessive pride or arrogance"—but the definition doesn't really do justice to the richness of its meaning. "Hubris" carries with it the flavor of breathtaking, blind, supreme arrogance—a condescending pridefulness so extreme that, like art or pornography, it is hard to define.

"Hubris" is a perfect fit with "secular humanism" as defined by the same authority as "belief in human-based morality." The *hubris* part is found in humanism's unreasonable faith in the power of nothing, a conclusion its apologists claim they arrived at using the power of reason—a power that *itself* arose from nothing.

That humanism is faith-based rather than rooted in science is found in the fact that for evolution to be true, established and observable scientific fact must be false. All genuine scientific theory is rooted in the bedrock principle outlined in the second law of thermodynamics,[76] which says among other things that all things break down with time.

By simply adding an incalculable period of time, evolutionary theory posits that the second law of thermodynamics suddenly and inexplicably works in reverse. This cannot be proven by any standard scientific method, so by definition it must be taken as an article of faith.

What Is "Morality"?

A basic tenet of secular humanism is that morality evolved in much the same way that everything else did. That is to say, over the course of time and through trial and error, a universal human moral code evolved.

What *is* morality? Again referring to my word processor's dictionary, it is "the rightness or wrongness of something as judged by acceptable moral standards." For this definition to make sense requires some kind of benchmark measure for what constitutes "right" and "wrong"—*and* it demands the existence of "an acceptable moral standard."

These concepts all exist outside the materialistic worldview of secular humanism. Morality can't be tasted, touched, heard, seen, or smelled. It can't be described materialistically. It can't even be objectively categorized. Secular humanism denies the existence of moral absolutes, but in so doing, removes any basis *for* a moral code. If there are no absolutes, then the concepts of right and wrong cannot exist independently: right or wrong...compared to *what?*

Something, therefore, can't be wrong in and of itself—it all depends on one's perspective. So the foundation upon which secular humanism rests—that of a human-based moral code—is as solid as the shifting sand. It is upon *that* foundation that humanism presumes to pontificate about the power of human reason.

I've No Mind, So You Don't Matter

The ability to reason is not the product of the brain. Grasshoppers have brains. (So do humanists.) But grasshoppers don't have *minds*— they can't reason. Neither can any other lower animals. The ability to reason is as uniquely human as the human mind.

How does a *mind* evolve—out of nothing?

According to secular humanism, man is a result of a continuous natural process; the mind is a projection of body and nothing more; man is molded mostly by his culture; there is no supernatural; and man has outgrown religion and any idea of God. Secular humanism says that man is inherently good—hence, the evolution of a moral code separating good from evil (or so said the drafters of the first Humanist Manifesto back in 1933).[77]

The bloodstained Nazi Holocaust, the Stalinist purges, Mao Tsetung's "cultural revolution," and Pol Pot's Cambodian genocide, etc. (that together claimed more than 100 million lives) forced the redrafting of the Humanist Manifesto II in 1974 to accommodate the shortcomings of the initial philosophy regarding the basic goodness of man.

The Humanist Manifesto II instead exhorts humanists to "enlarge our knowledge of the natural…no deity will save us; we must save ourselves."[78] How this salvation comes about or what exactly humanists hope to be saved from is unclear. The document goes on to say that "promises of immortal salvation or fear of eternal damnation are both illusory and harmful."

Having made that declarative statement, the writers of the Manifesto admit that, "*as far as we know*, the total personality is a function of the biological organism transacting in a social and cultural context" (emphasis added). Then, after openly acknowledging that they don't know what they are talking about, the authors say there is "no credible evidence that life survives the death of the body."

Is there "credible evidence" that Abraham Lincoln was assassinated in Ford's Theater on April 16, 1865? No one is alive today to testify as an eyewitness to the event. There are no photographs of John Wilkes Booth pulling the trigger or of Lincoln's actual assassination. The only evidence of the Lincoln assassination comes in the form of eyewitness accounts undisputed by other contemporary witnesses, with such accounts subsequently recorded by historians and passed down through the generations.

That is exactly the *same evidence* that testifies to the resurrection of Jesus Christ—eyewitness accounts undisputed by contemporary witnesses and subsequently recorded by historians for posterity. Therefore, if the evidence is sufficient to establish the historicity of the Lincoln assassination, it is sufficient to establish the historicity of the resurrection. And by *that* standard, there are literally *volumes* of credible evidence that life survives the death of the body.

Incredible Hubris of Humanism

The incredible hubris of humanism continued with the publication of the Humanist Manifesto III in 2003. Perhaps because when one believes in nothing, less is more, the Manifesto III is much shorter; it lists only six primary beliefs.

Think of it as a religious doctrinal statement supported entirely by faith in *itself.*

1. Empiricism: Knowledge of the world is derived by observation, experimentation, and rational analysis.

Hubris: Humanists cannot observe, experiment with, or rationally analyze the human mind; they can't even *define* it. The Terri Schiavo case proved that.[79] Science cannot recreate evolution or duplicate the big bang.

2. Evolution: Humans are the result of unguided evolutionary change.

Hubris: Since evolution cannot be proved empirically (as demanded by point number 1), these two doctrines are mutually exclusive.

3. Ethical Values: Morals and ethics are derived from human need and interest as tested by experience.

Hubris: Human needs and interests as tested by experience at various times are responsible for Joseph Stalin's purges, the Holocaust, Mao's Cultural Revolution, and Pol Pot's Cambodian genocide.

4. The Meaning of Life: Fulfillment is found in individual participation in the service of humane ideals.

Hubris: For some, maybe. But some find fulfillment in the service of communism; others find it in the service of themselves. Still more find it in the service of their deity.

5. Society: Humans are social by nature and find meaning in relationships.

Hubris: Humans are also antisocial in nature and are racist, segregationist, and sexist.

6. Happiness: Working to benefit society maximizes human happiness.

Hubris: The slogan that was displayed over the entrance to the Nazi death camps read *Arbeit Macht Frei*—German for "Work Makes You Free."[80]

Where Is Everybody?

According to evolutionary theory, mankind emerged on the planet some uncountable hundreds of thousands or millions of years ago.

My mother-in-law is eighty-eight (and given her current state of health and her genetic history, she could easily live to see one hundred). When she was born, in 1922, the earth's population was approaching 2 billion.[81]

According to the Population Reference Bureau's *2009 World Population Data Sheet*, the number of people on planet earth is projected to have reached 7 billion people in 2011.[82] Researchers are predicting that the global population will peak by the end of this century, at somewhere around 9 billion people, and will level off from there.[83]

You see the problem: We went from 2 billion to 7 billion people in just eighty years. The math doesn't support a human population that is millions of years old, or even tens of thousands of years old. It should have leveled off at 9 billion people or so many eons ago. But it didn't.

Cause and Effect

The quest for scientific knowledge boils down to a search for cause and effect. This scientific principle is known as the law of causality.[84]

Briefly, the law states that every effect must have a cause. This troubled the great Albert Einstein. Einstein's theory of relativity calculations indicated that the universe, rather than being static, was actually expanding. Einstein's understanding of the law of causality meant his findings indicated that the universe was not eternal; it had to have a beginning.

In 1927, astronomer Edwin Hubble (for whom the space telescope is named) observed what he called "a red shift" in the light between galaxies, confirming that Einstein's calculations had indeed disproved the cosmological constant.

The Big Bang Theory

The disproving of the cosmological constant means that since the universe is expanding, reversing the process makes it contract until it eventually disappears into nothingness. That forced the reformulation of scientific and evolutionary thinking, eventually exploding into the big bang theory—an effort to explain the creation of the universe without a Creator. That's no small trick, given the circumstances.

Interestingly, the big bang theory makes the same central assumptions that the Bible's creation story does. First, it had a beginning. Since it is expanding, it *had* to have a starting point. Prior to the beginning, it was without form and void—there was nothing. No universe. No matter. No stars. No space. No planets. No vacuum. Nothing.

"Nothing" is not a difficult concept to grasp—it is an *impossible* one. Nobody can imagine "nothing"—just try! The philosopher René Descartes tried to imagine nothing, only to come up with his famous words, *Cogito, ergo sum* ("I think, therefore, I am").

One cannot imagine nothing because it takes *something*—you— to do the imagining. "Nothing," in the truest sense of the word, is a scientific impossibility in the physical universe. And that is what science says preexisted the big bang—a scientific impossibility.

The Bible says that the universe and its contents were completed in six literal days. Science scoffs at that, but argues that during the big bang, what we know as time was compressed. The universe was at one point no bigger than a baseball, but it contained all the stars, planets, matter, etc., and began moving outward.

Time is compressed at the center and expands outwardly with the universe. So in six literal days—as measured from the center of the expanding universe—the stars could have traveled light years. After all, time is relative—that's what Einstein's theory of relativity is all about.

But the hubris of humanism will have none of *that*—it comes to close to the creation story, which is too fantastic. Humanists prefer the story in which something appeared out of nothing for no apparent reason and without a cause.

The Religion of Man

In 1948, the theory of evolution received two major boosts. The first was the introduction of the big bang theory that provided a pseudo-scientific explanation for the origin of the universe. The second was the *Brown v. Board of Education* decision, later established as a matter of law by the 1962 *Zorach v. Clauson* opinion.

The Supreme Court decided that in public schools, a period
of silence may be observed during which children can pray if they
wish—but the schools may not conduct devotional exercises, com-
pose prayers, read the Bible, or otherwise enter the field of religious
instruction. That was interpreted to mean that acknowledging any
divine hand in the creation of the universe or its contents was "entering the field of religious instruction."

The slippery slope of constitutional interpretation that reads
"freedom of religion" (a phrase not found anywhere in the U.S.
Constitution) as meaning "freedom from religion" began with the
case of *McCollum v. the Board of Education.*

Secular humanism is religion like Christianity, Buddhism, or
Taoism; the Supreme Court said so. Humanism is not only accepted
as a religion with full religious 501(c)(3) tax exemptions, but the
Supreme Court upheld Daniel Seeger's right to claim conscientious
objector status, exempting him from military service because of his
religious beliefs. His "religious belief"—as cited before the court—
was *secular humanism.*

Humanists are careful to disguise their religious beliefs as "science"
teaching the "theory" of evolution as "fact"—despite the absence of
any conclusive evidence to support it. The fact is that secular humanism is the only religious belief that is taught—by government mandate—in public schools.

The Missing Link

As I was working on this chapter, the *London Daily Mail* reported that
scientists have (once again) "discovered the missing link" (this time)
"between humans and apes."[85]

Scientists believe they have discovered the missing link between
humans and the ape-like creatures we evolved from.

The homonid, the evolutionary branch of primates that allegedly
led to humans, will be revealed when a two-million-year-old skeleton

of a child is unveiled this week. The skeleton was discovered in the Sterkfontein region of South Africa—an area known as the cradle of humanity—by Professor Lee Berger of the University of the Witwatersrand in Johannesburg, South Africa.

According to evolutionary scientists, every species has been evolving from some other species since the uncreated dawn of time. Every five or ten years, somebody shows up with a new "missing link" that "conclusively establishes"—often from a single bone fragment—the unguided evolutionary process.

It would seem that if evolution were a fact, we'd have found more evidence than that. In fact, if evolution were a process that took millions of years, we should be up to our necks in fossilized transitional life forms, or "links."

We have plenty of fossilized dinosaurs and lots of fossilized prehistoric fish, birds, insects, and so on. Logic would suggest an overwhelming percentage of those should be in transition—but *none* are.

We've already discussed the math problems with making mankind millions of years old; the same problems apply with the missing link(s). We should be drowning in them.

One Small Step for Fish...

A couple of years ago (2006), the scientific world was abuzz with the discovery of *Tiktaalik roseae,* the fossilized remains of a fish with a flattened, crocodile-like head and strong, bony fins that was also heralded as the "missing link."[86] The *Boston Globe's* headline announced that the discovery "Fills in a Piece of the Evolutionary Puzzle."[87] The *UK Independent* proclaimed, "Scientists Find Missing Link to Land Vertebrates."[88] The *London Times* called it the "fish that took the first step for mankind."[89]

In large part, the conclusion that Tiktaalik is the missing link arises from the initial conclusion that it was a fish in the process of turning *into* a crocodile. There appears to be no speculation that the find was a fossil of a previously undiscovered, crocodile-like species of fish or fish-like species of crocodile. The assumption that it was really a transitional life form was immediate and unshakeable…except by Dr. Neil Shubin, who discovered the fossil in the first place.

According to a *New York Times* story:

> While Dr. Shubin's team played down the fossil's significance in the raging debate over Darwinian theory, which is opposed mainly by some conservative Christians in the United States, other scientists were not so reticent. They said this should undercut the creationists' argument that there is no evidence in the fossil record of one kind of creature becoming another kind.[90]

One of my children totally demolished the evolution argument in such a simple and childlike way it makes me wonder how the idea ever even gained a foothold in the supposedly superior intellectual reasoning of secular humanism. He asked me, "Dad, if evolution is true, then why are there monkeys?"

Desperate Times Call for Desperate Measures

It takes a lot of effort to be a humanist—and it takes a lot of resilience to keep on despite the almost daily necessity to reevaluate one's faith system as new facts displace old theories. As we learn more about the complexities of DNA, I have every expectation that a Humanist Manifesto IV is right around the corner.

One can detect the need for such a document by looking at the desperate lengths to which secular science is willing to go and the stretches of logic that it is willing to entertain, provided it disproves the Bible or "undercuts the creationists."

A Florida State University professor of oceanography made international news recently with his "discovery" of how Jesus was able to walk on the surface of the Sea of Galilee.

> Doron Nof, a professor of oceanography, said a rare combination of water and atmospheric conditions in the Sea of Galilee two thousand years ago may offer a scientific explanation for one of the miracles recounted in the Bible. Nof said a patch of ice floating in the Sea of Galilee—which is actually a freshwater lake—would have been difficult to distinguish from unfrozen water surrounding it.[91]

Well, no wonder the apostle Peter began to sink; Peter didn't know where the ice floe was! That also explains why none of the Gospel writers mentioned the icy walkway. They couldn't see it, either.

Of course, that's not the only alternative explanation, since reality is no obstacle to theorizing. Maybe Jesus was wearing invisible wires and was being held up by a spacecraft hovering just above the clouds. Maybe He was standing on a barely submerged submarine? Or maybe He was wearing inflatable shoes.

The apostle Paul describes this mindset perfectly, writing: "And even as they did not like to retain God in their knowledge, God gave them up to a reprobate mind" (Rom. 1:28).

Any explanation but the obvious will do.

Nothing for Something

Secular humanism and its attending doctrines—atheism, scientific and social Darwinism, eugenics and its political offspring (primarily Marxism)—all argue that the foundation for their existence is based on their faith in the existence of nothing.

Humanists believe in man's creative ability, but they also believe that man himself evolved from "nothing" and was therefore created by "nobody." Since man is biologically no more than the lower animals, the value of any human life is set by society and is therefore adjustable.

The value of human life in China was set by Chairman Mao. It was set in Stalinist Russia by Joseph Stalin and in North Korea by Kim Il Sung. These are, or were, officially atheist states.

The value of human life in Venezuela, Nicaragua, Cuba, or Columbia is set according to the perceived need of the state, as determined by a small group of military/political elites in harmony with their Marxist/humanist principles.

The value of human life in the post-Christian democracies is determined by what amounts to mob rule—if the majority can be convinced that unwanted babies and uncared for elderly are better off dead, then abortion and euthanasia can become the law of the land.

In the United States, since the proclamation of the "death of God" in 1966, the Supreme Court has legalized abortion, several states have instituted a "right" to suicide, and schools have turned into war zones, neighborhoods into battlefields, and former divinity schools like Harvard and Yale into Marxist propaganda centers.

America was founded upon the principle of a Creator God. Under that principle, since a person's inalienable rights were granted by the Creator, only the Creator can take them away. But what if the Creator is dead? In such a case, trusteeship of our rights then falls to government. And what the government grants, the government can take away. Defying all the rules of logic and their own observation, humanism views this as "progress" or "political evolution"—and, therefore, as natural and good.

Like any other religion, humanism has its own clergy (evolutionary science), its own dogma (Darwinism), and its own cadre of evangelist/apologists (Richard Dawkins, Christopher Hitchens, etc.). I am endlessly fascinated with this third category, given the task before them. I've encountered such evangelists before, but to this day I cannot understand their motivation. Why would anyone want to convince someone else that there is no God, no accountability, and no hope beyond the grave? It is an offer of nothing; however, to accept it, one must reject the offer of something.

Such apologists generally argue that what they offer is "truth"… until you ask them to prove it. Since there is no such thing as "nothing," their proof invariably comes in the form of an attack on *something*—organized religion in general, and Christianity in particular.

Occam's Cuisinart

A principle of logic attributed to the medieval philosopher William of Occam, commonly referred to as "Occam's Razor" (also known as the "principle of parsimony") underlies all scientific modeling and theory building. Occam's Razor is a method by which to choose from a set of otherwise equivalent models of a given phenomenon the simplest explanation. In any given model, Occam's razor helps us "shave off" the concepts, variables, or constructs that are not really needed to explain the phenomenon.

By doing that, developing the model will become much easier, and there is less chance of introducing inconsistencies, ambiguities, and redundancies. In its shortest form, Occam's Razor states that one should not make more assumptions than the minimum needed.

To beat a dead horse to death, let me simplify it even more: The simplest explanation is logically the most likely to be correct.

That Does Not Compute

We hear a lot about DNA research and the potential it holds for unlocking the miraculous and promising to reveal the secrets to stopping or reversing the aging process, leading to much longer and healthier lives. The breakthrough in DNA research came when researchers discovered that each strand of DNA is actually a programmable biological computer. Here is an explanation from the How Stuff Works Web site:

Millions of natural supercomputers exist inside living organisms, including your body. DNA (deoxyribonucleic acid) molecules, the material our genes are made of, have the potential to perform calculations many times faster than the world's most powerful human-built computers. DNA might one day be integrated into a computer chip to create a so-called biochip that will push computers even faster. DNA molecules have already been harnessed to perform complex mathematical problems.[92]

The article goes on to say, "While still in their infancy, DNA computers will be capable of storing billions of times more data than your personal computer." Translated from geek-speak, the body is made up of billions of supercomputers so advanced that any *one* of them is faster, smaller, and more advanced than anything humans can hope to build.

Instead, scientists are using the already much more perfectly designed DNA computers that humanism says evolved by accident, like a tornado in a junkyard might accidentally combine the necessary elements to create a polished and running Rolls Royce whose dashboard clock is already in sync to the nanosecond with the Atomic Time Clock in Washington DC. (And *that* happens all the time. Where *did* you think Rolls Royces came from?)

The DNA supercomputers of which we are constructed and in which are encoded all the information about us, from eye color to the disease of which we are programmed to die, make us somewhat akin to the *Star Trek* android, Commander Data. In the TV series, Commander Data was an artificially constructed, super-advanced robot from the twenty-fourth century. But even then, Data was far from perfect; he was incapable of feeling emotion, and his moral code could be reprogrammed with the flip of a switch.

The series, created by celebrated humanist Gene Roddenberry, acknowledged that Data had a creator (a scientist that Data referred to as "Father") while simultaneously scoffing at the notion of a Creator that constructed humans using biological computers without any of Data's inherent flaws.

"Hubris" is the only word that fits.

Let's shave DNA with Occam's Razor and see how it looks. The body is constructed from billions of advanced, reprogrammable nano-computers so well designed that human scientists abandoned any effort to compete with the design, co-opting it instead.

The simplest and most logical explanation is either:

a) Each of those billions of supercomputers contained in every cell and programmed with every detail of physical existence built and programmed *themselves* (the way that tornadoes create Rolls Royces).

Or,

b) DNA was designed and preprogrammed as part of a deliberate act of creation by an intelligent and skillful Creator.

Like the annoying pitchman on the TV commercial said about the ShamWow reusable towel, "I dunno! It sells itself!"

The "Death" of God

The cover of the April 8, 1966, edition of *Time* magazine, in blood-red letters against a black background, asked the question, "Is God Dead?" before revealing in the accompanying article that indeed He is.

On July 13, 1966, Richard Speck broke into a townhouse in the Jeffery Manor neighborhood of Chicago armed only with a knife. One by one, he tortured, raped, and murdered the eight student nurses living there. He rounded them up in one room, then took each one out individually to an adjacent room as each of the rest waited for her turn to die.

Richard Speck wasn't America's worst mass murderer, or even its first. *That* honor went to Howard Unruh of Camden, New Jersey, who gunned down thirteen people in a twelve-minute shooting spree in 1949. But Unruh was psychotic and spent the rest of his life in an insane asylum.

In April, *Time* proclaimed the "death of God" and in July, Richard Speck appeared to confirm it. Speck was perfectly sane. He was also perfectly evil. And by modern serial killer standards, Richard Speck was an amateur. But Speck opened the floodgates, and through those floodgates poured the likes of Ted Bundy (forty victims), John Wayne Gacy (fifty-seven victims), Jeffrey Dahmer (fifteen victims), Gary Ridgway (seventy-one victims), Carl "Coral" Eugene Watts (eighty victims), Charles Manson, Henry Lee Lucas, Richard Ramirez…the list began with Speck in 1966, but one quickly loses count of how long that list has grown through the years.

"Surely," you protest, "you aren't blaming humanism for the Hillside Strangler?" Certainly not! I'm blaming humanism for the "death of God" movement, but not for the rise of evil. Since "God is dead," I'm arguing an effect without a cause—you know, like the big bang. It's perfectly scientific!

Dehumanizing Humanity

In the final analysis, humanism's most enduring contribution to the humanity it claims to serve is the dehumanization of mankind. If man is simply the product of unguided evolution, then the foundation to his claim to supremacy rests primarily in his position at the top of the food chain. Human values simply evolved over time and according to the needs of society, and will therefore continue to evolve. The ones we have now will do until newer and better values become necessary.

The concepts of right and wrong must therefore also exist on a sliding scale. Since they evolved over time and according to need, they must continue to evolve as well. It therefore follows that right and wrong are not constants, but are situational.

The thing that makes humans *special* and sets them apart from lower animals is therefore *also* continually evolving, and so we're only special as long as we remain at the top of the food chain. Our status as human beings is simply situational; life is therefore precious only insofar as it applies to the human collective. Consequently, when it comes down to a contest between human beings and the spotted owl, the odds favor *the owl!*

In this view, laws against murder evolved because we don't want to be murdered, not out of some inherent, God-given moral code. This allows for the permissibility of abortion as a matter of social or economic convenience, since the targets have no say in the matter.

I find little to distinguish humanism in all its various forms from the various other isms like Marxism, communism, atheism, fascism, and so on. All rest upon the same theory so beautifully summarized by Stalin as, "One death is a tragedy. A million deaths is a statistic."

What distinguishes mankind from the lower animals is more than our currently advantageous position on the evolutionary timeline. Man is created in the image of God, and it is that reflected glory that makes human life special. Remove that status, and with it goes the foundation for morality, truth, ethics, and reason.

The hubris of humanism is found in its unshakable faith in the existence of nothing, which science says *cannot* exist, by denying the existence of *something*, to wit, a Creator God. This unguided nothing, it reasons, is the source of human rights based on an ever-evolving moral code rooted in the belief in *nothing*—except that human beings came from nothing and are going nowhere.

It has been wisely said that those who stand for nothing will fall for anything. Or evidently, for nothing.

CHAPTER SIX

THE UNITED STATES, THE RAPTURE, AND GOD'S JUDGMENT

Is the United States Mentioned in Bible Prophecy?

By Michael Hile

Perhaps the two most frequently asked questions when Bible prophecy is brought up involve the role of America in the end times. Specifically, people want to know if the United States is mentioned in Bible prophecy and whether God will judge America. The U.S. is the dominant superpower in the world today; however, it appears mysteriously absent from the scene when the final prophecies in the Bible begin making their appearance. We should not assume that the U.S. will play a major role in the end-time scenario simply because of its current superpower status. On the other hand, we should be careful not to automatically exclude America from all of the prophetic Scriptures because of historic, traditional interpretations of certain passages.

Since the United States is arguably the most prosperous and powerful nation that has ever existed, why is there no mention of this great empire in the book of Revelation—especially since the Apocalypse appears to be on the horizon? The sobering conclusion we must arrive at, based on biblical evidence, is that the U.S. will not have a major role in the events that will take place during the final seven-year period of this age called Daniel's seventieth week. The role of the United States will have to greatly diminish in the future if we are in fact living in the end times, as many experts in Bible prophecy believe.

Although God is the only one who knows what the future holds for the United States and the rest of the nations of the world, some intriguing Scriptures in both the Old and New Testaments provide clues concerning specific nations or kingdoms that will arise before Christ returns to set up His Kingdom. These end-time nations and kingdoms may already be actively helping establish a global government that will eventually give rise to the Antichrist. Whether present or absent from the world scene, the United States appears to be playing a major part today in setting the stage for several end-time prophecies developing now.

Will God Judge America?

Will the United States collapse from economic problems, rampant moral decay, a series of natural disasters, pandemics, an electromagnetic pulse attack, nuclear war, or some other unforeseen catastrophe? Some think God's judgment upon this nation has already begun, as evidenced by the many natural disasters such as hurricanes, tornadoes, flooding, droughts, forest fires, mudslides, and environmental catastrophes that have been occurring throughout the country and offshore.

This nation has been in a cultural decline that began in the 1960s and has accelerated in recent years. Morals and family values have been disintegrating, and there is no indication that this trend will change without God's intervention. Without national repentance, these trends can be expected to continue. The prophet Jeremiah revealed

God's actions when a nation decides to forsake Him and go in the wrong direction:

> At what instant I shall speak concerning a nation, and concerning a kingdom, to pluck up, and to pull down, and to destroy it; if that nation, against whom I have pronounced, turn from their evil, I will repent of the evil that I thought to do unto them. (Jer. 18:7–8)

God can remove His hand of protection overnight and take away the blessings He has given a nation and its people. Contrary to what many Americans assume, the freedoms and blessings this nation enjoys are direct gifts from God to His people rather than the result of the creative ingenuity of its citizens. If we continue this downward spiral and do not begin turning back to the biblical principles that made this country great, God will judge this nation like He did Babylon more than twenty-five hundred years ago when the mysterious handwriting appeared on the wall of the king's palace: "God hath numbered thy kingdom, and finished it....Thou art weighed in the balances, and art found wanting" (Dan. 5:25–28).[93]

Where Is the United States Mentioned in the Scriptures?

Although the United States is not mentioned by name in the Bible, some believe its presence is inferred in the prophetic Scriptures due to the major political, economic, military, and technological roles it plays in the world today. Many passages have been linked to the U.S. by numerous Bible teachers, who cite references including the following:

- **Isaiah**—Chapters 13 and 14; chapter 18:1–2; chapters 21 and 24; chapter 47:5–6, 8, and 10–13; chapter 48.
- **Jeremiah**—Chapter 50:12, 16, and 23; chapter 51:13, 44, and 53.

- **Ezekiel**—Chapter 38:13 and 39:6.
- **Daniel**—Chapter 7:4.
- **Revelation**—Chapter 12:14; chapter 13:11–17; and chapters 17–19.

This study will focus on the prophecy of the "four great beasts" described in Daniel 7. The last chapter of Daniel tells us that his book would be "shut up" and "sealed" until "the time of the end," when many would run "to and fro" and knowledge would "be increased." The "wicked shall do wickedly" and will not understand what is happening (Bible prophecy), "but the wise shall understand" (Dan. 12:10). If we are close to "the time of the end," as the "signs of the times" indicate, we should anticipate an unsealing of these prophetic passages as we approach their time of fulfillment.

> But thou, O Daniel, shut up the words, and seal the book, even to the time of the end: many shall run to and fro, and knowledge shall be increased.... And I heard, but I understood not: then said I, "O my Lord, what shall be the end of these things?" And He said, "Go thy way, Daniel: for the words are closed up and sealed till the time of the end." Many shall be purified, and made white, and tried; but the wicked shall do wickedly: and none of the wicked shall understand; but the wise shall understand. (Dan. 12:4, 8–10)

The Prophecy of the Four Beasts

About nine years after King Nebuchadnezzar's death in 562 BC, Daniel received a vision of "four great beasts" (Dan. 7:1–28) that would arise out of the "great sea" (traditionally the Mediterranean Sea). This was in 553 BC, during the first year of the reign of Belshazzar, who was a great-grandson of Nebuchadnezzar and the fifth ruler in succession. The vision of the beasts was given to Daniel when he was nearly seventy years old.

In the first year of Belshazzar king of Babylon, Daniel had a dream and visions of his head upon his bed: then he wrote the dream, and told the sum of the matters. Daniel spake and said, "I saw in my vision by night, and, behold, the four winds of the heaven strove upon the great sea. And four great beasts came up from the sea, diverse one from another.

"The first was like a lion, and had eagle's wings: I beheld till the wings thereof were plucked, and it was lifted up from the earth, and made stand upon the feet as a man, and a man's heart was given to it. And behold another beast, a second, like to a bear, and it raised up itself on one side, and it had three ribs in the mouth of it between the teeth of it: and they said thus unto it, 'Arise, devour much flesh.' After this I beheld, and lo another, like a leopard, which had upon the back of it four wings of a fowl; the beast had also four heads; and dominion was given to it.

"After this I saw in the night visions, and behold a fourth beast, dreadful and terrible, and strong exceedingly; and it had great iron teeth: it devoured and brake in pieces, and stamped the residue with the feet of it: and it was diverse from all the beasts that were before it; and it had ten horns. I considered the horns, and, behold, there came up among them another little horn, before whom there were three of the first horns plucked up by the roots: and, behold, in this horn were eyes like the eyes of man, and a mouth speaking great things." (Dan. 7:1–8)

Daniel's vision took place about fourteen years before the mysterious handwriting appeared on the wall (Dan. 5:5), which signaled the demise of King Belshazzar and the end of the Babylonian dynasty. On October 12, 539 BC, Cyrus the Great, the Persian king, entered the city of Babylon and slew Belshazzar. After taking Babylon, the Medo-Persian Empire dominated Mesopotamia, "the land between the rivers," and the Middle Eastern nations for more than two hundred years, until Alexander the Great rose to power.

Three Views of the Four Beasts in Daniel 7

There are three major viewpoints concerning the "four great beasts" prophecy recorded in Daniel 7. The most prevalent thinking among conservative expositors is the traditional view. Other perspectives include the contemporary and futuristic views. All three positions will be defined; however, due to space limitations, only a condensed version of the contemporary view will be presented in order to show how it fits the prophetic model of the four great beasts. (For a more detailed examination of the three views, go to www.raptureready.com.) In all three views, the fourth beast is considered to be the final kingdom on earth (Antichrist's kingdom) before Christ returns to set up His Kingdom, so the fourth beast will not be included in the discussion with the first three beasts, unless needed for emphasis.

The Traditional View: The first three beasts are ancient kingdoms that existed more than two thousand years ago. The traditional view of Daniel 7 holds that the four beasts in this chapter are the same kingdoms as the five kingdoms that make up the great image in Daniel 2. Those kingdoms are the Babylonian, Medo-Persian, Grecian, Roman, and Antichrist's.

The Contemporary View: The first three beasts are kingdoms/nations that are present in the world today. The contemporary view of Daniel 7 holds that the four beasts are all future kings (verse 17) and kingdoms that will arise after this prophecy was received by Daniel, and that all four beasts will be present on earth when Christ returns after the end of Daniel's seventieth week. Those kingdoms are England (also Great Britain and the United Kingdom), the United States, Russia, a "leopard kingdom," and Antichrist's kingdom.

The Futuristic View: The first three beasts are kingdoms/nations that will arise shortly before Christ's return. The futuristic view of

Daniel 7 holds that the four beasts are all future kingdoms that are yet to be determined. They will arise shortly before the fourth beast's kingdom (Antichrist's) and will be incorporated into Antichrist's kingdom as depicted by the leopard, bear, and lion composite beast in Revelation 13:2.

England, the United States, and Russia in Prophecy
The Contemporary View of Daniel Chapter 7

Could the United States be present in the prophetic Scriptures, and we have failed to identify correctly the lion with eagle's wings and the other creatures listed in Daniel's prophecy of the "four great beasts"? Not only does the evidence point to the presence of the United States (Dan. 7:4) in the book of Daniel, but the kingdoms and empires of England and Russia (Dan. 7:4 and 5) also appear to be represented as major powers during the end times (Rev. 13:1–2).

> Daniel spake and said, "I saw in my vision by night, and, behold, the four winds of the heaven strove upon the great sea. And four great beasts came up from the sea, diverse one from another. The first was like a lion, and had eagle's wings: I beheld till the wings thereof were plucked, and it was lifted up from the earth, and made stand upon the feet as a man, and a man's heart was given to it." (Dan. 7:2–4)

If God wanted the superpowers of England, the United States, and Russia to be represented in the Bible, and specifically in Daniel 7, how would He describe them and what code words or symbols would He use? From a human perspective, He would have to determine which kingdoms would be selected and the order in which He would bring these three kingdoms (empires) onto the world stage. He would also have to determine in advance what their national symbols would be and the proper order for their appearance. The symbols of the first great beast (the lion with eagle's wings) in Daniel 7 coincides perfectly with the symbols (the lion and the eagle) of the two great powers (England and the United States) that have dominated the world in commerce and military power for more than two hundred years. Did these historical events randomly happen, or did God orchestrate all these things and bring them about in order to show his power and glory (Isaiah 42:5–9)?

The Lion Dominates the World

England (the lion) was the world's leading commercial and military power during the nineteenth and early twentieth centuries (World War I), and the United States (the eagle) has taken over those roles from the mid-twentieth century (World War II) through the early twenty-first century. At its height, England was the largest empire in history. From 1815 to 1914, a period referred to as Britain's "imperial century" by some historians, Britain dominated commerce around the globe and was a formidable force on the oceans and seas, as it oversaw its numerous colonies throughout the world.[94] England could easily qualify as a great beast (the lion), with her vast empire reaching around the globe and covering more square miles of territory than any kingdom that has ever existed.

If God wanted to depict two great and diverse empires (kingdoms) that would be united in one super-kingdom but would later separate to form two super-kingdoms, how would He describe that scenario using twenty-five-hundred-year-old language like that found in the book of Daniel? Could it be possible that God would choose the kingdom of England (the lion) to be the dominant superpower that would give rise to a new, future superpower, the United States of America (the eagle), that would, in its formative years, rebel against British rule and be torn (as eagle's wings ripped from the lion) from the mother country (the Revolutionary War, 1775–1783)? The founding fathers of our country were compelled by necessity, and perhaps destiny, to form a new government (constitutional republic) based upon the human rights of the individual (the Declaration of Independence and the Bill of Rights) in a land of freedom and opportunity (government of the people, by the people, and for the people) that would prove to be a lighthouse of refuge for those seeking a new way of life.

The United States Adopts the Bald Eagle

On June 20, 1782, the American bald eagle was selected to occupy a prominent place on the Great Seal of the United States. A few years later, the bald eagle was nominated to become the nation's official bird when George Washington, the first president of the United States, took office on April 30, 1789.

> The first was like a lion, and had eagle's wings: I beheld till the wings thereof were plucked, and it was lifted up from the earth, and made stand upon the feet as a man, and a man's heart was given to it. (Dan. 7:4)

The eagle's wings (the United States) being plucked from the lion (England) during the Revolutionary War is perhaps an appropriate analogy of what happened when the United States was permanently separated from England at the treaty of Paris in 1783. The plucking of the eagle's wings from the lion and being made to stand upon the feet as a man was a vivid depiction of the formation of the United States government during the Revolutionary War (also the War of American Independence) and the years that followed.

If God wanted to portray the humanitarian efforts of America in the Bible in a way that was opposite to the nature of wild beasts, what symbol would He use? Perhaps the representation of our nation "as a man, with a man's heart given to it" would symbolize the benevolent nature of this country and the major role it has played in helping evangelize the world through the saving knowledge of Jesus Christ.

Spreading the "good news" message to all the other beasts on the earth (i.e., kings, rulers, peoples, multitudes, nations, and tongues) would change some of their beastly and stony hearts (those who rebel and harden their hearts), and they would receive a new heart from God (see Dan. 4:16, 5:21, 8:4; 2 Pet. 2:12; Jude 10; Titus 1:12; and Ezek. 11:19, 36:26).

The Eagle Dominates the World

The depiction of the eagle's wings being plucked from the lion and made to stand as a man, with a human heart given to it, is an accurate depiction of the United States' role in helping other nations during their time of need. America has not devoured other nations and taken their people and property like Babylon, the Medo-Persians, and the Grecian empires. We have provided more humanitarian aid to other countries during periods of emergency than any other nation (kingdom) in history.

When natural disasters such as earthquakes, tsunamis, hurricanes, tornadoes, floods, droughts, and pestilences have devastated other countries and territories, America has responded with billions of dollars in assistance and foreign aid to help feed the homeless, provide needed medicines and assistance, and help rebuild infrastructures. We have led the way in providing humanitarian aid to rebuild war-torn nations and help other countries, islands, territories, and provinces recover from natural disasters and other catastrophes.

The symbol God chose for the first beast in Daniel 7:4, the lion with eagle's wings, matches perfectly with the history of England and the United States. What is the probability that those two nations would randomly become the dominant global empires in the world since the early nineteenth century—and that the national symbols just happen to be the lion and the eagle? Or, could it be possible that England and the United States are fulfilling preordained roles that are setting the stage for God's sovereign plan for the end times, and their identities have been mysteriously cloaked (sealed up) in the lion and eagle symbols of the first beast in Daniel's vision?

The Decline of the American Empire

Bible prophecy teachers have taught for decades that there is no scriptural evidence that the United States will be present and involved with the last gentile government that will rule over "the whole earth" in "the end times" (Dan. 7:23). That presumption, however, does not exclude the U.S. from having an active, stage-setting role in developing many of the technologies and weapon systems that will be used during the end times.

Since America is the leading economic and military superpower in the world today and many of the end-time prophecies in the Bible are now taking center stage to be fulfilled before Christ's return, the decline of the American empire may be sooner than we think rather than later. The foundations of the United States are crumbling (Psa. 11:3) as the Supreme Court, Congress, and president race to destroy the Christian values and moral principles upon which this nation was founded. Why are America and the nations of the world madly pursuing a new world order that forsakes God and excludes Him from its deliberations and plans (Gen. 11:1–9, Psa. 2)?

If the eagle in Daniel 7:4 represents the United States and that animal is absent in the end-times prophecy described in Revelation 13:1–2, the role of America will have to diminish greatly before the global government system is fully implemented during Daniel's seventieth week. From a prophetic perspective, the United States is the leading candidate for the "sudden destruction" described in 1 Thessalonians 5:3 that takes place after the Rapture of all believers from the earth. If the U.S. (the eagle) ceases to be the dominant leader in the world due to the "sudden destruction" or other unforeseen cataclysms, Russia (the bear), with its large conventional army and vastly superior nuclear arsenal, will be poised to exert its influence and dominion throughout the world—especially in the Middle East and eastern European arenas.

The Big, Bad Bear Rises to Power

If the United States were, for some reason known only to God, removed overnight from its dominant position in the world, what nations would become the new leaders on the world scene? Economically, Japan, China, and Germany would, based upon the 2009 GDP (Gross Domestic Product—*CIA Factbook*). Militarily, Russia and China are at the top and are about the same strength in terms of conventional weapons; however, Russia greatly exceeds China's firepower when nuclear warheads are included in the comparison.[95]

> And behold another beast, a second, like to a bear, and it raised up itself on one side, and it had three ribs in the mouth of it between the teeth of it: and they said thus unto it, "Arise, devour much flesh." (Dan. 7:5)

In the absence of the United States, Russia would quickly fill the void as the world's top military superpower. Russia would hold a strategic, military advantage over other countries, and it could use intimidation and blackmail to push its global agenda. The increasing worldwide demand for oil to operate industry and commerce will be important factors in determining Russia's course of action and could be one of the "hooks" that pulls Russia into the Middle East for the Gog and Magog war (Ezek. 38:4). Russia would possibly focus on influencing the near Middle East, Africa, and Western nations, while China would concentrate on the far Middle East and eastern nations of Asia (kings of the east).

The Decline of the Russian Empire

Russia will make its fatal mistake when it comes down "upon the mountains of Israel" (Ezek. 38 and 39) to "take a spoil" and "take a prey." God will destroy most of the Russian army (Ezek. 39:2), and its role in world affairs will greatly diminish; however, Russia will continue to have a position of authority (dominion) during the end times, as indicated by the bear's presence in Daniel 7:12 and Revelation 13:2.

Russia's decreased military presence, after its defeat on the mountains of Israel, will give rise to a future, "leopard" kingdom (Dan. 7:6) that will dominate for a short time before the fourth beast (Antichrist's kingdom) rises to power and unites the leopard (third beast), the bear (second beast), and the lion (first beast) to form the multifaceted beast described in Revelation 13:1–2 that will "be diverse from all kingdoms, and shall devour the whole earth, and shall tread it down, and break it in pieces" (Dan. 7:23).

> And I stood upon the sand of the sea, and saw a beast rise up out of the sea, having seven heads and ten horns, and upon his horns ten crowns, and upon his heads the name of blasphemy. And the beast which I saw was like unto a leopard, and his feet were as the feet of a bear, and his mouth as the mouth of a lion: and the dragon gave him his power, and his seat, and great authority. (Rev. 13:1–2)

Do the Three Beasts Represent England, the United States, and Russia?

If God wanted to describe in a prophecy the major kingdoms that would rule over the earth during "the time of the end," how would He go about doing that with His prophets, who lived more than two thousand years ago and lacked many of the words and expressions we take for granted today? Perhaps God has already done that with the symbols of the lion, the eagle, the bear, and the leopard used in Daniel 7 and the leopard, the bear, and the lion used in Revelation 13.

Is it possible that the real identities of the first three beasts in Daniel 7 are England (the lion), the United States (the eagle), and Russia (the bear), and that the understanding of this prophecy has been "closed up and sealed" until the "end times" arrive (Dan. 12:8–10)? If the beasts described in Daniel (the lion, the eagle, the bear, and the leopard) and Revelation (the leopard, the bear, and the lion) have already arrived on earth and are "alive" and ruling over a portion of their "dominion" in the world today, we must be living during the time Daniel talked about, and we are beginning to see the unsealing of his book that was written for those living near "the time of the end."

A Plausible End-Time Scenario

The United States has entered into the most dangerous period of time since the Declaration of Independence was signed and the U.S. Constitution was adopted. The enemies of this country, however, are not coming from outside the borders of this great nation as in the past; rather, they are coming from the inside—much like what happened when the old Roman Empire collapsed. Numerous bad decisions made by the three branches of government (legislative, judicial, and executive) in recent years are beginning to take effect, and are jeopardizing the freedoms and protections this nation has enjoyed for more than two centuries. If America continues down the same path during the current decade, it will be difficult for this nation to recover from the moral and economic damage that has been done.

From his first day in office, U.S. President Barack Obama has been promoting the spread of Islam in America and around the world while taking action to marginalize and destroy the Christian heritage, morals, and values this nation was founded upon. Even though he has claimed to be a Christian, his speeches and actions have repeatedly promoted Islam and other world religions while ignoring and undermining the values and principles taught in the Bible. Should people believe what their current administration tells them, or should they believe what that administration is actually doing?

> Beware of false prophets, which come to you in sheep's clothing, but inwardly they are ravening wolves. Ye shall know them by their fruits. Do men gather grapes of thorns, or figs of thistles? Even so every good tree bringeth forth good fruit; but a corrupt tree bringeth forth evil fruit. A good tree cannot bring forth evil fruit, neither can a corrupt tree bring forth good fruit. Every tree that bringeth not forth good fruit is hewn down, and cast into the fire. Wherefore by their fruits ye shall know them. Not every one that saith unto me, "Lord, Lord," shall enter into the kingdom of heaven; but he that doeth the will of My Father which is in heaven. (Matt. 7:15–21)

The Blessing...or the Curse?

The most dangerous policy the United States has been following in international and foreign affairs is turning against Israel and trying to divide up its land—actions that are specifically forbidden by God in many Old Testament passages (see, for example, Gen. 22:15–18, Num. 6:22–27, Joel 3:1–2, and Zech. 12:1–3, 8–9). Ironically, America, who has in the past been Israel's closest ally, has been leading the way in this diabolical endeavor through so-called peace negotiations between Israel and the Palestinian people. This negotiating bloc of nations is called the Quartet (the United States, Russia, the United Nations, and the European Union). God told Abram (whose name was later changed to Abraham) that those who blessed Israel would be blessed and those who cursed Israel would be cursed:

Now the LORD had said unto Abram, "Get thee out of thy country, and from thy kindred, and from thy father's house, unto a land that I will shew thee: And I will make of thee a great nation, and I will bless thee, and make thy name great; and thou shalt be a blessing: And I will bless them that bless thee, and curse him that curseth thee: and in thee shall all families of the earth be blessed." (Gen. 12:1–3)

The demise of the United States could very well come as a result of the "peace and security" negotiations taking place with Israel and the Palestinians, which were prophesied by the apostle Paul in 1 Thessalonians 5:1–3 nearly two thousand years ago. The "sudden destruction" described in this verse is specifically aimed at the nations, groups, or entities promoting "peace and security" throughout the world—which includes the U.S.

For when they [the Quartet nations] shall say [in their public speeches and writings], "Peace and safety" [code words used by the Quartet promoting peace and security between Israel and the Palestinians]; then [in God's timing—immediately after the Rapture] sudden destruction [cataclysmic disaster] cometh [will be poured out] upon them [the Quartet nations], as travail [birth pangs] upon a woman with child [increasing in frequency and intensity]; and they [the Quartet nations] shall not escape [God's judgment]. (1 Thess. 5:3)

The Rapture and the Rapid Rise of Russia

Sandwiched between today's headlines and the return of Jesus Christ at the end of the age will be the most astonishing global catastrophe since the Flood of Noah's day. The Rapture of the church will be the most surprising and shocking event to occur worldwide in human history, and it will immediately separate the believers in Christ, who will be whisked away to heavenly pleasures, from the unbelievers, who will be left behind to face the consequences of a world gone mad that hates God and everything He stands for (Psa. 2).

The removal of the saints from this earth will take place just before the "sudden destruction" comes upon those who ignore God's clear warning signs (1 Thess. 4:13–18, 5:1–11). With all believers removed from the planet and the United States taken out of the way, a major paradigm shift will occur among the nations of the world that will usher in a new world order headed up by the Antichrist. After the U.S. (the eagle) is removed from its position of dominance, Russia (the bear) will arise and dominate the world scene. Events will then shift back to Europe, Asia, and the Middle East for the remaining events of the last days described in the Scriptures.

As we see many of the prophecies predicted in the Bible coming alive in our times, such as the return of Israel to its land after almost two thousand years of dispersion, the formation of a global government, the ability to number and track every person in the world, the development of the Russian and Islamic alliance, and the alignment of all the nations of the world against Israel, we should be watchmen on the wall (Ezek. 33:1–16) who are watching, warning, and winning others to Christ before "the great and dreadful day of the Lord" arrives (Mal. 4:5, 1 Thess. 4:13–18, 5:1–11).

These approaching prophetic events casting their shadows backward into our times serve as an early warning system reminding us that we should be getting our spiritual houses in order and taking care of the Master's business (Mark 13:33–37). That involves making sure we have trusted in Jesus Christ as our personal Savior so that whether we go up at the Rapture or die of natural causes, we will have made our "calling and election sure" (2 Pet. 1:10; Phil. 2:12).

Living During the Times of the Signs

The evidence is overwhelming that we are living during "the times and seasons" of the Lord's return. Believers are admonished to "watch...and be ready," as Matthew 24:42–51 tells us, and we should be informing our families and loved ones about what is happening in the world from a prophetic perspective. All of the signs of the times we see developing suggest that the Rapture is imminent and that we are approaching the day and hour set by God the Father (Acts 1:7) when we will "be caught up together...to meet the Lord in the air: and so shall we ever be with the Lord" (1 Thess. 4:17).

Although no sign is given in the Scriptures concerning the day and hour of the Rapture, some believe Hebrews 10:25 implies that we will be able to see the **day of the Rapture** (followed by the Day of the Lord) approaching: "Not forsaking the assembling of ourselves together, as the manner of some is: but exhorting one another: and so much the more, **as you see the day approaching**" (emphasis added). Anticipation of the approaching Rapture of God's saints seems to be implied in Luke 21:28: "And when these things begin to come to pass, then look up, and lift up your heads; for your redemption draweth nigh."

One of the rewards in heaven that we each can qualify for is the "crown of righteousness" the Lord will personally give all those who "love His appearing" (2 Tim. 4:8). Charles H. Spurgeon, famous pastor of the Metropolitan Tabernacle in London, described the spiritual mindset that should be present in those who are seriously watching for the Lord's return.

> While I am at work, my Master may come. Before I get weary, my Master may return. While others are mocking at me, my Master may appear; and whether they mock or applaud, is nothing to me, I live before the great Task-master's eye, and do my service knowing that He sees me, and expecting that

by-and-by He will reveal Himself to me, and then He will reveal me and my right intention to misrepresenting men. May the Lord keep you waiting, working, watching.[96]

It is "high time" for the saints of God to "wake up," "comfort one another," "exhort and edify one another," and "lift up our heads" as we see the day of "our redemption" drawing near (Rom. 13:11–14). Those who are not prepared and miss the Rapture will be in big trouble! Don't be one of them!

CHAPTER SEVEN

ABORTION

Blood Sacrifice to "Gods" of Planet Earth

By Joseph Chambers

T he aborting of unborn children is the darkest act of human existence. The Islamic terrorists who march around the world looking for ways to destroy all religions and governments that differ
from Islam are not any more vile than a mother who destroys her own
child in her womb. The pro-abortion doctors and liberal politicians in
our Western world who support this depraved industry might well be
judged by the Creator more seriously than the Islamic terrorists. How
did we descend to accepting the mindset that murdering an unborn
child is acceptable? Could this fall have started when we stopped saying "mother with child" and started saying "pregnant woman?" This
terrible tragedy of sacrificing millions of children cannot be understood without understanding Bible prophecy.

First, let's reflect on the sacred facts concerning a mother's womb,
and then consider some statements of what occurs during the act

of abortion.[97] We will limit the description to the most common methods.

The Sanctity of Life from Conception

Before we consider the methods of abortion, let's look at the ethical reality of childbearing and the sacred facts surrounding the establishment of life in a mother's womb. The Creator of this universe could speak each life into existence as He did with Adam and Eve and simply "eject" new people into our world. Instead, He made men and women His partners in multiplying and spreading the human family. While we are partners with God in many of His actions, such as bringing converts into the spiritual family, this alliance is especially unique: A husband and wife physically unite to plant a seed of life in a very safe location of the mother's body. This life, shortly after the egg is fertilized, becomes a separate entity from the mother and begins the physiological process of developing towards a self-sustaining existence. But miraculously, the womb of the mother is so sacred that the life inside instantly possesses an eternal soul as well. There can be no point in the child's development that a soul somehow "occurs"; this eternal soul can only be counted from conception.

To summarize: The Creator has given mothers and fathers the divine capacity to set a life—and soul—in motion. The womb of the mother is somehow similar to a "holy of holies," where the eternal existence of the child grows as the body to house the soul develops. To call this marvelous transaction anything but sacred is impossible. Understanding the Creator's grand design for human life and its extension of itself reaches far beyond just biological facts. To consider disrupting this holy process by invading the safe dominion of the mother's womb and mutilating the life within should be unthinkable. Whether the child lives or dies, the father and mother will face this soul in eternity. The biblical acts of our eternal existence do not allow for anything less. It is truly awesome.

Abortion Procedures in the Various Stages of Gestation

Now, with a firm grasp of the spiritual and biological realities of new life within a mother's uterus, we'll turn our attention to the infinitely more difficult-to-read-about topic of physically ending that life.

First Trimester

Abortion performed during the first trimester of a woman's pregnancy is usually carried out with a "manual vacuum aspiration." In some cases, an electric vacuum is used. A long, thin tube is inserted into the uterus and, when suction is created, the developing child is drawn out. Often, a tool called a curette is used in order to make certain that none of the baby's parts are left in the mother that would cause infection or require surgery.

A different procedure is necessary for an abortion performed between the sixth and fourteenth week of the pregnancy. Labeled a "suction curettage" method, it is described on the www.pregnancycenters.org Web site as the following:

> This is the most common surgical abortion procedure. Because the baby is larger, the doctor must first stretch open the cervix using metal rods. Opening the cervix may be painful, so local or general anesthesia is typically needed. After the cervix is stretched open, the doctor inserts a hard plastic tube into the uterus. He then connects this tube to a suction machine. The suction pulls the fetus' body apart and out of the uterus. The doctor may also use a loop-shaped knife called a curette to scrape the fetus and fetal parts out of the uterus. (The doctor may refer to the fetus and fetal parts as the "products of conception.")[98]

A third method of ending the life in a mother's womb during the first trimester is the administration of RU486 (Mifepristone) medication, also known as the "abortion pill."

This drug is only approved for use in women up to the forty-ninth day after their last menstrual period. The procedure usually requires three office visits. On the first visit, the woman is given pills to cause the death of the embryo. Two days later, if the abortion has not occurred, she is given a second drug which causes cramps to expel the embryo. The last visit is to determine if the procedure has been completed.[99]

Second Trimester

It is extremely evident that a second-trimester abortion—called dilation and evacuation (D and E)—is far more serious than a first-trimester abortion, and is certainly more dangerous for the mother. While the length of the pregnancy is reported using different time periods, the D and E is generally performed from thirteen to twenty-four weeks after conception. By this stage of pregnancy, the child has developed greatly, has a clear heartbeat, and bears all the marks of a person. Pictures of these babies after they've been aborted—either whole or in parts—are unbearable to look at. The following partly describes the procedure:

> This surgical abortion is done during the second trimester of pregnancy. At this point in pregnancy, the fetus is too large to be broken up by suction alone and will not pass through the suction tubing. In this procedure, the cervix must be opened wider than in a first trimester abortion. This is done by inserting numerous thin rods made of seaweed a day or two before the abortion. Once the cervix is stretched open, the doctor pulls out the fetal parts with forceps. The fetus' skull is crushed to ease removal. A sharp tool…is also used to scrape out the contents of the uterus, removing any remaining tissue.[100]

Third Trimester

A typical procedure performed during the third trimester is called dilation and extraction (D and X), also referred to as partial-birth abortion. These ominous terms should be enough to change the mind of a mother concerning the destruction of her child. This procedure may be used from twenty weeks into the pregnancy to full term (forty weeks). This is basically a three-day procedure that begins with the injection of medication into the baby's heart to stop it from beating. The abortionist must use an ultrasound to locate the heart for this process. During the first two days, there is a gradual enlarging of the mother's cervix by laminaria ("sticks of seaweed which absorb fluid and swell dilation"[101]). On the third day, the abortionist bursts and drains the amniotic sac, then uses the dilation and evacuation procedure to remove the child. Here is an excerpt from the www.americanpregnancy.org Web site describing what a woman undergoing the procedure can expect to happen to her unborn child once her water breaks:

> The fetus is rotated and forceps are used to grasp and pull the legs, shoulders, and arms through the birth canal. A small incision is made at the base of the skull to allow a suction catheter inside. The catheter removes the cerebral material until the skull collapses. Then the fetus is completely removed.[102]

More details about the stomach-turning procedure are explained in the following excerpt:

> Under the Intact D & X method, the largest part of the fetus (the head) is reduced in diameter to allow vaginal passage. According to the American Medical Association, this procedure has four main elements. First, the cervix is dilated. Second, the fetus is positioned for a footling breech. Third,

the fetus is partially pulled out, starting with the feet, as far as the neck. Fourth, the brain and material inside the skull [are] evacuated, so that a dead but otherwise intact fetus can be delivered via the vagina.

Usually, preliminary procedures are performed over a period of two to three days, to gradually dilate the cervix using laminaria tents.... Sometimes drugs such as pitocin, a synthetic form of oxytocin, are used to induce labor. Once the cervix is sufficiently dilated, the doctor uses an ultrasound and forceps to grasp the fetus' leg. The fetus is turned to a breech position, if necessary, and the doctor pulls one or both legs out of the birth canal, which some refer to as "partial birth" of the fetus. The doctor subsequently extracts the rest of the fetus, leaving only the head still inside the birth canal. An incision is made at the base of the skull, a blunt dissector (such as a Kelly clamp) is inserted into the incision and opened to widen the opening, and then a suction catheter is inserted into the opening. The brain is suctioned out, which causes the skull to collapse and allows the fetus to pass more easily through the birth canal. The placenta is removed and the uterine wall is vacuum aspirated using a cannula.[103]

What Must Our God Think?

Every leg, arm, or other body part torn from a baby's body in the process of eliminating an unborn child is recorded in God's great world of knowledge. Every fingerprint that sets apart a living soul is uniquely planned long before conception in the womb. No two fingerprints of all the billions created have ever been duplicated. The Creator, who uses a mother's womb as His workshop and her love as His partnership, has designed every part. At some time in His ageless past, He planned every soul and designed every life. He said, "All souls are mine." They may be torn from His heart, but they will never be removed from His knowledge.

The Holy Ghost inspired a clear statement of this fact. The Spirit said:

> For thou hast possessed my reins: thou hast covered me in my mother's womb. I will praise thee; for I am fearfully and wonderfully made: marvellous are thy works; and that my soul knoweth right well. My substance was not hid from thee, when I was made in secret, and curiously wrought in the lowest parts of the earth. Thine eyes did see my substance, yet being unperfect; and in thy book all my members were written, which in continuance were fashioned, when as yet there was none of them. (Psa. 139:13–16)

More beautiful words could never be written! Human life is not just another animal; evolution is the world's biggest lie! The Sovereign God has a plan for His human family, and no living soul is exempt. Every part of the physical body was designed by the Creator. He did not just create Adam and Eve and leave the rest of the world's population to the process of addition. Each living soul is uniquely designed and individually planned. Any other possibility defies common sense.

Jesus Christ was conceived by the Holy Ghost in Mary's womb (see Matt. 1:18 and Luke 1:35), and immediately His presence affected both Mary and others around her. Elizabeth and her son— six-months after conception—were filled with the Holy Ghost by the presence of Mary and her womb-borne "Savior and Deliverer" (see Luke 1:39–45). This kind of activity in the wombs of these mothers testifies to the glory of an unborn child! That our God would choose to send even His ONLY Son to redeem mankind by using His creative ingeniousness of a mother's womb forever proves the existence of life from conception. Jesus Christ is eternal, and there was no nine-month lapse in His conscious existence. He did not come to live on earth when He was born; He came when He was conceived by the Holy Ghost in Mary's womb.

The blood of every murdered baby is crying from the earth! Can you hear the moans of sorrow? The Heavenly Father can. When Cain killed Abel, the Father cried to this first murderer, "Where is Abel thy brother?" Cain answered back with a lie and an excuse, "I know not: Am I my brother's keeper?" Then, God spoke awesome words: "What hast thou done? The voice of thy brother's blood crieth unto me from the ground" (Gen. 4:9–10). The judgments of God are gathering like a pent-up storm that is soon to be unleashed. Blood, the innocent blood of the multitude of little ones who were never allowed to see the light of day, is crying…and God is listening.

All God asks of us is to weep in repentance and stand up in defense that we may end this sacrifice of our babies! Jeremiah said that "crying and sighing" was our duty in the face of every abomination of sin. If we will both "weep in repentance" and "stand in defense," our God will continue to raise up pastors and political leaders who will put their careers on the line for the unborn. *Roe v. Wade* has a death warrant that is being signed by the praying people of America. The anger and mindless actions of the liberals in America are a testimony that the death warrant against that landmark Supreme Court Decision of January 22, 1973, may soon be served.

The Guilty Church World

It seems impossible that those in our "church world" have allowed this to happen. Christian churches are in almost every part of America; their real estate value totals in the billions of dollars. Many ministers live in the comfort of an elite class, spending extravagantly on comfort, education, missions, social events, and advertisements. How and when did we forget the moral challenges of the entire Holy Bible? Jesus Christ was crucified because He disrupted the comfort of the compromised. He neither owned a camel to ride on nor had a bed to sleep on, but He stormed the gates of hell.

Dr. Francis Schaeffer said it perfectly in his book, *The Great Evangelical Disaster:*

> Accommodation, accommodation. How the mindset of accommodation grows and expands. The last sixty years have given birth to a moral disaster, and what have we done? Sadly, we must say that the evangelical world has been part of the disaster. More than this, the evangelical response itself has been a disaster. Where is the clear voice speaking to the crucial issues of the day with distinctively biblical, Christian answers? With tears we must say it is not there and that a large segment of the evangelical world has become seduced by the world spirit of this present age. And more than this, we can expect the future to be a further disaster if the evangelical world does not take a stand for biblical truth and morality in the full spectrum of life. For the evangelical accommodation to the world of our age represents the removal of the last barrier against the breakdown of our culture. And with the final removal of this barrier will come social chaos and the rise of authoritarianism in some form to restore social order.[104]

Sacrificing to the "Gods" of Confusion

As the church world has departed from separation from the world, the world's ways have captured the church. No one believed that allowing all the innocent-appearing compromises would culminate in the sacrifices of children in abortions, but it did and always does. The god of this world is never satisfied with partial worship; he wants our all. To give him an inch is the spiritual equivalent of giving him all, because that's his game. When we open the door, he then has right of possession.

The families of God have always lived in the midst of corruption and evil influences. It is impossible to escape the presence of sin and satanic powers as long as we are living on this side of the resurrection and final redemption. When Jesus prayed His pastoral prayer for the disciples, He framed that prayer to show our vulnerability.

> And now I am no more in the world, but these are in the world, and I come to thee. Holy Father, keep through thine own name those whom thou hast given me, that they may be one, as we are. (John 17:11)
>
> I have given them thy word; and the world hath hated them, because they are not of the world, even as I am not of the world. I pray not that thou shouldest take them out of the world, but that thou shouldest keep them from the evil. They are not of the world, even as I am not of the world. (John 17:14–16)

We are in the midst of absolute filth. Satan is the god of this world (2 Cor. 4:4). Our families stand in victory only when we live out the prayer in the above paragraph. We are *in* the world but not *a part of* it. There is absolutely no other way to build our Christian homes but by constantly standing vigil over their foundations and principles. As the children of Israel were traveling through the wilderness toward the Promised Land, the Lord warned them of these evil influences and what they would do to the houses of Jewish families:

> The graven images of their gods shall ye burn with fire: thou shalt not desire the silver or gold that is on them, nor take it unto thee, lest thou be *snared* therein: for it is an abomination to the LORD thy God. Neither shalt thou bring an abomination

into thine house, lest thou be a *cursed thing like it*: but thou shalt utterly detest it, and thou shalt utterly abhor it; for it is a cursed thing. (Deut. 7:25–26, emphasis added)

The families of the Lord must learn to abhor every semblance of evil and wickedness reflected on the ungodly side of the world system. When we translate the terms of the above Scripture into modern language, it paints a very clear picture. The phrase "graven images of their gods" easily reflects the gods of music and the vulgar dress that accompanies the music culture. The celebrity sports culture has permeated the American lifestyle until we put up with sports figures who are absolute moral perverts and stadiums that are nothing but big beer-and-gambling-party houses. We tolerate the utter desecration of the Day of the Lord, the day Jesus was resurrected and the day that was established as our Sabbath, yet most people treat it as a "holiday" rather than a "holy day." This powerful warning in Deuteronomy stated that the abominations of the world will make your home *a cursed thing* and would create a *snare* to your family. Ministries like Bill Gothard's, mine, and many others have documented how children and young people have been snared and led to rebellion by the presence of evil in the home. Movie star pictures on a bedroom wall; toys, games, and entertainment with witchcraft influence; and decorating or dressing in the attire of godless people, etc., will snare the lives of those who live under these abominations. We cannot take fire into our bosoms and not be burned.

It is impossible to name all the many items, expressions, and images that have come to represent the work of demon spirits in our culture. Secular television is saturated with the filth of immorality and pagan influences. A good part of recent Hollywood productions has used themes from varying religious ideas and heathen cultures. We cannot bring these snares into our homes without consequence.

God's warning to the ancient children of Israel is certainly a warning to our modern lives today as well. Satan's techniques have not changed. We are approaching his last effort at world control, and we're going to see evil manifested in an unparalleled fashion. Our homes must become places of spiritual light. Truth must be an open book so that our children are protected. Satan is like a cockroach: He hates the light and flees when it is made manifest.

Satan Always Wants Blood in the End

Our world has fallen so far from the truth of the Bible that the sacrifice of blood is the final price Satan demands. Some people think the church has recently turned away from the truth to this point of darkness, but we started at least fifty years ago. I remember hearing A. W. Tozer preaching here in Charlotte, North Carolina, about forty years ago. He stated that he had preached himself out of the pulpits of his own denomination. Can we grasp what has happened? It's almost impossible to believe that our churches say almost nothing about four thousand babies being aborted every day in America. Between the *Roe v. Wade* decision of January 22, 1973 and 3:30 PM on March 23, 2010—the time I completed writing this chapter—we have murdered 5,477,630 babies. Now, add four thousand for every day since that date. That is approximately one dead baby every twenty seconds.

In their book, *Entertaining Spirits Unaware,* authors David Benoit and Eric Barger stated:

> It is obvious that if we think that the "civilized world" is rid of such horrors [as sacrificing human lives], we need to think again. The spirit of Molech is alive and well in America today. Satan's desire to kill, steal, and destroy (John 10:10) is vividly displayed through both the emotional and physical acts of child abuse and the ultimate practice inspired by this horrific god/abortion. Abortion may not be carried out in consideration of an actual deity, but they are surely an act

of human sacrifice, taking life on the altar of convenience to appease the god of "self" and sexual promiscuity.[105]

No doubt abortion is an act of worship to the god of the "adamic nature." By birth, man's nature is capable of hideous actions, and when it is untaught and unchanged by divine grace, it normally descends deeper and deeper into vileness. I have often said that man does not have to be possessed by spirits or demons, but can digress to being a demon himself. If a holy angel can become a demon—and a multitude did—then a human can become of a similar nature.

The people of the nation Israel were God's chosen people, and they experienced great miracles of care and protection. Consider the Red Sea crossing, the Great Flood of water in the desert, and the fire that covered a mountain and left it burnt black until this present hour. Those are only three of a supernatural list. Yet, the Israelites turned from God to offer their children as sacrifices to the fire in worship of Molech. Listen to the prophet Jeremiah bemoan their descent into false worship to a vicious false god:

Because of all the evil of the children of Israel and of the children of Judah, which they have done to provoke me to anger, they, their kings, their princes, their priests, and their prophets, and the men of Judah, and the inhabitants of Jerusalem. And they have turned unto me the back, and not the face: though I taught them, rising up early and teaching them, yet they have not hearkened to receive instruction. But they set their abominations in the house, which is called by my name, to defile it. And they built the high places of Baal, which are in the valley of the son of Hinnom, to cause their sons and their daughters to pass through the fire unto Molech; which I commanded them not, neither came it into my mind, that they should do this abomination, to cause Judah to sin. (Jer. 32:32–35)

It is amazing how quickly human nature can turn from the miracles of a true faith and begin to worship false gods. As in the book of Acts, the apostle Luke warned us of this descent:

> Then God turned, and gave them up to worship the host of heaven; as it is written in the book of the prophets, "O ye house of Israel, have ye offered to Me slain beasts and sacrifices by the space of forty years in the wilderness? Yea, ye took up the tabernacle of Moloch, and the star of your god Remphan, figures which ye made to worship them: and I will carry you away beyond Babylon." (Acts 7:42–43)

Man is incurably idolatrous unless he is possessed of a vibrant faith and a disciplined will. A multitude of Americans are claiming to worship the God of biblical revelations and are worshipping Molech at the same time. I do not believe it is possible for Spirit-led believers to offer their unborn children on an abortion clinic altar. I shall not forget when my wife, Juanita, was carrying our children: Both of us would woo and whisper to these little ones growing in their sacred chamber. As the time of their birth drew near, we planned names and enjoyed every thought of their soon arrival. As my children grew into young adults, I would weep every time I thought of their departure from our home. They were absolutely dear to us from the moment their mother knew she was "with child." (Remember how all of us used to speak of pregnancy: "with child." It was unacceptable to say the word "pregnant" in public. Isn't it amazing how far we have come!)

Conclusion

We are saved by grace alone, but sin must be identified. One of the major problems in the church of America is that we have played down the effects of sin. The church world has done this in the name of grace. Since we are saved by grace and not by our righteousness, then sin is considered of little consequence. The modern way is to talk about grace, love, and positive things, and to leave off sin and the dark side of life. Satan loves this kind of thinking.

While we have watched the church world play this little game, sin has infiltrated our schools, our culture, our homes, and our churches. Just like Lot in Sodom, the righteous will survive and ultimately escape the impending judgment, but the web of evil that has ensnared our houses, our children, and our youth will still be in place. Those lives caught in this web (like Lot's family) will be the crowd that will not hear the warning of the judgment to come.

Let's sprinkle again our houses with Christ's blood as we remind our families that they must remain in the house to be protected. How do we sprinkle this blood? By faith! The Old Testament worshippers used a hyssop branch, but we live and act by faith. That blood is sprinkled as you trust Him only and cling to His cross with abandonment. We bring nothing to the altar of His sacrifice except total trust. Declaring ourselves helpless, we trust only in Him. We must teach this trust to our families over and over again.

CHAPTER EIGHT

END-OF-DAYS DEMONS
IN HIGH PLACES

By Thomas Horn

The English theologian George Hawkins Pember, in his 1876 masterpiece, *Earth's Earliest Ages*, analyzed the prophecy of Jesus Christ that says the end times would be a repeat of "the days of Noah." Pember outlined the seven great causes of the antediluvian destruction and documented their developmental beginnings in his lifetime. The seventh and most fearful sign, Pember wrote, would be the return of the spirits of Nephilim, "the appearance upon earth of beings from the Principality of the Air, and their unlawful intercourse with the human race."

Jesus Himself, in answering His disciples concerning the signs of His coming and of the end of the world, said it would be "as the days of Noe were" (Matt. 24:37). The implication is, just as it was before the Flood when the spirits of Nephilim were powerful upon earth (Gen. 6:4), mankind would experience an end-times renaissance of the influence of these entities. From Scripture we are made to understand the purpose of this latter-day wave of supernaturalism includes deception (2 Tim. 3:13), and the effect upon mankind would be so successful that heresy and delusion would become firmly entrenched—even within institutionalized Christianity. In writing of this scenario, Paul prophesied to Timothy that "in the latter times, some shall depart from the faith, giving heed to seducing spirits, and doctrines of devils" (1 Tim. 4:1).

Based on contemporary developments, the foretold increase in demonism and its influence within secular and religious society is rapidly unfolding in this century—abruptly, dramatically, and suspiciously. In a recent edition of *Prophecy in the News* magazine, biblical scholar Gary Stearman agreed, stating in disturbing language how the manifestation of these powers are quickening now because the world is under conditions "in which the influence of God's Holy Spirit is diminishing."[106] This is apparent not only in metaphysics, but within science and technology, where genetic engineering and transhumanist aspirations seem literally hell-bent on repeating what the Watchers did in giving birth to the spirits of Nephilim as in the days of Noah.

The First Time Nephilim Appeared on Earth

As far back as the beginning of time and within every major culture of the ancient world, the astonishingly consistent story is told of "gods" that descended from heaven and materialized in bodies of flesh. From Rome to Greece—and before that, to Egypt, Persia, Assyria, Babylonia, and Sumer—the earliest records of civilization tell of the era when powerful beings known to the Hebrews as "Watchers" and in the book of Genesis as the *benei ha-elohim* ("sons of God") mingled themselves with humans, giving birth to part-celestial, part-terrestrial hybrids known as "Nephilim." The Bible says this happened when men began to increase on earth and daughters were born to them. When the sons of God saw the women's beauty, they took wives from among them to sire their unusual offspring. In Genesis 6:4, we read the following account: "There were giants [Nephilim] in the earth in those days; and also after that, when the sons of God came in unto the daughters of men, and they bare children to them, the same became mighty men which were of old, men of renown."

When this Scripture is compared with other ancient texts, including Enoch, Jubilees, Baruch, Genesis Apocryphon, Philo, Josephus, Jasher, and others, it unfolds to some that the giants of the Old Testament such as Goliath were the part-human, part-animal, part-angelic offspring of a supernatural interruption into the divine order and natural development of the species. The apocryphal book of Enoch gives a name to the angels involved in this cosmic conspiracy, calling them "Watchers." We read:

> And I Enoch was blessing the Lord of majesty and the King of the ages, and lo! the Watchers called me—Enoch the scribe— and said to me: "Enoch, thou scribe of righteousness, go, declare to the Watchers of the heaven who have left the high heaven, the holy eternal place, and have defiled themselves with women, and have done as the children of earth do, and have taken unto themselves wives: Ye have wrought great destruction on the earth: And ye shall have no peace nor forgiveness of sin: and inasmuch as they delight themselves in their children [the Nephilim], The murder of their beloved ones shall they see, and over the destruction of their children shall they lament, and shall make supplication unto eternity, but mercy and peace shall ye not attain." (1 Enoch 10:3–8)

According to Enoch, two hundred of these powerful angels departed "high heaven" and used women (among other things) to extend their progeny into mankind's plane of existence. The Interlinear Hebrew Bible (IHN) offers an interesting interpretation of Genesis 6:2 in this regard. Where the King James Version of the Bible says,

"The sons of God saw the daughters of men that they [were] fair," the IHN interprets this as, "The benei Elohim saw the daughters of Adam, that they were *fit extensions*" (emphasis added). The term "fit extensions" seems applicable when the whole of the ancient record is understood to mean that the Watchers wanted to leave their proper sphere of existence in order to enter earth's three-dimensional reality. They viewed women—or at least their genetic material—as part of the formula for accomplishing this task. Departing the proper habitation that God had assigned them was grievous to the Lord and led to divine penalization. Jude described it this way: The "angels which kept not their first estate, but left their own habitation, he hath reserved in everlasting chains under darkness unto the judgment of the great day" (Jude 6).

Besides apocryphal, pseudepigraphic, and Jewish traditions related to the legend of the Watchers and the "mighty men" born of their union with humans, mythologized accounts tell the stories of "gods" using humans to produce heroes or demigods (half-gods). When the ancient Greek version of the Hebrew Old Testament (the LXX or Septuagint) was made, the word "Nephilim"—referring to the part-human offspring of the Watchers—was translated *gegenes*, a word implying "earth born." This same terminology was used to describe the Greek Titans and other legendary heroes of partly celestial and partly terrestrial origin, such as Hercules (born of Zeus and the mortal Alcmena), Achilles (the Trojan hero son of Thetis and Peleus), and Gilgamesh (the two-thirds god and one-third human child of Lugalbanda and Ninsun).

These demigods were likewise accompanied in texts and idol representation by half-animal and half-human creatures like centaurs (the part-human, part-horse offspring of Apollo's son, Centaurus), chimeras, furies, satyrs, gorgons, nymphs, minotaurs, and other genetic aberrations. All of this seems to indicate that the Watchers not only modified human DNA during the construction of Nephilim, but that of animals as well, a point the book of Enoch supports, saying in the seventh chapter that the fallen angels "sinned" against animals as well as humans. Other books such as Jubilees add that this interspecies mingling eventually resulted in mutations among normal humans and animals whose "flesh" (genetic makeup) was "corrupted" by the activity, presumably through crossbreeding (see 5:1–5; 7:21–25). Even the Old Testament contains reference to the genetic mutations that developed among humans following this time frame, including "men" of unusual size, physical strength, six fingers, six toes, animal appetite for blood, and even lion-like features (2 Sam. 21:20; 23:20).

But of all the ancient records, the most telling extra-biblical script is from the book of Jasher, a mostly forgotten text referred to in the Bible in Joshua 10:13 and 2 Samuel 1:18. Jasher records the familiar story of the fall of the Watchers, then adds an exceptional detail that none of the other texts is as unequivocal about, something that can only be understood in modern language to mean advanced biotechnology, genetic engineering, or "transgenic modification" of species. After the Watchers had instructed humans "in the secrets of heaven," note what Jasher says occurred: "[Then] the sons of men [began teaching] the mixture of animals of one species with the other, in order therewith to provoke the Lord" (4:18).

The phrase "the mixture of animals of one species with the other" does not mean Watchers had taught men hybridization, as this would not have "provoked the Lord." God made like animals of different breeds capable of reproducing. For example, horses can propagate with other mammals of the equidae classification (the taxonomic "horse family"), including donkeys and zebras. It would not have "provoked the Lord" for this type of animal breeding to have taken place, as God Himself made the animals able to do this.

If, on the other hand, the Watchers were crossing species boundaries by mixing incompatible animals *of one species with the other*, such as a horse with a human (a centaur), this would have been a different matter and may cast light on the numerous ancient stories of mythical beings of variant-species manufacturing that fit perfectly within the records of what the Watchers were accomplishing. Understandably, this kind of chimera-making would have "provoked the Lord" and raises the serious question of why the Watchers would have risked eternal damnation by tinkering with God's creation in this way. Yahweh had placed boundaries between the species and strictly ordered that "each kind" reproduce only after its "own kind." Was the motive of the Watchers to break these rules simply the desire to rebel, to assault God's creative genius through biologically altering what He had made? Or was something of deeper significance behind the activity?

Some believe the corruption of antediluvian DNA by Watchers was an effort to cut off the birth line of the Messiah. This theory posits that Satan understood the protoevangelium—the promise in Genesis 3:15 that a Savior would be born, the seed of the woman, and that He would destroy the fallen angel's power. Satan's followers therefore intermingled with the human race in a conspiracy to stop the birth of Christ. If human DNA could be universally corrupted or "demonized," they reasoned, no Savior would be born and mankind would be lost forever. Those who support this theory believe this is why God ordered His people to maintain a pure bloodline and not to intermarry with the other nations. When men breached this command and the mutated DNA began rapidly spreading among humans and animals, God instructed Noah to build an ark and to prepare for a flood that would destroy every living thing. That God had to send such a universal fiat like the Flood illustrates how widespread the altered DNA eventually became. In fact, the Bible says in Genesis 6:9 that only Noah—and by extension, his children—were found "perfect" in their generation. The Hebrew word for "perfect" in this case is *tamiym*, which means "without blemish" or "healthy," the same word used in Leviticus to describe an unblemished sacrificial lamb. The meaning was not that Noah was morally perfect, but that his physical makeup—his DNA—had not been contaminated with Nephilim descent, as apparently the rest of the world had become. In order to preserve mankind as He had made them, God destroyed all but Noah's family in the Flood. The ancient records including those of the Bible appear to agree with this theology, consistently describing the cause of the Flood as happening in response to "all flesh" having become "corrupted, both man and beast."

While I believe the theory of DNA corruption as an intended method for halting the coming of Christ has merit, an alternative or additional reason the Watchers may have blended living organisms exists in a theory I postulated in my book, *Apollyon Rising 2012: The Lost Symbol Found and the Final Mystery of the Great Seal Revealed.* In that book, I speculated that the manipulation of DNA may have had a deeper purpose—namely to create a hybrid form that neither the spirit of man nor God would inhabit, because it was neither man nor beast, and thus provided an unusual body made up of human, animal, and plant genetics known as Nephilim, an earth-born facsimile or "fit extension" into which the Watchers could extend themselves.

Signs of "the Days of Noah" in Modern Science?

I believe Watcher technology is echoed today in recombinant DNA science, where a transgenic organism is created when the genetic structure of one species is altered by the transfer of a gene or genes from another. Given that molecular biologists classify the functions of genes within native species but are unsure in many cases how a gene's coding might react from one species to another, not only could the genetic structure of the modified animal and its offspring be changed in physical appearance as a result of transgenics, but its sensory modalities, disease propensity, personality, behavior traits, and more could be changed as well.

Many readers will be astonished to learn that in spite of these unknowns, such transgenic tinkering is already taking place in most parts of the world, including the United States, Britain, and Australia, where animal eggs are being used to create hybrid human embryos from which stem cell lines can be produced for medical research. On

March 9, 2009, President Barack Obama signed an executive order providing federal funding to expand this type of embryonic research in the United States. Not counting synthetic biology, where entirely new forms of life are being brewed, there is no limit to the number of human-animal concoctions currently under development in laboratories around the world. A team at Newcastle and Durham universities in the United Kingdom recently announced plans to create "hybrid rabbit and human embryos, as well as other 'chimera' embryos mixing human and cow genes." The same researchers more alarmingly have already managed to reanimate tissue "from dead human cells in another breakthrough that was heralded as a way of overcoming ethical dilemmas over using living embryos for medical research."[107] In the United States, similar studies led Irv Weissman, director of Stanford University's Institute of Cancer/Stem Cell Biology and Medicine in California, to create mice with partly human brains, causing some ethicists to raise the issue of "humanized animals" in the future that could become "self aware" as a result of genetic modification. Even former president of the United States, George W. Bush, in his January 31, 2006, State of the Union address called for legislation to "prohibit...creating human-animal hybrids, and buying, selling, or patenting human embryos." His words fell on deaf ears, and now "the chimera, or combination of species, is a subject of serious discussion in certain scientific circles," writes Joseph Infranco, senior counsel for the Alliance Defense Fund. "We are well beyond the science fiction of H. G. Wells' tormented hybrids in *The Island of Doctor Moreau;* we are in a time where scientists are seriously contemplating the creation of human-animal hybrids."[108]

Not everybody shares Infranco's concerns. A radical, international, intellectual, and quickly growing cultural movement known as "transhumanism" supports the use of new sciences, including genetic modification, to enhance human mental and physical abilities and aptitudes so that "human beings will eventually be transformed into beings with such greatly expanded abilities as to merit the label 'posthuman.'"[109]

I have personally debated leading transhumanist Dr. James Hughes on his weekly syndicated talk show, *Changesurfer Radio*. Hughes is executive director of the Institute for Ethics and Emerging Technologies and teaches at Trinity College in Hartford, Connecticut. He is also the author of *Citizen Cyborg: Why Democratic Societies Must Respond to the Redesigned Human of the Future*, a sort of bible for transhumanist values. Dr. Hughes joins a growing body of academics, bioethicists, and sociologists who support:

> Large-scale genetic and neurological engineering of ourselves… [a] new chapter in evolution [as] the result of accelerating developments in the fields of genomics, stem-cell research, genetic enhancement, germ-line engineering, neuro-pharmacology, artificial intelligence, robotics, pattern recognition technologies, and nanotechnology…at the intersection of science and religion [which has begun to question] what it means to be human.[110]

While the transformation of man to posthuman is in its fledgling state, complete integration of the technological singularity necessary to replace existing Homo sapiens as the dominant life form on earth is approaching an exponential curve. In a *Reuters* article dated November 9, 2009, titled "Scientists Want Debate on Animals with Human Genes," just how far scientists have come and how far they intend to go was apparent. The news piece started out, "A mouse that can speak? A monkey with Down's Syndrome? Dogs with human hands or feet? British scientists want to know if such experiments are acceptable," and continued with revelations that scientists in Britain are comfortable now with up to 50 percent animal-human integration. The article hinted that not all of the research is being kept at the embryonic level and that fully mature monstrosities may be under study as "some scientists in some places may want to push boundaries." *National Geographic Magazine* predicted this in 2007 when it said that within ten years, the first transhumans would walk the earth. Legendary writer Vernor Vinge added recently that we are entering a period in history when questions like "What is the meaning of life?" will be nothing more than engineering questions. "Within thirty years, we will have the technological means to create superhuman intelligence," he told *H+ Magazine.* "Shortly thereafter, the human era will be ended."[111]

In preparation of the post-human (new Nephilim) revolution, Case Law School in Cleveland was awarded a $773,000 grant in April 2006 from the National Institutes of Health to begin developing guidelines "for the use of human subjects in…the next frontier in medical technology–genetic enhancement." Maxwell Mehlman, Arthur E. Petersilge professor of law, director of the Law-Medicine Center at the Case Western Reserve University School of Law, and professor of bioethics in the Case School of Medicine, led the team of law professors, physicians, and bioethicists over the two-year project "to develop standards for tests on human subjects in research that involves the use of genetic technologies to enhance 'normal' individuals."[112] Following this study, in 2009, Mehlman began offering university lectures such as "Directed Evolution: Public Policy and Human Enhancement" and "Transhumanism and the Future of Democracy," addressing the need for society to comprehend how emerging fields of science will, in approaching years, alter what it means to be human and what this means to democracy, individual rights, free will, eugenics, and equality. Other law schools, including Stanford and Oxford, have hosted similar "Human Enhancement and Technology" conferences, where transhumanists, futurists, bioethicists, and legal scholars have been busying themselves with the ethical, legal, and inevitable ramifications of posthumanity.

As the director of the Future of Humanity Institute and a professor of philosophy at Oxford University, Nick Bostrom (www. NickBostrom.com) is another leading advocate of transhumanism who, like the Watchers before him, envisions remanufacturing humans with animals, plants, and other synthetic life forms through the use of modern sciences. When describing the benefits of man-with-beast combinations in his online thesis, "Transhumanist Values," Bostrom cites how animals have "sonar, magnetic orientation, or sensors for electricity and vibration," among other extra-human abilities. He goes on to include how the range of sensory modalities for transhumans would not be limited to those among animals, and that there is "no fundamental block to adding, say, a capacity to see infrared radiation or to perceive radio signals and perhaps to add some kind of telepathic sense by augmenting our brains."[113]

Bostrom is correct in that the animal kingdom has levels of perception beyond human. Some animals can "sense" earthquakes and "smell" tumors. Others, like dogs, can hear sounds as high as forty thousand hertz—and dolphins can hear even higher. It is also known that at least some animals see wavelengths beyond normal human capacity. Incidentally, what Bostrom may also understand and anticipate is that, according to the biblical story of Balaam's donkey, certain animals see into the spirit world. At Arizona State University, where the Templeton Foundation is currently funding a series of lectures titled Facing the Challenges of Transhumanism: Religion, Science, Technology[114] transhumanism is consequently viewed as possibly effecting *supernatural,* not just physical, transformation. Called "the next epoch in human evolution," some of the lecturers at ASU believe radical alteration of Homo sapiens could open a door to unseen intelligence. As a result, ASU launched another study in 2009 to explore communication with these "entities." Called the SOPHIA project (after the Greek goddess), the express purpose of the study is to verify communication "with deceased people, spirit guides, angels, other-worldly entities/extraterrestrials, and/or a universal intelligence/God."[115]

Imagine what this could mean if government laboratories with unlimited budgets working beyond congressional review were to decode the gene functions that lead animals to have preternatural capabilities of sense, smell, and sight, and then blended them with Homo sapiens. Among other things, the ultimate psychotronic weapon could be created for use against entire populations—genetically engineered "Nephilim agents" that appear to be human but who hypothetically see and even interact with invisible forces.

While the former chairman of the President's Council on Bioethics, Leon Kass, does not elaborate on the same type of issues, he provided a status report on how real and how frightening the dangers of such biotechnology could imminently be in the hands of transhumanists. In the introduction to his book, *Life, Liberty and the Defense of Dignity: The Challenges of Bioethics,* Kass warned:

> Human nature itself lies on the operating table, ready for alteration, for eugenic and psychic "enhancement," for wholesale redesign. In leading laboratories, academic and industrial, new creators are confidently amassing their powers and quietly honing their skills, while on the street their evangelists are zealously prophesying a posthuman future. For anyone who cares about preserving our humanity, the time has come for paying attention.[116]

The warning by Kass of the potential hazards of emerging technologies coupled with transhumanist aspirations is not an overreaction. One law school in the UK where students are taught crime scene investigation is already discussing the need to add classes in the future devoted to analyzing crime scenes committed by posthumans. The requirement for such specially trained law enforcement personnel will arise due to part-human, part-animal beings possessing behavior patterns not consistent with present-day profiling or forensics understanding. Add to this other unknowns such as "memory transference" (an entirely new field of study showing that complex behavior patterns and even memories can be transferred from donors of large human organs to their recipients) and the potential for tomorrow's human-animal chimera issues multiplies. How would the memories, behavior patterns, or instincts, let's say, of a wolf affect the mind of a human? That such unprecedented questions will have to be dealt with sooner than later has already been illustrated in animal-to-animal experiments, including those conducted by Evan Balaban at McGill University in Montreal, where sections of brain from embryonic quails were transplanted into the brains of chickens and the resultant chickens exhibited head bobs and vocal trills unique to quail.[117] The implication from this field of study alone suggests transhumans will likely bear unintended behavior and appetite disorders that could literally produce lycanthropes (werewolves) and other nightmarish nephilim traits.

As troubling as those thoughts are, even this contemplation could be just the tip of the iceberg. One-on-one, interpersonal malevolence by human-animals might quickly be overshadowed by global acts of swarm violence. The possibility of groups of "transhuman terrorists" in the conceivable future is real enough that a House Foreign Affairs (HFA) committee chaired by California Democrat Brad Sherman, best known for his expertise on the spread of nuclear weapons and terrorism, is among a number of government panels and think tanks currently studying the implications of genetic modification and human-transforming technologies related to future terrorism. *Congressional Quarterly* columnist Mark Stencel listened to the recent HFA committee hearings and wrote in his March 15, 2009, article, "Futurist: Genes Without Borders," that the conference "sounded more like a Hollywood pitch for a sci-fi thriller than a sober discussion of scientific reality...with talk of biotech's potential for creating supersoldiers, superintelligence, and superanimals [that could become] agents of unprecedented lethal force."[118] George Annas, Lori Andrews, and Rosario Isasi were even more apocalyptic in their *American Journal of Law and Medicine* article, "Protecting the Endangered Human: Toward an International Treaty Prohibiting Cloning and Inheritable Alterations," when they wrote:

The new species, or "posthuman," will likely view the old
"normal" humans as inferior, even savages, and fit for slavery
or slaughter. The normals, on the other hand, may see the
posthumans as a threat and if they can, may engage in a
preemptive strike by killing the posthumans before they
themselves are killed or enslaved by them. It is ultimately
this predictable potential for genocide that makes species-
altering experiments potential weapons of mass destruction,
and makes the unaccountable genetic engineer a potential
bioterrorist.[119]

Observations like those of Annas, Andrews, and Isasi cause one to
wonder if this is not how the servants of Antichrist move with such
compassionless brutality in rounding up to destroy all who refuse to
receive the mark of the Beast.

Not to be outpaced in this regard by rogue fringe scientists or even
bioterrorists, DARPA (Defense Advanced Research Projects Agency)
and other agencies of the U.S. military have taken inspiration from the
likes of J. R. R. Tolkien's *Lord of the Rings,* and in scenes reminiscent of
Saruman the wizard creating monstrous Uruk-Hai to wage unending,
merciless war, billions of American tax dollars have flowed into the
Pentagon's Frankensteinian dream of "super-soldiers" and "Extended
Performance War Fighter" programs. Not only does this research envision "injecting young men and women with hormonal, neurologi-
cal, and genetic concoctions; implanting microchips and electrodes
in their bodies to control their internal organs and brain functions;
and plying them with drugs that deaden some of their normal human
tendencies: the need for sleep, the fear of death, [and] the reluctance
to kill their fellow human beings," but as Chris Floyd, in an article for
CounterPunch a while back, continued:

Some of the research now underway involves actually altering the genetic code of soldiers, modifying bits of DNA to

fashion a new type of human specimen, one that functions like a machine, killing tirelessly for days and nights on end... mutations [that] will "revolutionize the contemporary order of battle" and guarantee "operational dominance across the whole range of potential U.S. military employments."[120]

To illustrate how serious they are about this plan, DARPA included in its budget for 2011 funding for science that will lead to "editing a soldier's DNA."[121] The same budget provides $6 million for the creation of "BioDesign," a mysterious artificial life project with military applications in which DARPA plans to eliminate the randomness of natural evolution "by advanced genetic engineering and molecular biology technologies to produce the intended biological effect," the 2011 budget states. The language in this section of the report actually speaks of eliminating "cell death" through creation of "a new generation of regenerative cells that could ultimately be programmed to live indefinitely." In other words, whatever this synthetic life application is (*Wired* magazine described it as "living, breathing creatures"), the plan is to make *it* immortal.[122]

In keeping with our study, imagine the staggering implications of such science if dead Nephilim tissue were discovered with intact DNA and a government somewhere was willing to clone or mingle the extracted organisms to make Homo-Nephilim. If one accepts the biblical story of the Nephilim as real, such discovery could actually be made someday—or perhaps already has been and was covered up. As an example of this possibility, in 2009, blood was extracted from the bone of a dinosaur that scientists insist is eighty million years old. Nephilim would have existed in relatively recent times comparably, making clonable material from dead biblical giants feasible. The technology to resurrect the extinct species already exists, and cloning methods are being studied now for use with bringing back Tasmanian tigers, woolly mammoths, and other extinguished creatures. *National Geographic* also confirmed this possibility in its May 2009 special report, "Recipe for a Resurrection," quoting Hendrik Poinar of McMaster University in Ontario, an authority on ancient DNA who served as a scientific consultant for the movie *Jurassic Park*, saying: "I laughed when Steven Spielberg said that cloning extinct animals was inevitable. But I'm not laughing anymore.... This is going to happen. It's just a matter of working out the details."[123]

The ramifications of using science to revive extinct animals or Nephilim may also play a key role in the kingdom of Antichrist. This is because as interbreeding begins between transgenic animals, genetically modified humans, and species as God made them, the altered DNA will quickly migrate into the natural environment. When that happens (as is already occurring among genetically modified plants and animals), "alien" and/or animal characteristics will be introduced to the human gene pool and spread through intermarriage, altering the human genetic code and eventually eliminating humanity as we know it. This is what happened before the Great Flood, according to many theologians, and perhaps that has been the whole idea for the end-times as well—to create a generation of genetically altered "fit extensions" for the resurrection of underworld Nephilim-hordes in preparation of Armageddon.

Does a curious verse in the book of Daniel hint at this? Speaking of the last days of human government, Daniel said: "They shall mingle themselves with the seed of men: but they shall not cleave one to another, even as iron is not mixed with clay" (Dan. 2:43).

While Daniel does not explain who "they" that "mingle themselves with the seed of men" are, the personal pronoun "they" caused Chuck Missler and Mark Eastman, in their book, *Alien Encounters,* to ask: "Just what (or who) are 'mingling with the seed of men?' Who are these non-seed? It staggers the mind to contemplate the potential significance of Daniel's passage and its implications for the future global governance."[124]

Daniel's verse troubled Missler and Eastman because it seemed to indicate that the same phenomenon that occurred in Genesis chapter 6, where non-human species or "non-seed" mingled with human seed and produced Nephilim, would happen again in the end times. When this verse from Daniel is coupled with Genesis 3:15, which says, "And I will put enmity between thee and the woman, and between thy *seed* [*zera,* meaning "offspring," "descendents," or "children"] and her *seed,*" an incredible tenet emerges—that Satan has seed, and that it is at enmity with Christ.

We Have Entered the Days of Noah

Christians cannot review the abbreviated information in this chapter, or this book as a whole, without concluding that Satan is indeed engaged in an unprecedented conspiracy to revive supernaturalism such as existed in Noah's day. Though countless multitudes may never perceive them, these "principalities…powers…rulers of darkness…and spiritual wickedness in high places" (Eph. 6:12) form the unseen arena under which unregenerate mankind is currently organized. Within this demonic influence, scientists, politicians, philosophers, and even some preachers are being orchestrated within a great evil scheme toward an epic end-times event—the return of the days of Noah.

In more than thirty important biblical passages, the Greek New Testament employs the term *kosmos* describing the unseen government hard at work behind current earthly administrations. At Satan's desire, archons command this hidden, geopolitical sphere, dominating *kosmokrators* (rulers of darkness who work in and through their human counterparts) who, in turn, command spirits of lesser rank until every level of human government is touched by this influence. It is this dominion, not flesh and blood, that is building a world system under Satan's control (see Eph. 6). If we could see through the veil into this invisible world, we would find there an underworld sphere writhing with Nephilim anticipating their return (see Job 26:5).

In the same way the ancient records say Watchers traded military and occult knowledge for use of human biology, today's humanist scientific communities are striking a Faustian deal with the devil, whether they know it or not. This repeat performance by modern scientists to cross over the species barrier in direct violation of God's divine order is, in my opinion, the million-pound elephant standing at the center of modern prophecy research. It behooves the church to sit up, pay attention, and engage these issues while there is still time, as we are undoubtedly witnessing the unfolding of biblical prophecy in fulfillment of the days of Noah, the preeminent sign that the departure of the church is at hand.

CHAPTER NINE

MEDIA

Priests of Last-Days Madness

By Don McGee

T he perception that we are living in the last days of the church dispensation is commonly acknowledged by students of Bible prophecy whose interpretation of Scripture is literal. The greatest sign of that era is the reestablishment of the Israeli state in 1948. The increasing belligerency of the Arab consortium of nations against Israel, along with the growing isolation of that Jewish state among the nations of the world, makes it easy to see how the entire Gentile world is near the point of abandoning Israel to her enemies.

Add to that the growing proliferation of weapons of mass destruction by Communist and Islamic nations and the dramatic effort to acquire them by those who do not have them, and you have a world ready to fall headlong into a morass of armed madness—a situation that will eventually escalate into a showdown against God.

However, there is another sign indicating not only that the world is sliding down the slippery slope of full-blown rebellion against God, but that the Rapture of the church is imminent. That sign, somewhat blurry to the biblically untrained eye, is obvious to those who can see beyond the secular interpretation of current events. Not surprisingly, it has to do with the influence of media, its anti-God agenda, and the resulting spiritual, moral, and social degradation of Western culture.

Nothing influences this post-modern society as does the media with its extraordinary ability to deliver information, and to deliver it with a biased perspective. Karl Marx once said that religion is the "opium of the people,"[125] but that was long before the era of instant communication and video broadcasts. Should he be able to speak today, perhaps he might say dark-ages religion has been replaced by twenty-first-century media as the "opium of the people."

What makes the media so vital to modern culture? Quite simply, society is unable to function as quickly, efficiently, and effortlessly without it. But such convenience can also be an injurious thing when the impact it has on its society's value systems is negative. Unfortunately, the almost universal influence of modern media is that it distances man from his Creator.

Also, we must not forget another aspect of twenty-first-century media: the world of entertainment. Whereas the news media is expert at influencing people's opinions about current events, those in the entertainment industry are expert in directly influencing the way people act and react—that is, the way they live.

A Disclaimer

Before going farther, a disclaimer is in order. To avoid issuing a blanket indictment against all media, it must be said that some members of the media do not allow themselves to become tools of evil. From their corporate boards and officers to their field journalists and news anchors, their collection and analysis of news events is professional and reliable. Such organizations and their people do not always necessarily subscribe to the biblical worldview, but neither do they censure and discredit those who do. These, however, are the rare exceptions to twenty-first-century opinion-makers.

Ethical principles can, at times, be found in radio, TV, periodicals, and others sources of information. But even among sources that claim to have conservative scruples and a biblical worldview, there are those with slanted views who attempt to deceive and influence their audiences. To discern the difference between genuine and counterfeit teachers, writers, publishers, etc., people must compare their claims with the plain sense of the Bible, as did the noble Bereans (Acts 17:10, 11).

In addition to comparing a group's values to orthodox biblical doctrine, it is also advisable to investigate its attitude toward money. When organizations and individuals constantly ask for money, or when they refuse to issue a financial report, something could be very wrong. When it comes to using other people's money, integrity demands that there must be no hidden closets.

As part of the above disclaimer, it must be said that there are some entertainers, politicians, athletes, and other icons of power and success who decline to endorse any aspect of the anti-God agenda. Because they have biblical worldviews, they are faithful in marriage and ethical in business, and thus refuse to become involved in actions that dishonor God. These, too, are the rare exceptions to the way things are today.

The Obvious

With that stated, we now look at some things that are very obvious. First, the world is not becoming a better place to live, no matter the decades of humanist teaching and influence. The infamous Rodney King and his rather juvenile question during the 1992 Los Angeles riots—"Can we all get along?"—is in reality rhetorical and demands an obvious and strongly answered, "No, we cannot get along!"[126]

At least part of the reason for this is simple. The dog-eat-dog theory of evolution has so ingrained the last several generations that being our brother's keeper is often seen as being financially or professionally detrimental. In this modern secular world, it is more expedient to see other people as the enemy, or at the very least as potential competitors. Taking care of "number one" is each day's order of business, and since evolution essentially denies the existence of God, nobody has to worry about ethics or eventual accountability. Sure makes things easier that way.

On the international level, the world is not becoming more pacifist-oriented, and that is in spite of UN efforts, peace treaties, and conferences. If an unbiased observer were to objectively examine current world events, it would be clear that a potentially cataclysmic war of some kind is on the near horizon. It is evident that the saber-rattling of a number of third-world Islamic and Communist nations is escalating. With this escalation of fear-mongering and war talk, it is also clear that even third-rate demagogues are gaining access to the same arsenals of mass destruction as those of the superpowers. Of course, the frightening thing is that no one seems to be able to do much about it.

The second observation, and perhaps more alarming than the first, is the fact that an objective look at things also shows that the media is deeply involved in social engineering and the construction of collective conscience. It seems this is all happening with outright, in-your-face impunity. Historically, most powerful entities—both public and private—have been held to at least some degree of accountability, but the situation regarding media influence is different. It is basically free from all constraints, including those of conscience. The media in America, under the protection of the First Amendment, is able to support any agenda, good or bad, and it does so with very little accountability. Like it or not, the media is the most powerful mover and shaker in the entire world.

So, exactly what is the media?

Though the media is multi-faceted, the common denominator across the board is the influence each of its components has upon society. News outlets—including news magazines, radio, television, newspapers, Internet blogs, etc.—all affect their consumers and subscribers. If such influence were not present, no one would advertise goods and services through those media. In addition to news outlets, there are television programming, music, motion pictures, and other forms of entertainment available twenty-four hours per day, each day of the year. And, each of those facets of media wields a high level of influence on social mores.

Do the worlds of business and politics believe the media can influence consumers and voters? Without doubt they do! When a company spends $2.4 million on a thirty-second Super Bowl add or when a TV spot for the final *Seinfeld* program sells for $2 million,[127] we can conclude that somebody, somewhere, with a lot of money believes in media influence. And, they exploit it for maximum benefit!

Further, those who wish to sell products or impose an ideology upon others understand the power of celebrity status. Entertainers and athletes are paid vast sums of money to endorse particular products or services. Some product manufacturers pay to have their products and logos seen in movies, even if the appearance is brief and benign. However, if that same product is worn, drank, smoked, driven, eaten, or in any way part of a popular actor's character on the screen, the value of the appearance is further enhanced. A good example of this was the instant popularity of the Pontiac Trans Am sports car after the very high-profile role it had in the 1977 movie *Smokey and the Bandit.*[128]

The American media has been referred to as the "fourth branch of government" because some consider its influence to be not very different from that of the constitutional triad of civil government—that is, the executive, legislative, and judicial branches. This kind of influence did not come into its own until the latter part of the twentieth century. Only then did politicians fully realize how they could exploit press releases, news conferences, political speeches, fact-finding trips, etc., to their advantage. It is obvious much of the exploitation seen in media today is actually a misrepresentation of the truth, but that does not matter. As long as the politician benefits from the positive image shown to his or her constituency, the effort is deemed successful. The important thing was, and is, the ability to influence the voter. And when it comes to influence and public image, any good politician understands that perception is more important than fact.

This unofficial, yet very revealing, name given to the media is based upon the belief that the media's responsibility to the public is "essential to the healthy functioning of the democracy."[129] When the founding fathers incorporated freedom of the press into the First Amendment to the U.S. Constitution, they established a means by which government actions could be made public and private opinions could be published without fear of government retaliation. Though the authors of our Constitution could not imagine twenty-first-century technology, the basic principle of an unhindered media was the idea.

The ultimate benefit of the media is contingent upon its integrity. Said another way, if that which is published is sound and proper, then the public can make sound and proper decisions. The state of life of the consuming public is based upon the truth and validity of what is presented by the media. Various elements of society make crucial decisions with long-range consequences based upon the information they receive from various media outlets; when that information is slanted or distorted, the result is dysfunction. Society then becomes diseased and impaired and reproduces itself with ever-increasing flaws. At some point down the line, social structure falls apart because its pillars become rotten to their cores. Those pillars include morality, civil government, education, etc., and today people with the biblical worldview can see that they are catastrophically compromised.

The basic purpose of media is to inform, and the responsibility of news outlets is to present facts to their subscribers without bias. The interpretation and application of those facts is supposed to be at the discretion of the user. This, of course, is the ideal, and is a rare state of affairs today.

The fact of the matter is that it is very difficult to find news sources that are totally free of biased opinions. At the very least, many sources construct the delivery of news and information in such a way as to guide, even subliminally, the viewer's conclusion. It is in this way that the media becomes a powerful propaganda tool.

The same can be said for the entertainment media. Its original purpose was to entertain, using wholesome means to give people some temporary respite from the often-difficult challenges of labor, raising families, and contributing to the stability and welfare of their communities, villages, towns, and cities. That noble purpose has been replaced with a less-than-noble agenda by powerful social and political engineers who have no scruples whatsoever about the broken lives and lost souls they leave in their wake. They understand that a society that is spiritually, and thus morally, crippled is one easy to control and exploit.

In most every society, mass media is the most effective vehicle for propaganda and its propaganda value is in direct proportion to the gullibility, ignorance, and *laissez-faire* attitude of the targeted masses. There is hardly any end to the influence the media can have when people choose to have no convictions regarding the issues governing the day. One of the best examples of this is what happened in Nazi Germany under the heavy hand of Dr. Joseph Goebbels.

Goebbels was a powerful and persuasive orator, a strong anti-Semite, and Adolf Hitler's minister of propaganda. Though his PhD was in eighteenth-century romantic drama, his real expertise was in the field of propaganda. He practically invented the type of propaganda that is sometimes called "the big lie." That is, if a lie is sufficiently outrageous and is repeated many times, the masses will eventually believe it.[130] Goebbels controlled both the German press and the entertainment industry, and he used them to turn the "final solution" plan into the actual "final solution" effort. His use of media-delivered propaganda worked very efficiently in the Nazi attempt to turn the collective German public's opinion against its Jewish neighbors and friends, as initially seen in the 1938 pogrom against the Jews called *Kristallnacht*, or "Night of Broken Glass." That was the beginning of the end of any sense of official acceptance of Jews in Germany.

Satan's Use of Modern Media

With a tool so effective, let there be no doubt that Satan has used, and is using, all forms of media to their fullest. There is no means so effective at molding public opinion as the media, and the fact that the media is willing to be involved in the spiritual and moral manipulation of Western culture just makes it easier. There are several battlefronts Satan is exploiting in his untiring effort to destroy everyone and everything connected to God, and each of them is served to a gullible public by some form of media. Further, it seems there are those with special expertise in each category who work tirelessly in order to influence anyone who might cross their paths.

Think about the modern assault against God by the secular world. Satan, who appears as an "angel of light" (2 Cor. 11:14), has used the secular media to deceive the spiritually immature. Whether it is TV, movies, the news, the Internet, periodicals, or radio, etc., he is assaulting and corrupting the minds of people at every opportunity.

How is he doing this? He is using the same tactic he used against Eve in Genesis 3:1; he causes his target to question what God has said. To Eve, he said, "Yea, hath God said, 'Ye shall not eat of every tree of the garden?'" To modern man he says the same thing, but the critical issue today is not about a food prohibition. It is usually about something like fornication, abortion, homosexuality, or the Bible.

Just as the speaking serpent was not a repulsive, slithering snake when he approached Eve in the Garden of Eden, Satan does not use outwardly abhorrent means to reach people today. Rather, his tools of choice are revered and popular celebrities. Consider three examples.

Walter Cronkite

The first example has to do with an event that happened more than forty years ago. It regards a February 1968 editorial by the venerable Walter Cronkite concerning the Tet Offensive during the Vietnam War. After soundly defeating the Communist enemy in every major battle during the Tet Offensive, and after killing more than forty-five thousand of their troops, Cronkite was able to put a negative spin on the American victory in a simple thirty-second broadcast.[131] Though many believe his conclusions were inaccurate, his comments are believed to be largely responsible for turning public opinion away from U.S. involvement in the war and demanding withdrawal. Of course, the North Vietnamese took note of this weak spot in American resolve and exploited it completely.

How could one man command so much influence? The answer is in two parts. First, Walter Cronkite was considered by most in America as the epitome of objective journalism. That role was amplified by his characteristic grandfatherly voice and his patient demeanor. Who, the country might have asked, can issue an accusation against such a fine, mannerly gentleman? Because of his kind demeanor and convincing delivery, anyone who would find fault with him was looked upon with disdain, as one might look upon a vagabond barging in on a group of refined ladies celebrating high tea.

The second reason for Walter Cronkite's influence with the American public was his effective use of mass media. Cronkite and his colleagues of the 1970s were on the cutting edge of rapid visual communication. The Vietnam War was the first to be brought into American living rooms each evening at six o'clock. Nothing like this had ever been seen before. By the use of television and audio/visual reports from the battlefield, American viewers became enamored with the news and impressed with this seemingly kind and knowledgeable newsman delivering it. By exploiting this somewhat emotional connection, the national media-beast created an aura whereby viewers surrendered their own ability to discern things and adopted the views of the one doing the reporting. This surrender of personal insight and judgment had little to do with facts and much to do with emotional appeal and some warped sense of consolation offered by Cronkite. The result was the eventual end of American involvement in Southeast Asia.

Ellen DeGeneres

The second example has to do with a current moral issue and a popular celebrity who is deeply involved in it. Who better to convince women that lesbianism is socially, morally, and spiritually acceptable than Ellen DeGeneres (especially when she uses Oprah Winfrey as a very willing prop when delivering the message)?[132] Not only does Ellen DeGeneres appear nicely dressed and professionally styled from head to toe, but every effort is made to present her in a wholesome light in spite of her sexually perverted, lesbian lifestyle. The idea is for her down-home, all-American, girl-down-the-street persona in the television studio to somehow void the shadowy, twisted immorality in her soul as she delivers her message on how a lesbian relationship can be as loving, fulfilling, and socially acceptable as that between a man and a woman.

That God flat-out condemns such perversion without regard to cultural context is not relevant to the social engineers and their media conduits. The fact that for millennia every civilized society has condemned it is not relevant either. The goal is to take perversion, dress it up, and present it to a spiritually and morally crippled society while blurring the ultimate and very real consequences of a culture that has been infected with the pathogen of amorality.

The goal is for members of the viewing audience to come away with a dangerous question in their minds: How can something that appears so loving and that it endorsed by someone so celebrated be so wrong? In essence, the media and its celebrity puppets bring God's commandments into question, and the intended conclusion is that if it feels so good, then it just has to be right. This teaches people, especially young people, that what makes a choice right or wrong completely depends upon one's personal desires, not upon the antiquated commands of God, which can be ignored with impunity. The edge Satan has in this particular attack through the media is that it is easy to instill upon people just about any corrupt ideology if they are without a biblical foundation.

Kathy Griffin

Look at one more example. This one demonstrates just how far the anti-God crowd has gone. No doubt the sewer-bottom of such blasphemous behavior happened on September 15, 2007, when Kathy Griffin—actress, stand-up comedian, militant atheist, and homosexual/lesbian rights advocate—in her Creative Arts Emmy award acceptance speech said, "Now, a lot of people come up here and thank Jesus for this award. I want you to know that no one had less to do with this award than Jesus. He didn't help me a bit." [133] Griffin then used a blasphemously vulgar description of a salacious act to express her contempt for Jesus Christ.

On that night, Griffin's notoriety came together with a high-profile media event to become a grand slam for those anti-God activists determined to undermine any semblance of public decorum and respect. How many up-and-coming actresses and comedians took note of this performance and chose to put it into their own repertoire? Is there any way to calculate how many young people were impressed with the "humor" of her statement while never pausing to consider its blasphemous nature and the eventual consequences?

That is a powerful case in point because it lends itself to the establishment of a godless path a person might take for life, one that will inevitably end in the lake of fire. The bottom line is that this anti-God hate message could never have been delivered so effectively without the means of media and the luminary who gave it a "respectable" human face.

———•———

In the Old Testament, the Levitical priests functioned as mediators between God and His people, in essence giving human support to God's divine order. It was not that God needed any man's validation. Rather, it was about the encouragement offered when the priests stood before the people and said, in a manner of speaking, "Yes, what God has commanded is good!"

The popular icons of the modern media have become somewhat like those Old Testament priests—certainly not like them regarding concern for God and His commandments, but like them in that they stand between two entities. With great fanfare, they introduce the warped practices of this new system of godlessness and offer their personal and full endorsement to the applause and acceptance of the spiritually ignorant masses listening to their every word.

After pouring every form of filth and degradation possible into our homes via TV, music, movies, periodicals, and news commentaries, the entertainment elite present their supportive views and recommendations to millions of people just waiting for such an endorsement. You see, when someone of celebrity status vouches for a particular ideology, it goes a long way in reducing guilt (if there is any conscience at all) and provides what is hoped to be a credible excuse just in case there might happen to be a day of accountability sometime in the distant future. The subtle lie implanted into evil hearts is that God, if there even is a God, understands how these things work and makes allowances for those whose choices were at the recommendation of celebrated others. Besides that, what loving God would send people to hell anyway?

The Modern Public Education System

At this point, we need to briefly consider another somewhat modern means of influencing human thinking that has become a type of media in itself: the modern public education system. Public education has not always been so rife with anti-Godism. However, the growing wave of early twentieth-century secularism began to have its impact by the middle of the century. In 1962, prayer was removed from public schools, and by the next year the Bible was also thrown out. Many of us can testify to the fact that serious problems began when God was "dismissed" from the classroom.

Why was the classroom chosen as the battlefield for the hearts and minds of America's children? It is all about getting children when they are very young, when their windows of learning are wide open, and then implanting into their minds secular and godless ideology without the kids having to "unlearn" anything having to do with God. This is made very easy because it happens to coincide with the very time parents are often wrapped up in career-building plans instead of being attentive to their children's developing sense of right and wrong. This time in their lives offers the best opportunity for creating the next generation of secularists and is the premier means of social reconstruction.

Think about it: Each school year, children spend almost two hundred days sitting in public school classrooms being told what to believe—mostly by teachers who have no concern whatsoever for the biblical values system. Considering the fact that most children are seldom, if ever, exposed to Bible teaching (either in a church setting or under the in-home tutelage of their parents), they go into classrooms with open minds susceptible to the theory of evolution, same-sex education, multi-cultural studies, American history revisionism, and a host of other curricula whose purpose is to establish religion-neutral kids who will grow up to be godless adult secularists.

From the home-front perspective, the parental attitude is often that of apathy. As long as the school keeps the kids several hours each day and prepares them to get into a public university, many parents are not the least concerned with what worldview their children adopt. Additionally, many modern parents want their teens to be sexually savvy so that sufficient precautions can be taken to prevent a somewhat embarrassing situation coupled with an expensive abortion procedure. It is easier that way, you see.

The priests of the modern public education media are non-Christian classroom teachers, and especially the cadre that trains those same teachers. Educators with graduate degrees and post-graduate degrees in education are generally involved in college and university classrooms and are more deeply immersed in the humanist philosophies of John Dewey[134]—"the father of American education" and an original signer of the Humanist Manifesto in 1933[135]—and others of his ilk.

The Church Media

We live in what could be called the "image generation," and this has spilled over even into what could loosely be called "the church." Worship is now largely defined as performances by singers and their bands whose obvious purpose is to draw attention to themselves. Sermons too often are now feel-good messages that have titles with the words "Three Steps to…" or "The Key to Positive…". Rarely are sin and judgment mentioned because those are negative terms. Many modern preachers no longer declare the immutable word of God from pulpits, but stand on massive stages dressed in overpriced Armani suits. Their presentations are supported by digital enhancements, orchestrated programs, and expensive props as they talk about what amounts to disgusting cultural drivel.

In many churches, the people in the pews or chairs are no longer referred to as "the congregation," but as "the audience." And often, the preachers "perform" by trying to outdo the other guys. In fact, some preachers are no longer known as heralds, but as celebrities.

The world of the media is so all-encompassing that even the church is now part of it. Though the church (a somewhat loose term in this context) might not condone immorality in its official meetings, that same church does precious little to take a stand against it. The result is that a form of silent endorsement is given by the media-church, and this gives a de-facto approval to that which God disapproves.

Conclusion

Where would anti-Godism be without the modern media? No doubt it would be alive and well in every strata of society, but not with the degree of acceptance it enjoys today. It would be lurking in the shadows of cheap, back-alley dives and brothels, and would be seen in those movies clandestinely produced, marketed, and viewed. But, it would not enjoy such obvious acceptance by so many people. Business leaders and administrative supervisors would recognize the negative impact such conduct has upon families, relationships in a work environment, and productivity. Prime-time television would not be open to the blasphemous words and sexual antics of philanderers, home wreckers, sexual deviants, and other strains of moral reprobates. Entertainment awards ceremonies would be fit for family viewing.

Further, while it has become in vogue to portray most every form of religious degeneracy in a favorable light in the media (all in the name of political or social correctness), seldom, if ever, is Christianity treated with the same forbearance. In the media, American Indian shamans, Buddhist monks, Hindu priests, Moslem imams, Wiccan high priests, etc., are not simply to be held in high regard, but in higher regard than Christian leaders. Television sitcoms and comedians make derogatory jokes and disparaging comments about Christians and their belief system, but nothing of the kind is said about idolatrous pagans.

Of course, all this anti-Christian bias is denied—but with thinly veiled smiles. Acting as if they are shocked by such charges, some secularists take loud issue with the accusations that liberal political and social correctness are the reasons for so much Christian-bashing. On the surface, the accusations are dead on, for Christians are indeed viewed as social and intellectual Neanderthals deserving of disaffection.

From another perspective, anti-Christian hatred is not solely based upon moral support for secular political and social attitudes. The real reason for the anti-Christian bias is pure, unadulterated hatred for God, His people, and the Bible. Just the mention of Jesus is hateful to many in the secular world. The word "Jesus" is far more than just a mere word, or even a mere name. It is the Name that infuriates the unseen dimension of demonic activity that plagues this world that is so shackled by the bonds of the evil one. The reason for this deep, primeval hatred is the clear fact that the demons know that this very same Jesus will one day judge them for their rebellion and sentence them to the infernal regions for all eternity without recourse (Matt. 8:29).

Yet there is a bright spot! In the study of this intensely wicked and open war upon all things Christian, one ray of hope is plainly visible: the indisputable fact that the church's departure is imminent. It is not simply "soon," for that implies it won't happen now, but in the near future. The word "imminent" is a far better word to express the moment in which we are living.

Never before have things been so homogenized. That is, historically, all things that have pointed to the great cataclysmic events on the near horizon have stood independently. That's no longer the case. Every godless current event is now part of a deceitful end-times scenario wherein each loses its distinctiveness in order to come together in a single homogenous blend that declares these are the last days. Call it synergism, in which the total effect is greater than the sum of the effects when taken separately. Technology is no longer simply about technology; entertainment is no longer simply about entertainment; apostasy is no longer simply about apostasy. They have all come together with a single focal point—the disparagement of God.

He, being God, has characteristically orchestrated their blasphemous mockery into a brilliant, flashing sign that boldly declares for the entire world to see, "The Rapture is imminent!"

Amen.

Come, Lord Jesus.

CHAPTER TEN

TURNING TO FABLES

The Emergent, Laodicean Church

*For the time will come when they will not endure sound doctrine;
but after their own lusts shall they heap to themselves teachers,
having itching ears; And they shall turn away their ears from
the truth, and shall be turned unto fables.*

2 Tim. 4: 3, 4

By Alan Franklin

There are more than 450,000 churches in America.[136] Many other nations are littered with buildings people call churches. Yet the Western world is in a moral and spiritual mess, spiraling to destruction. Many churches are not giving clear moral guidance or making a difference in society; they are not being salt and light to a sin-sick world.

The apostle Paul predicted that in the time prior to the return of our Lord, biblical doctrine would not be favorably received. Even so, churches are often full, their parking lots are packed, and their TV ministries are watched by millions. What do many of these churches stand for, other than the gospel of success? If the church stands for nothing, it will fall for anything—and it has.

"Easy-believism" has replaced hard truth as "prostitutes"—men and women for whom the Word is the way to great riches—preach in numerous pulpits. There has been a great falling away from the fundamental truths of Christianity. In fact, the very word "fundamental" has acquired a bad reputation (even though all it means to Christians is belief in the essential truths of the Bible). Many bishops and ministers deny the foundation of our faith: the virgin birth, the atoning death of Christ, and His resurrection. A counterfeit Christianity has much of the church in its grip today.

In our book, *Goodbye America, Goodbye Britain,* my wife, Pat, stated the following:

> Alan and I were once accused of being "fundamentalists" by someone trying to smear us. I took it as a compliment, a badge of honor, the only one I'm ever likely to get and the only one I want. A Christian fundamentalist is one who believes that the Bible is the Word of God, one who tries to follow Jesus. It has nothing to do with politics.[137]

The fundamental beliefs of born-again believers include the following tenets:

- The Bible was inspired by God, and Scripture is inerrant (true, without error). It is the Maker's "manual"—God's Holy Book not only telling us how He created everything and how it will all end, but also showing us how we should live.
- The Lord Jesus was born of a virgin. He is fully God and fully man. The death of the Lord Jesus on the cross atoned for our sins. We are saved by faith in Him alone, not by any good works.
- The Lord Jesus died, was buried, and rose again.

- The miracles of our Lord were historical realities.
- The Lord Jesus Christ will literally return in glory to reign on this earth for a thousand years.

Many Christians object to the last point; however, we cannot compromise on the literal truth of the Bible—even on the parts that are unpopular today. Truth divides, whereas ecumenism—the coming together of the lukewarm, Laodicean church from many different denominations—is leading to the formation of the united, "great whore" church of Revelation 17.

Catholicism Leading the Way

There is a move towards global religion matching the coming-together of governments, world regions, the world's money, and big business. Leading this false religion will be the pope, because numerous—formerly Protestant—denominations have declared that they either acknowledge him as head of the church or are prepared to work with Catholics, burying centuries of discord. The Roman Catholic Church, the only church with embassies and diplomats around the world, will for a time work hand in glove with the coming world government.

Many prominent media personalities, often those beloved of the "right," are Catholics. The world admires these attractive announcers, as well as the beautiful Catholic buildings and the respectful behavior of the huge crowds that gather at the Vatican. Everyone, it seems, likes being associated with wealth and success, but they don't realize that they are simply being "softened up" for the end-times deception that is almost upon us—the deception that will compel everyone to choose between worshipping the Antichrist and being executed (see Rev. 13:15).

Pat, who was raised as a Roman Catholic, points out that Catholics are already worshipping the communion wafer, believing that Jesus is mystically present in the object. The Bible tells us repeatedly not to worship anything man-made, so this is pure idolatry. If people can be persuaded to kneel down and worship a little white wafer as if it were God, how will they avoid venerating the one the Bible calls the "man of sin"? If you are part of a church that meets in a building featuring statues and religious objects, you might prayerfully consider whether to come out of it; you might be in the wrong church. The roots of some churches of this sort are in the pagan worship of ancient Babylon. The ancient pagans were physically scattered by God when He confused the language at Babel. Now, both religious and political Babylon are being rebuilt—primarily in Europe, but also in America and elsewhere. The great "whore church" of Revelation is being created right before our eyes, and it crops up in unexpected situations and places. Alongside it is the New Age movement, which also has its roots in Babylonian mysticism.

Ecumenism

Despite these obviously evil influences, there is a vast movement today to bring churches together in the spirit of ecumenism. In most towns of the West, true and false churches come together as if they had everything in common, even though they share only the name "Christian." In our book—*Cults and Isms: True or False?*[138]—my wife and I go into great detail about false faiths and the true gospel, and we stress that you should investigate the people you choose to follow; they just might be leading you over a spiritual cliff.

Clearly, doctrine divides. Catholics, Methodists, Presbyterians, Anglicans, and Baptists cannot *all* be right. If we join together to march, which "Jesus" are we marching for? If homosexual priests are "right," then the Bible is wrong. If priests must be celibate, then the Bible is in error. (All believers are said in 1 Peter 2:9–10 to be members of "a royal priesthood, a holy nation, a peculiar people…which in time past were not a people, but are now the people of God.") If the Bible is fallible, why follow it? We might as well follow a cookbook and brew up our own unholy stew.

I would say that most Christians today follow this ecumenical line, criticism of which gets us charged with being unloving and having a critical spirit. God is not pleased when light aligns with darkness in pseudo-unity, so churches together can pray to a god of their own imagination. Remember, the Lord our God is a holy God, and His doctrinal truths are not to be compromised. In ages past, saints were martyred for refusing to compromise on biblical truth, and the same thing is happening in the third world today.

The Emergent Church

One movement bringing a mishmash of mysticism and Catholicism into the mainstream Protestant churches is the emergent church (something from which Christians need to "emerge"!). It appeals to those who favor sensory experiences, altars, statues, pictures, incense, candles, and vestments. In other words, it is the road back to Rome via contemplative spirituality.

Roger Oakland, founder of Understand the Times, gave two insightful addresses to our church in England on the emerging church movement. He has written a book about the subject, *Faith Undone,*[139] and on the author's notes posted on his Web site, he states:

> In the not-too-distant future, most evangelical pastors will have to decide whether to support or reject the spirituality behind the emerging church. If this movement continues unfolding at the present pace, mainstream Christianity will be completely restructured, and the biblical gospel of Jesus Christ will be considered obsolete....
>
> Sad to say, the emerging church is far more than a fleeting fad and much more than the complaints of a group of young leaders. It is indeed a *new way of being Christian* and its objective is to usher in a new reformation throughout the world.

Those who refuse to embrace this direction will be considered spiritual oddballs who are hindering a unified one-world spirituality that is promoted as the answer for peace.… Behind this new kind of worship, this new kind of church is a strategic apostasy and maneuver by the prince of this world, the enemy of our souls, to literally take apart the faith of millions—it will be nothing less than faith undone.[140]

Emerging church leaders speak approvingly of getting wisdom from a Trappist monk and a Buddhist monk, and they even favor getting insights into Jesus from an Eastern perspective.[141] The apostle Paul said:

I marvel that ye are so soon removed from him that called you into the grace of Christ unto another gospel: which is not another; but there be some that trouble you, and would pervert the gospel of Christ. But though we, or an angel from heaven, preach any other gospel unto you than that which we have preached unto you, let him be accursed. (Gal. 1:8)

Prosperity Gospel

Let's turn to the money making tub-thumpers, the name-it-and-claim-it brigade that preaches the false prosperity gospel and pollutes the airwaves from many a godless TV channel. Pat and I know them well. When we were younger and less discerning, we shoveled thousands of dollars at them, for we believed that surely these were men and women of God. We now know that "through covetousness shall they with feigned words make merchandise of you" (2 Pet. 2:3). Pat wrote the following under the heading "The Sheep Are Being Fleeced" in *Goodbye America, Goodbye Britain*:[142]

When we warn Christians about specific people, sometimes their jaws literally drop as they realize the famous men they think are so wonderful are nothing more than charlatans. Please investigate the people you follow! Don't be gullible! The bad guys (and sometimes women) are building their bank balances on your hard-earned money. Type their names into a search engine after the words "critics of." See what their critics are saying about them. The good guys have critics too. But may God grant you the discernment to see through that. Not all the false teachers are rich—they only wish they were, and they are trying their best to get you to give, give, give. To them!

Here's one pretty good indicator—do they constantly harp on about giving? Is it always in their sermons and talks? Do they brag about money? Then stop following them. Let them spend their own money on their television programs, etc.—you keep yours. The good guys would rather die than enrich themselves from the preaching of the gospel.

God's Word to the Wise about Wealth

Does God really want us to become rich? Here is what His Word says about the matter of wealth; these are some good quotes with which to confront the "money" preachers:

- "My kingdom is not of this world" (John 18:36).
- "It is easier for a camel to go through a needle's eye, than for a rich man to enter into the kingdom of God" (Luke 18:25).
- "The love of money is the root of all evil: which while some coveted after, they have erred from the faith, and pierced themselves through with many sorrows" (1 Tim. 6:10).
- "Go to now, ye rich men, weep and howl for your miseries that shall come upon you. Your riches are corrupted, and your garments are moth-eaten. Your gold and silver is cankered; and the rust of them shall be a witness against you, and shall eat your flesh as it were fire. Ye have heaped treasure together for the last days" (James 5:1–3).

- "Having food and raiment [clothing], let us be therewith content" (1 Tim. 6:8).
- "Lay not up for yourselves treasures upon earth…for where your treasure is, there will your heart be also" (Matt. 6:19, 21).
- "How hardly shall they that have riches enter into the kingdom of God!" (Luke 18:24).
- "Set your affection on things above, not on things on the earth" (Col. 3:2).
- "This know also, that in the last days perilous times shall come. For men shall be lovers of their own selves, *covetous*" (2 Tim. 3:1–2, emphasis added).
- "Labor not to be rich" (Prov. 23:4).

Pat has pointed out that it's important to obtain "a good Bible commentary like William Macdonald's *Believer's Bible Commentary*, which clearly explains the truth behind Scriptures that are twisted by today's 'miracle men.' Deceivers," she says, "are taking Scripture out of context and using it in ways the Lord never intended. Most believers today have never had a good grounding. They need a good basic course in the Bible, not a once-a-week bless-up about success and prosperity."[143]

Performance Church

Hypnotic rock music, falsely labeled "Christian," sets the mood in many outwardly successful churches today. Too many become pale parodies of rock concert halls when "charismania" sweeps in. Hey, man, it's "performance church." Loud rock music is heard in many Sunday services, with the beat encouraging people to get up, fling themselves about, and lose their inhibitions. In fact, having inhibitions and not wanting to leap about wildly was almost considered a sin in one church Pat and I attended where people were encouraged to get up and start dancing. Those who did not were said to be "standing on their dignity." I remember one Sunday when I refused to take off my shoes and socks after a woman announced that we were standing on "holy ground" and should remove our footwear. Those of us who stayed shod were considered by others there to be "missing the move of the spirit," or even "quenching the spirit." Some spirits—not the Holy Spirit—need quenching! Like so many others, we had become enmeshed in the charismatic movement. Needless to say, we left that church many years ago.

We are told by God's Word to come out of the world, not to conform to it. When the church tries to ape the world, it looks foolish, like a middle-aged vicar joining in a youth club rock dance. Shortly after I became a Christian, my wife and I took my mother along to a so-called Christian outreach at Guildford Civic Hall in the county of Surrey, England. I was astounded to see a full rock group line up on stage, complete with massive sound system. Oddly enough, I had once been in a successful Guildford-based rock group billed as "Surrey's top group." The scene of many a Primevals' (that was the name of our group) triumph had been at this venue. I had played the drums on that stage scores of times at New Year's Eve dances and so forth. The setting was familiar to me. The sounds were familiar, too. It was just like any other "rave night" at the Civic, with lots of noise, teenage couples lying together on the floor and shouting out to each other, and a general air of raucous licentiousness.

The three of us were in the front row, and the sound level was so shattering that I don't really think Mother ever quite realized what was going on. She certainly wasn't saved that day. Who could have been? This is not the way the world will ever turn to Christ.

Music has a powerful effect. So-called evangelist Todd Bentley of Fresh Fire Ministries used hypnotic rock music to pull in and excite the crowds at his extended pseudo-revival in Lakeland, Florida, in 2008. When an obvious buffoon like Bentley struts around on stage flaunting his tattoos—and bellowing "Bam!"—you wouldn't think it would take much discernment to realize that the antics are not of

God. But you would be wrong. Gullible Christians flocked to view this disgrace for more than six months—and those of us who "dared" to point out that these fiascos were not scriptural were criticized.

Another minister who has used rock music in his presentations is Rick Warren, arguably the best-known Christian in the west. Zondervan—the publishing company for his best-selling books, including *The Purpose-Driven Church* and *The Purpose-Driven Life*— is owned by media mogul Rupert Murdoch, who publishes sleazy newspapers like the *Sun* and *News of the World* in Britain, owns major Internet gaming sites, and serves as chairman of News Corporation, which features porn channels on one of its associated networks. (Although it does not own these channels in Britain, it provides them with a platform.)

According to Warren, he is Murdoch's pastor. An article on World Net Daily states:

> Author-pastor Rick Warren is under fire for failing to discipline media giant Rupert Murdoch for owning and expanding pornographic channels for satellite TV. The Australian-born owner of Fox Broadcasting and cable TV networks isn't a member of Warren's twenty-thousand-member Saddleback Church, but Warren is on record as claiming to be Murdoch's pastor.[144]

Rick Warren's Global Peace Plan

On Sunday, April 17, 2005, Warren launched a so-called global peace plan to enlist "one billion foot soldiers for the kingdom of God." According to Let Us Reason Ministries and many other sources,[145] in a talk that day given to thirty thousand people in Anaheim, California, the man dubbed "America's pastor" announced what he called the "most important series of messages" ever taught in twenty-three years at Saddleback Church. The plan he outlined is designed to change the world; eradicate poverty, disease and ignorance; and overcome spiritual emptiness and self-serving leadership. He called the plan no less than a new reformation...a reformation of purpose: "what the church does in the world."[146]

The Let Us Reason report continued:

> [Warren] believes [the peace plan] will herald in a new worldwide spiritual awakening in the twenty-first century. But before he made the announcement, he decided to have some fun and surprised the audience when he said: "I've always wanted to do this in a stadium." He then sang Jimi Hendrix's hit song, "Purple Haze." As the audience erupted into laughter, the church band joined in playing back-up to it.
>
> "Purple Haze" is...about an LSD trip.... Frankly, I find the song quite revealing and fitting for what Warren has been doing. Sometimes God shows us what is under the surface. [It's] amazing that people would approve of this as he launched his plan to change the world.
>
> [Warren] then went on to unveil and outline the PEACE Plan: "Our goal will be to enlist one billion foot soldiers for the Kingdom of God, who will permanently change the face of international missions to take on these five 'global giants' for which the church can become the ultimate distribution and change agent to overcome: spiritual emptiness, self-serving leadership, poverty, disease, and ignorance (or illiteracy)," he said.[147]

The above statements are not in accordance with what the Bible teaches about the end times, nor with reality. Jesus warned of earthquakes, disasters, famines, and disease hitting the earth with increasing frequency. Far from influencing the world, true Christians are hated, despised, and flung into jail—or worse. The reality is an apostate church, led—in the case of the Anglican community—by a druid!

(The Archbishop of Canterbury was inducted as a druid in a centuries-old Celtic ceremony in August, 2002.)[148] Eastern religions are sweeping the world, together with militant Islam. "Taking the world for Christ" is a California daydream. The concept is not prophesied anywhere in the Bible—but then, Rick Warren thinks that the study of prophecy is a distraction from sharing our faith. Dominionist-inclined Christians have some reality checks coming their way. Perhaps Murdoch could commission a book on this?

Mega churches like those that follow the Purpose-Driven program don't like to be negative, so hell, judgment, repentance, and sin are not likely to be mentioned. The jargon, in fact, calls sinners "pre-Christian people." This "seeker-friendly" approach shows a church in love with the world. Yet Christians are told by God through His Word to come *out* of the world and take the church *into* the world—not the other way around. Until sin is acknowledged, there can be no redemption and no future hope for tens of millions of lost souls who think they are saved by "going to church."

In an article reprinted on our Web site, www.thefreepressonline.co.uk, author and talk radio host Jan Markell said this of Warren and his "purpose":[149]

> On July 5, the *Washington Times* online reported that Pastor Rick Warren told his Islamic audience, the Islamic Society of North America (ISNA), that he envisions "a coalition of faith." Whether Pastor Warren knows this or not, this is just another term for the coming one-world religion outlined in Revelation 13. It is further outlined in Revelation 17. I have not taken on the issue of Rick Warren all that often, but after reading what the *Washington Times* has to say about his message to a group of spiritually lost Muslims, I feel I must address this in an open letter to the man many say is the most influential pastor in America and some would say the world.

Pastor Warren, you pleaded with eight thousand Muslim listeners on Saturday, July 4, to work together to solve the world's greatest problems by cooperating in a series of interfaith projects. You said, "Muslims and Christians can work together for the common good without compromising my convictions or your convictions." Pastor Warren, you needed to compromise the convictions of the Muslims in attendance. To just say that "My deepest faith is in Jesus Christ" was not enough to a thoroughly lost crowd. The hour is too late to withhold a gospel message without which they will face a Christless eternity, and you will be held accountable. The "world's greatest problems" will always be with us and the Bible says so in Matthew 26:11. Sin is at the root of them. I have to conclude you are more interested in ecumenical unity and solving AIDS, poverty, and other social issues.

Miracle Men

As for the big-name Word of Faith/prosperity gospel/miracle men, the Bible has them pegged: "They speak great swelling words of vanity, they allure through the lusts of the flesh" (2 Pet. 2:18). Beware of their "wonders," especially when they make people fall down "under the power of the spirit." Remember, we are warned about lying signs and wonders. I know there is power in the occult; I was involved in it. Those who litter the floors of their churches with heaps of prostrate people are using occult power, whether they know it or not. Eastern gurus have always done this: A former Hindu, descended from a long line of witch doctors in Nepal, told me that they do exactly the same. This is Satan making fools of Christians at gatherings like the Toronto Vineyard fiasco that began in January 1994. Avoid such lunacy! Remember that deception is a major sign of the end times, and the Lord warned about it several times in Matthew 24, which summarizes end-time conditions.

Fast-Food Faith

While some churches are going mad, others hold services that are just plain short. To get congregants in and out fast, the worship leaders serve up a quick hymn sandwich, a prayer, announcements, and a little homily about doing good—and those in attendance are out the door in time to beat the lunch crowds at local restaurants. I lived near one denominational church where the Sunday service—taught, if that is the word, by a woman minister—was completed within the hour. In the foyer of the building was a poster advertising a yoga class. This is not a church that can withstand false teaching, let alone the power of Antichrist with his lying signs and wonders.

Pat and I touch on many false faiths in our book, *Cults and Isms: True or False?* As a result, I am often accused of being negative or worse. After a recent talk I presented on the end times, I was challenged by a man in attendance who said the message was nothing but doom and gloom—and too depressing. He wanted something to cheer him up—a positive message. Perhaps he had come from one of the churches teaching that a church triumphant will somehow "Christianize" the world and present it gift-wrapped so our Lord can come back and rule. The Bible teaches the exact opposite: There will be apostasy, deceit, and a great falling away. Men's hearts will grow cold. But God is in control, with His hand on the helm of history, and He has a wonderful future worked out for those who love Him. The King—and the Kingdom—are coming!

The Blessed Hope

The book of Revelation is actually incredibly positive...but only if you are a Christian. It describes how the present world will end, when the one who created it returns in triumph to rule and reign, bringing us—His saints—with Him. Christians through the ages have looked forward to this time, the time of the return of our "blessed hope."

Oddly enough, as we actually move into the end times that are prophesied, fewer churches bother to teach on the amazing events that are drawing near.

We are in exciting times, and momentous things are already happening. The pending Rapture gives us a sense of urgency. Knowing the signs of the times, we must get right with God—and encourage others to do so. In Revelation, the only book of the Bible that promises us a special blessing, Christ says: "And behold, I am coming quickly. Blessed is he who heeds the words of the prophecy of this book" (22:7). About a third of the Bible was prophetic when written, and around 90 percent of the prophecies have already come true. We now look to the final, climactic time when the last ten percent are revealed as true predictions.

Maranatha!—Come, Lord Jesus!

CHAPTER ELEVEN

ARMIES OF APOCALYPSE ARISE

By Phillip Goodman

Have you asked Jesus Christ into your life to be your personal Savior? Right now is the time, for the Russian-Islamic invasion of Israel is imminent and the time is short. The Bible predicts in Ezekiel 38–39 that a massive Russian and Muslim force will invade Israel in the last days. There is strong biblical support that the Russian-Islamic invasion of Israel is the stage-setting event for the end-time Tribulation. And there is scriptural evidence that the invasion is in fact imminent! Ezekiel writes:

> Thus saith the Lord God; "Behold, I am against thee, O Gog, the chief prince of Meshech and Tubal: And I will turn thee back, and put hooks into thy jaws, and I will bring thee forth, and all thine army...thou shalt be visited: in the latter years thou shalt come into the land that is brought back from the sword, and is gathered out of many people, against the mountains of Israel.... Thou shalt ascend and come like a

storm, thou shalt be like a cloud to cover the land, thou, and
all thy bands, and many people with thee.... And thou shalt
come up against my people of Israel…it shall be in the latter
days, and I will bring thee against my land…and I will rain
upon him, and upon his bands, and upon the many people
that are with him, an overflowing rain, and great hailstones,
fire, and brimstone." (Ezek. 38:3–9, 16, 22)

Ours is the first generation ever to be in prime position to see
the prophecy of "Gog, of the land of Magog" launch forth from the
pages of the Bible and from the northernmost regions of the earth.
Jesus said that when these things "begin," He is near. Are you ready
to meet Jesus?

A Probable Scenario

Ezekiel's prophecy offers the prospect of an amazing scenario involving a series of events that frames the climax of human history for this
current age. What makes this scenario credible is that it will answer
one of prophecy's most perplexing questions, one that has puzzled
prophecy watchers for years: How will it be possible for the Jews to
rebuild the Third Temple on the site now occupied by the third-most-
holy shrine in the Muslim world, the Mosque of Omar—also called
the Dome of the Rock?

Here is a probable event schedule of how the Russian-Islamic
invasion of Israel will set the stage for the end of the age and the
Tribulation Period leading to the return of Jesus Christ:

1. Russia and the Middle Eastern Islamic nations will realize that
the security of Israel, believed to be impenetrable by the Israelis, can
be breached.

2. Russia will then lead a massive coalition of multinational forces
to invade Israel in the wake of the "peace" agreement. In defense of
Israel, God will miraculously destroy the Russian-Islamic allied forces.

3. The reaction in Israel by many Jews will be a new faith in Messiah Jesus. And there will be a recognition from the nations that Israel's God has acted and resides in their midst.

4. Most in the nations will "know that [God is] the LORD," (Ezek. 38:23) but without true faith (Rom. 1:21). The Antichrist will be one of those. He will muster the world's support and demand that peace be made for Israel and the Temple be rebuilt on its original site. The decimation of the Muslim nations as a result of their participation in the Russian invasion will negate any opposition they raise to the rebuilding of the Temple on the site now occupied by the Dome of the Rock.

5. The Antichrist will then rise to his moment of destiny and proclaim the divine right of the Jews to rebuild the Third Temple. He will strike a seven-year "peace" covenant and order the rebuilding to begin. The Tribulation will commence at that point.

The Land of Magog, and Many Nations With You

Who are the people and nations that will invade Israel? How do we know the leading nation will actually be Russia? Some Bible scholars have used the linguistic science of etymology to tie the terms "Rosh" (Ezek. 38:2 NAS and NKJV) with Russia, and "Meshech" and "Tubal" with Moscow and Tobolsk, two of the principal cities of modern-day Russia. But the strongest evidence is to be found in the phrase "the land of Magog":

1. The first-century Jewish historian Josephus wrote that Magog (Noah's grandson through Japheth) was the forefather of the Scythians. "Magog founded those that from him were named Magogites, but who are by the Greeks called Scythians."[150]

2. The Scythians settled in Russia in the lands surrounding the Black and Caspian seas and constituted one of the tribal ancestors of today's Russians.

[The Scythians] remained lords of the Russian steppe from the seventh to the third century BC.[151]

Modern Russians sometimes call themselves Scythians.... No doubt some of the old Scythian stock was absorbed[152]....

Historical references confirm that during the sixth century BC, the Scythians actually dominated the land that was later to become Russia.[153]

3. Therefore, one can accurately read Ezekiel 38:2 as Gog of "the land of Magog, which is the land of Scythia, which is the land of Russia."

From the Remote Parts of the North

There is more evidence that Russia is the lead nation because we read that "thou shalt come from thy place out of the north parts" (Ezek. 38:15; i.e., "far, extreme, uttermost north").

In biblical geography, Jerusalem is directionally at the center of the nations. In other words, all nations radiate outward from Jerusalem in various directions like spokes on a wheel: "Thus says the Lord GOD, 'This is Jerusalem: I have set it in the midst [center] of the nations and countries that are round about her'" (Ezek. 5:5). Israel is "the people that are gathered out of the nations...that dwell in the midst of the land" (Ezek. 38:12; Luke 24:47).

The land of Magog is said in Ezekiel 38:15 to be situated "out of the north parts" (remote parts of the north). Russia is caught squarely on the needle of the compass here—the hard facts of the global grid locate Moscow directly to the far north of Jerusalem.

Furthermore, the time frame for the rise of the Russian state to superpower status has paralleled the birth of the state of Israel. This cannot be a historical "coincidence." Russia is the lead nation in Ezekiel's vision of the latter-day invasion of Israel.

Being out of the remote north, the Russians will, of course, follow a path south to Israel. And today that path is being charted, secured, and prepared. Russia has already acquired two ports in Syria, the country immediately north of Israel. Syria is a Muslim nation. So is Turkey, which is the next country just north of Syria. And today,

Turkey's semi-friendly relations with Israel are deteriorating. The only other country between Syria-Turkey and Russia is Georgia, and Russia invaded and took parts of Georgia in 2008.

One of Russia's strategic goals includes increasing control of energy pipelines to Turkey, which has Turkish territory attached to it. With a Russian path carved through Georgia, Turkey, and Syria, the next stop is Israel!

And Many Peoples with You

What is the identity of the other nations named in Ezekiel's Magog prophecy? "Libya" and "Ethiopia" are clearly identified and have their modern counterparts in Libya and Ethiopia-Sudan, respectively. The other names have been thoroughly researched by Mark Hitchcock in his classic book, *After the Empire*, which is based on his doctoral dissertation. The following information is gleaned from that work.

Rosh—The ancient Sarmatians, who were known as Rashu, Rasapu, Ros, and Rus, are the people Ezekiel called "Rosh" in Ezekiel 38:2. The Sarmatians originally inhabited the land around the Caspian Sea, which is territory inhabited by eight of the former Soviet republics—Armenia, Georgia, Azerbaijan, Kazakhstan, Kirghizia, Uzbekistan, Turkmenistan, and Tajikistan...six of these former republics are Muslim nations.[154]

Meshech and Tubal—At every point in the history of Meshech and Tubal, these two nations occupied territory in the modern nation of Turkey. To ascribe any other location to them is totally inconsistent with the clear facts of ancient history.[155]

Gomer—Josephus, the ancient Jewish historian, identified the people of Galatia with Gomer. He said that the people the Greeks called the Galatians were the Gomerites. The Galatians, of course, lived in an area that today is in the west-central part of Turkey.[156]

Beth-togarmah—This is always associated with a city or district within the boundaries of the modern nation of Turkey.[157]

Persia—The modern nation of Iran is ancient Persia. The name "Persia," which was written all over the pages of ancient history, was changed to "Iran" in foreign usage in March 1935.[158]

In view of Hitchcock's study, it is apparent that nearly all of the nations that join with Russia are Muslim countries. Thus, the term "Russian-Islamic invasion of Israel," which is used throughout this chapter, and Ezekiel's terms "Gog and Magog" or simply "Magog" are interchangeable.

In the Latter Days—But When?

When will the Gog-Magog (Russian-Islamic) invasion of Israel occur? Will it occur at the end of the Millennium, or at the start? Or will it occur at the end of the Tribulation (Armageddon), in the middle, or at the start—or even sometime before the Tribulation? Using biblical timing clues to guide us in a process of elimination, we find that the stage is being set and the LORD IS NEAR!

At the End of the Millennium

Will the Magog invasion occur at the end of the Millennium? Is the Ezekiel 38 Gog-Magog the same as the Gog-Magog of Revelation 20:8–9 that comes at the end of a thousand years of the reign of Christ on the earth? No, because the Ezekiel Magog invasion will cause the Jews to awaken spiritually. "So will I make my holy name known in the midst of my people Israel" (Ezek. 39:7). Yet, throughout the thousand years of the Millennium, the Jews are in fact **already** wide awake spiritually. "And they shall teach no more…'Know the Lord': for they shall all know me, from the least of them unto the greatest of them…as the waters cover the sea" (Jer. 31:34; Isa. 11:9).

Why, then, is the millennial revolt in Revelation 20 also referred to as Gog-Magog? The answer is that the godless memory of the Ezekiel invasion is applied to the millennial Gog-Magog, just as the godless memory of Egypt and Sodom are applied to a degenerate Jerusalem in Revelation 11:8. But the different timing of the two events is required by the fact that Ezekiel's Magog causes Israel to "know the Lord," but when Revelation's Magog comes at the end of the Millennium, Israel will have already known the Lord for a thousand years.

At the Start of the Millennium

Some have proposed that the Magog invasion will happen at the start of the Millennium. However, this can't be the case because the Magog invasion is an attack by unbelievers and warring nations: "And I will bring thee forth, and all thine army...all of them clothed with all sorts of armour...all of them handling swords" (Ezek. 38:4). Yet, for one, no unbelievers will be permitted to enter the millennial kingdom, for "except a man be born again, he cannot see the kingdom of God" (John 3:3). Second, no warring nations can arise during the Millennium, for war is not an option since "nation shall not lift up a sword against nation, neither shall they learn war any more [during the Millennium]" (Mic. 4:3). Why, then, do we see the uprising of "Gog and Magog" in Revelation 20 during the Millennium? The reason is that the "Gog and Magog" event of Revelation chapter 20 is not a war, it is a doomed insurrection. God will instantly judge the Satan-led revolt and prevent a war.

At the End of the Tribulation

Will Magog invade Israel at the end of the Tribulation? No, because the Magog invasion will occur when Israel is at peace: "After many days...thou [Gog-Magog] shalt come into...Israel...they shall [be] dwell[ing] safely" (Ezek. 38:8). Yet at the end of the Tribulation, Israel will be doing anything but "dwelling safely." Throughout the second half of the Tribulation, Israel will be the direct target of history's worst nightmare, the Great Tribulation (Jer. 30:7; Matt. 24:21). The prerequisite that Israel will be in a secure state when Magog attacks is not the case at the end of the Tribulation, because Israel will be in the crosshairs of the nations at Armageddon.

At the Middle of the Tribulation

Will the Magog invasion come in the middle of the Tribulation? No, because Ezekiel's Magog invasion is the prophecy of an unsuccessful invasion into the Holy Land. We read that "all the heathen shall see my judgment that I have executed [the destruction of Magog], and my hand that I have laid upon them" (Ezek. 39:21). Yet in the middle of the Tribulation, Scripture records a successful invasion into the Holy Land by the Antichrist, when the Jews will be forced to "flee into the mountains" (Matt. 24:15–16). Thus, at the middle of the Tribulation, the Jews will escape a successful invader (Antichrist). But the Magog invasion portrays the Jews as being protected from an unsuccessful invader (Magog).

At or Near the Beginning of the Tribulation

By the process of elimination, we arrive at the beginning or just before the Tribulation. Will Magog invade at that point? Yes, because the Magog invasion will happen when Israel is "dwelling safely [securely]" (Ezek. 38:8). There are two possibilities here. The Bible records a time of "security" for Israel in the false peace covenant confirmed by the Antichrist at the very outset of the seven-year Tribulation. "And he [Antichrist] shall confirm the covenant [of peace] with many [Israel] for one week [seven years]" (Dan. 9:27). This false peace covenant clearly qualifies as the prerequisite that Israel will be "living securely" when Magog attacks.

But another time period also finds Israel "living securely," and that time is now. Israel is living securely now. Here is the evidence for that assertion, first from the Bible, and then as confirmed by history.

When My People Are Living Securely

The Bible says that "On that day when My people Israel are living securely," the Russian-Islamic (Magog) forces will invade Israel (Ezek. 38:14). The prerequisite to the Magog invasion is that Israel will be "living securely." When will that be? We find the answer in the Bible's four-part capsule history of the Jews since their dispersion from the land in AD 70.

The first part, summarized in Deuteronomy 28:64–68, begins with the AD 70 expulsion of the Jews from their land and continues through centuries of persecution culminating in the Holocaust of World War II. The second part of Jewish history picks up with the return of the Jews to their land in 1948 until our current time (Ezek. 38:8). The third part foretells of the ultimate Jewish holocaust yet to come called Jacob's (Israel's) Trouble and known as the Great Tribulation (Jer. 30:5–7; Matt. 24:21–22). Finally, the fourth part prophesies that Jewish history will culminate in the restoration of all Jews to their land under their everlasting King, Jesus Christ (Zech. 14:9–11).

In parts one and three, the Jews are in a radically unsecure state. In parts two and four, they are living "securely." But part four is the everlasting kingdom of security. Therefore, part two, with Israel living "securely" today, is Ezekiel's reference and must serve as the springboard for the Russian-Islamic invasion of Israel.

Deuteronomy 28 sums up part one of Jewish history since AD 70. It is a graphic prophecy of the entire AD 70—1945 span of Jewish persecution.

> And the LORD shall scatter thee among all people, from the one end of the earth even unto the other.... And among these nations shalt thou find no ease, neither shall the sole of thy foot have rest: but the LORD shall give thee there a trembling heart, and failing of eyes, and sorrow of mind: And

thy life shall hang in doubt before thee; and thou shalt fear day and night, and shalt have none assurance of thy life. In the morning thou shalt say, "Would God it were even!" and at even thou shalt say, "Would God it were morning!" for the fear of thine heart. (Deut. 28:64–68)

Nineteen centuries of Jewish suffering culminated in the Holocaust during the Second World War, when 6 million Jews disappeared in the Nazi death camps: "Neither shall the sole of thy foot have rest…thy life shall hang in doubt before thee…and thou shalt fear day and night, and shalt have none assurance of thy life." All of this couldn't be more graphic in describing Jewish "unsecurity" throughout that period.

Part two of post-AD 70 prophetic history saw the Jews return to the land of Israel. Ezekiel 38, our Magog passage, prophesied that miraculous event, which was fulfilled in 1948.

The land that is brought back from the sword, and is gathered out of many people, against the mountains of Israel, which have been always waste: but it is brought forth out of the nations, and they shall dwell safely all of them. (Ezek. 38:8)

Note especially this phrase, "they shall [be] dwell[ing] safely" [after Israel is regathered to its land, the people will be "living securely"]. The evidence shows that time to be now. Here is why: Take another look at the four parts of Israel's prophetic history above. First, there were nineteen hundred years of pure fright prompted by constant terror and "death camps." It was all capped by the infamous Holocaust.

Next, look at part three of the nation's history (yet future), the "time of Jacob's Trouble," the Great Tribulation (Jer. 30:7; Matt. 24:21–22). Sandwiched in between is part two of the Jewish story—the return to the land in 1948—continuing up until today. Now, it is no stretch of the imagination to say that there is no comparison between the security of today's Israel and, on the one hand, the Holocaust, and on the other hand, the Great Tribulation. By comparison, Israel today is absolutely secure.

Here is a sure test of this assertion: Ask any Christian tour leader to Israel what he tells his group about "tour safety in Israel" today. I've heard them, and I myself said the same on a tour I led to Israel in 2004: "Today the streets of Israel are safer than the streets of Chicago and New York!" And it is the truth. The same couldn't have been said about a visit to the Jews in the 1945 Nazi death camps or at any time in the preceding nineteen hundred years! Nor could the same be said about a "tour" to Israel during the coming Tribulation. Every Christian tour leader proclaims that, today, Israel is secure—terrorists and the 1948, '54, '67, and '73 wars notwithstanding. Those wars actually enhanced Israel's security.

In 1948, Israel came out of nineteen centuries of extreme "insecurity"! During the Tribulation, the Jews will return for a short time to an even more intense period of "unsecurity." But today, Israel is sandwiched into a brief period—by comparison—of super-security! Interestingly, when we observe the use of the word used by Ezekiel 38:8 for "safely" ["securely"], the Hebrew *betach*, we find it defined as "properly, a place of refuge, security, safety."[159] That is exactly what the state of Israel has represented for Jews worldwide since its inception in 1948. Today, then, Israel is a secure land of "refuge" from the nightmare of the previous centuries of Jewish suffering.

Now let's look at what history says about the fulfillment of these prophecies, keeping in mind Ezekiel's prophecy that when Magog invades, Israel will be living "securely."

Prophecy historian John Walvoord wrote:

> The sad condition of being scattered to the ends of the earth has persisted until the twentieth century, and with it has come untold sufferings to the people of Israel climaxing in the terrible scourge of Hitler who murdered some six million of the people of Israel.[160]

Notice that Walvoord says that this first period of Jewish "unse-curity" was **climaxed** by the Holocaust. It came to an end with the founding of Israel in 1948. "The world was shocked that such bar-barism could take place in the twentieth century" and so the world demanded a place of refuge for the surviving Jews—a national home-land—a return to the land of Israel.[161] The world's response was that "a Jewish national homeland was finally brought into being by a hor-rified, conscience-stricken international community which viewed Israel as a **necessary refuge** for Jews throughout the world."[162]

In light of both their previous history (Holocaust) and their future history (Tribulation), Israel today is far and away "secure." Jews worldwide continue to migrate, right along with the tourists, to their "secure place." "Having their own country was…a practical answer to the problem of having a **secure place** to go to."[163] Israeli Prime Minister Benjamin Netanyahu affirmed that fact with this statement: "Israel was founded to protect Jewish lives."[164] Max Dimont, the great historian of the Jews, acknowledges that "the state of Israel today is a citadel of Judaism, a **haven of refuge.**"[165]

Israel's only other time of living "securely" will be in the eter-nal kingdom when "the LORD shall be king over all the earth…and there shall be no more utter destruction; but Jerusalem shall be **safely inhabited**" (Zech. 14:9–11, emphasis added).

Summarizing the above, we find that after AD 70, the Bible tells of **two times** of security in Israel's future, and Israel is in the first one **now**. And it is this time of Israel living "securely" that sets the stage for the Russian-Islamic invasion of Israel. Therefore, the Russian-Islamic invasion of Israel is an imminent event; it could happen any day!

A False Security

This raises the question: Why would Magog attack Israel if it is actu-ally secure in its armed forces? The answer we glean from Scripture is that there are three perspectives on what it means to be secure: the perspective of Israel; that of Israel's enemy, Gog-Magog (Russia); and that of the Lord. Obviously, in Ezekiel 38, Israel believes that it is living "securely." But from Magog's perspective, that security can be breached, or else there wouldn't be the risk of an attack. And from the Lord's perspective, any security apart from trust in Him is a false security. Israel's confidence in the Israeli Defense Forces (IDF) apart from the Lord is a false security, and no one, including Israel's superb defense forces, will receive the glory that is due to God alone, for "My glory will I not give to another" (Isa. 42:8).

That Israel trusts in its own security is evident in this simple statement by Israeli Prime Minister Benjamin Netanyahu in response to the ever-present "peace" negotiations: "We want peace, but not at the price of security."[166]

Netanyahu believes that "peace" and "security" are not one and the same. He is right. The Ezekiel 38 prediction of Israel's condition at the time of the Russian-Islamic invasion is not one of peace, but one of security. Netanyahu obviously believes that Israel is presently secure by virtue of its military power. The source of that security? Netanyahu continued by making an admiring reference to a statement by Israeli patriot Theodore Herzl a century earlier. On June 11, 1901, Herzl said, "Do not rely on the help of foreigners nor on that of benefactors.... A people that wants to stand upright must put all its trust in **itself alone**." Israel's perspective on living "securely" is the same one it had when it was driven out of the land two thousand years ago, which is summed up in Ezekiel 33:26: "Ye stand upon your sword...shall ye possess the land?"

Then there is the perspective of the Russian-Islamic arch enemy. It sees Israel's security "walls" wide open for a breach, for then "shall things come into thy mind, and thou shalt think an evil thought, And thou shalt say, 'I will go up to the land of unwalled villages" (Ezek. 38:10–11). If the Russian-Islamic invaders really believed that the IDF was an impenetrable wall of defense, with unbreachable "gates" of security, then of course they wouldn't attack in the first place! But the prophecy says that then "shall things come into thy mind," and

they will view Israel as "living dwelling without walls, and having neither bars nor gates" (Ezek. 38:11).

The third perspective on Israel's security is the Lord's—the only
one that matters. "'Not by might, nor by power, but by My spirit,'
saith the LORD of hosts" (Zech. 4:6).

Regarding the belief that Israel (and many Christians) have that
Israel is secure behind the Israeli Defense Forces, the Bible declares
something else:

"There is no king saved by the multitude of an host [a mighty
army]: a mighty man is not delivered by much strength" (Psa. 33:16).

"For I will not trust in my bow, neither shall my sword save me"
(Psa. 44:6).

"Some trust in chariots, and some in horses: but we will remember the name of the LORD our God" (Psa. 20:7).

Israel's trust in itself and its IDF gives rise to a false security that
the nation is protected behind "walls" and "barred gates." However,
then "shall things come into thy mind," and as a result, the Russian-
Islamic coalition will have a different perspective: Israel will be ripe
for an invasion because Russia "shalt say, I will go up to the land of
unwalled villages; I will go to them that are at rest, that dwell safely,
all of them dwelling without walls, and having neither bars nor gates"
(Ezek. 38:11). As to why Israel will find itself in this predicament,
parallel phrases in the Bible about safety, security, "walled villages,"
and "bars and gates" give us the answer.

1. Israel dwells ALONE among hateful neighbors in the Mideast.
The Babylonians attacked a "secure" Arabian people precisely because
they were isolated, alone without allies. Israel did the same to the city
of Laish in the days of the Judges because they also were living in an
isolated false security, without allies to help them.

Nebuchadnezzar king of Babylon has formed a plan against
you and devised a scheme against you. "Arise Arise, get you

up unto the wealthy nation [Arabia-dwellers] that **dwelleth without care**," saith the LORD, "which **have neither gates nor bars**, which **dwell alone**." (Jer. 49:30–31, emphasis added)

Then the five men departed, and came to Laish, and saw the people that were therein, how they **dwelt careless**, after the manner of the Zidonians, **quiet and secure**...and they were far from the Zidonians, and had **no business with any man** [dwelt alone]. (Judg. 18:7, emphasis added)

2. Israel is "complacent" about its security. Jeremiah's indictment of the complacent ("careless") women of Jerusalem came as a warning about false security before Jerusalem's destruction by Babylon.

Rise up, ye women that **are at ease** [safe and secure]; hear my voice, ye **careless** daughters; give ear unto my speech." (Isa. 32:9, emphasis added)

3. Israel is prideful of being self-sufficient. God is not in the equation. Babylon trusted in its self-security in the same way. So did the Assyrian super-city of Nineveh two centuries earlier.

Therefore hear now this [Babylon], thou that art given to pleasures, that **dwellest carelessly** [securely], that sayest in thine heart, "**I am, and none else beside me** [self sufficient]; I shall not sit as a widow, neither shall I know the loss of children." (Isa. 47:8, emphasis added)

This is the rejoicing city [Nineveh] that **dwelt carelessly** [securely], that said in her heart, "**I am, and there is none beside me**." (Zeph. 2:15, emphasis added)

4. Israel is arrogant about its own strength. With that same attitude in the eighth century BC, Israel fell to the Assyrians.

> Woe to them that are at ease in Zion, **and trust** [feel secure] in the mountain of Samaria....The Lord GOD hath sworn by Himself..."I abhor the **excellency of Jacob** [arrogance of Jacob]...therefore will I deliver up the city with all that is therein.... Ye which rejoice in a thing of nought, which say, 'Have we not taken to us horns **by our own strength?**'" (Amos 6:1, 8, 13, emphasis added)

5. From our Ezekiel 38 passage on the Russian-Islamic invasion of Israel, we find a remarkable similarity in the phrasing of the "security" conditions in the first four above.

> But it is brought forth out of the nations, and they shall dwell safely [are **living securely**] all of them.... And thou shalt say, "I will go up to the land of **unwalled villages**; I will go to them that are **at rest**, that **dwell safely**, all of them **dwelling without walls, and having neither bars nor gates.**" (Ezek. 38:8, 11, emphasis added)

However, God will use the Russian-Islamic invasion of Israel to raise a remnant of believing Jews who "shall know that I am the LORD their God from that day and forward" (Ezek. 39:22). These will be the one hundred and forty-four thousand Jewish "firstfruits" of salvation (Rev. 7:1–8; 14:4). They will testify to the rest of Israel during much of the Tribulation Period. After God miraculously destroys Magog, Israel will begin a transition to an everlasting trust in the Lord, and by the end of the Tribulation that follows, "all Israel shall be saved" and Israel's false walls of security will then be changed to this: "Jerusalem will be inhabited **without walls**....'For I,' saith the LORD, 'will be unto her a **wall of fire** round about, and will be the glory in the midst of her.'" (Zech. 2:4–5, emphasis added)

"Security" in a Premillennial Millennial Kingdom?

Some have proposed that Israel will use its IDF military superiority to hammer all of the surrounding Arab nations, capturing their oil fields and vast petrol wealth and actually expanding Israel's borders in the process to gain the territory promised to it in the millennial kingdom, from the Mediterranean to the Euphrates River. The biblical basis claimed for this scenario is Psalm 83. In that passage, Israel defeats a host of surrounding nations that have been perpetual enemies of God's chosen people. These peoples, which include Lebanon, Jordan, Gaza, the tongue of Egypt, etc., are the Arab groups that immediately surround Israel. It is assumed that since they are not specifically mentioned in the list of Ezekiel's invading Magog nations, nations that form a more distant circle of countries surrounding Israel, then the Psalm 83 and Ezekiel 38 prophecies must be two different wars.

The theory proposes that once Israel has captured the territories of Lebanon, Jordan, Syria, and the others of Psalm 83—all the way over to Iraq—it is only then that the outer parameter of Ezekiel's Magog-Persian-led nations can come down upon Israel's expanded territory. The goal of the Russian-Islamic invaders is to "take a spoil" (Ezek. 38:12). Supposedly, that is the oil fields spread throughout the Mideast, but now, according to this scenario, under Israel's control. The instrument of this exceeding great conquest of the Mideast by Israel is the IDF, identified as the "exceeding great army" that emerges out of the valley of dry bones in Ezekiel 37:10.

The Israeli Defense Forces are then internationally glorified as the world's premier military force. And Israel gains a premillennial version of its divinely deeded millennial kingdom. The theory goes on to say that only then is Israel in a truly secure state, and consequently it is only then that Ezekiel's Magog invasion can occur.

But this theory has serious problems:

1. The realization of Israel's extended kingdom boundaries is to come after the return of Christ (Dan. 2:44, 7:26–17; Matt. 25:31–34).

2. The target of Ezekiel's Magog invasion is not the supposed expanded territories of Israel comprised of the entire Mideast oil fields, but rather a very specific geographic identifier called "the mountains of Israel" (Ezek. 39:2–4). The "mountains of Israel" territory is not the expanded Mideast, but rather the spine of Israel proper, the mountain range connecting the entire country north and south. More about "the mountains of Israel" shortly.

Also, it seems that in the Ezekiel invasion, the "spoil and plunder" is not the motive of the invasion, but is rather a pretext. Satan's plan has never been to get the goods, but rather to get the people and the land. The text itself infers this. In the very context of the "spoil" passage, we read the following:

> Thus says the Lord GOD, "It shall also come to pass, that at the same time shall things come into thy mind, and thou shalt think an evil thought…to turn thine hand upon the **desolate places** [the land] that are now inhabited, and upon **the people**." (Ezek. 38:10–12, emphasis added)

Then, to confirm that the real goal of the invasion is to wipe out God's chosen people from their God-given land, God Himself makes it clear what the real target is: "And thou shalt come up against **my people** of Israel, as a cloud to cover the land; it shall be in the latter days, and I will bring thee against **my land**" (Ezek. 38:16, emphasis added).

3. The "exceeding great army" of Ezekiel 37:10 is not today's Israeli Defense Forces, but rather the army of Jews raised up by the Lord to join with Him at His Second Coming in the war against the nations

at Armageddon. Ezekiel 37 gives a very careful and clear sequence of the restoration to life of the "dry bones" of Israel. First, there is the vision of Israel as a vast valley of "dry bones," which is the graveyard of the nations into which Israel was dispersed for nineteen hundred years (37:1–2). Next comes the reassembling of the bones into flesh-covered bodies, physically alive (37:7–8) but still spiritually dead, and interpreted by the passage itself as "the whole house of Israel" returned to its homeland (37:11–12). Only in the final phase of events does the salvation of Israel occur, when the "breath" (37:8–9), which is "my spirit" (37:9, 14), is imparted to Israel by God. At that point—the time of Israel's salvation is at the time of the Second Coming of Christ (Rom. 11:26; Zech. 12:10)—Israel will become the "exceeding great army" in Ezekiel 37:10. In Zechariah 12:6–10, we see the true mission and correct sequence of the "exceeding great army" when, at the return of Christ and empowered by "my spirit," it is said of Israel:

> In that day will I make the governors of Judah like an hearth of fire among the wood, and like a torch of fire in a sheaf; and they shall devour all the people round about, on the right hand and on the left.... In that day shall the LORD defend the inhabitants of Jerusalem; and he that is feeble among them at that day shall be as David; and the house of David shall be as God, as the angel of the LORD before them.... And I will pour upon the house of David, and upon the inhabitants of Jerusalem, the spirit of grace and of supplications. (Zech. 12:6–10)

The Israeli Defense Forces (IDF) are not the "exceeding great army" of Ezekiel chapter 37.

4. To say that the Psalm 83 prophecy must be an entirely different event that must precede the Magog invasion because the Ezekiel and Psalms passages have a different listing of nations ignores the fact that the Bible, when describing an event, sometimes lists only the leader nations, and at other times lists only the follower nations. Joel's

account of the war of Armageddon in chapter 3 lists only the follower nations (Tyre, Sidon, Philitia, Egypt, Edom, etc.), and Isaiah 11 adds to that list Moab and Ammon. Both passages are clearly set at the time of Armageddon. Both passages leave out the leader nations (as does Psalm 83), as well as any mention of the Antichrist, the ten kings, or the "kings of the east" (Rev. 17:12; 16:12). It is probable that the Psalm 83 nations are those "many people with thee" and "all thy company that are assembled unto thee" follower nations under the "guard" (Ezek. 38:6–7) of the Magog-leader nations listed by Ezekiel.

5. Finally, Israel doesn't have to capture the entire Middle East to place itself in the secure position that is required before Magog can invade. Israel already perceives itself today as a people who "dwell safely" and are living "securely." We made that case at length earlier. Furthermore, though Israel today certainly is not at peace with its Islamic neighbors, Israel is secure. That's not to confuse "peace" with "security": Remember our earlier quote from Israeli Prime Minister Benjamin Netanyahu, who very aptly made the point when he said, "We want peace, but not at the price of security."[167]

Against the Mountains of Israel

Finally, for further confirmation that the Russian-Islamic invasion of Israel is an imminent, any-moment event, we read this:

> And I will turn thee back…and will cause thee to come up from the north parts, and will bring thee upon **the mountains of Israel**…. Thou shalt fall upon **the mountains of Israel**, thou, and all thy bands, and the people that is with thee: I will give thee unto the ravenous birds of every sort, and to the beasts of the field to be devoured. (Ezek. 39:2–4)

It is against "the mountains of Israel" that the Russian-Islamic forces will come, and it is upon "the mountains of Israel" that the

Russian-Islamic forces will fall. Magog is not invading the expanded greater Mideast lands of an enlarged Israel. Nor does Magog fall on the sands somewhere in the Iraqi desert. The target is the "people" and the "land," and the people are identified as Israelis who live on a land called "the mountains of Israel." So one question becomes very important: How does Ezekiel use this term, "the mountains of Israel"?

Invariably, Ezekiel means literal mountains when he refers to the "mountains of Israel." In his passage foretelling the restoration of Israel (chapters 33–48), he couples "mountains of Israel" with other physical characteristics such as "land," "pasture," etc. (33:28, 34:14, 36:4, 36:6, 37:22). It is upon "the mountains of Israel" that Russian-Islamic invaders will in the future fall in a great slaughter (39:2–4; 17).

Here is the timing issue with "the mountains of Israel." When Israel returned to the land in 1948, not all the original homeland came under Jewish control. That only happened in phases through a series of Israeli-Arab wars over the next twenty years. Two geographic criteria are required by Ezekiel 38 and 39 before the Russian-Islamic invasion can occur. The first one, that Israel must be returned to the land (38:8), happened in 1948. But the second one, that Israel must possess "the mountains of Israel," was not possible then because "the mountains of Israel" were in fact under the territory of Jordan. However, in the 1967 war, Israel took East Jerusalem and "the mountains of Israel" that constitute much of what is today known as the West Bank (of the Jordan River). It is only since 1967, then, that the geographic criteria for Ezekiel's Magog invasion have been met. Israel now occupies "the mountains of Israel." And since Israel is living "securely" in those mountains, then the Russian-Islamic invasion of Israel could happen at any time. The fulfillment of Ezekiel's Magog prophecy is imminent! (For more on the Russian-Islamic invasion of Israel, go to www.prophecywatch.com.)

This chapter opened with a question: Have you asked Jesus Christ into your life to be your personal Savior? As you can see, the time is short, and the time is imminent. Jesus said, "When ye shall see all these things, know that it [the end of the age and the coming of Jesus Christ] is near, even at the doors" (Matt. 24:33).

As you conclude your reading about the Russian-Islamic invasion of Israel, with that event right at the doorstep of our generation, ask Jesus into your life now if you haven't already. If you have already done so, make a new commitment to live for Him at this epoch time in world history, reach out in love to your family and those around you, and tell them of Jesus the Savior!

CHAPTER TWELVE

THE TEMPLE MOUNT TEMPEST

By Todd Baker

The Temple Mount (*Har haBáyit* in Hebrew) in Jerusalem, where the two temples of the God of Israel stood and where the present Islamic mosque, the golden Dome of the Rock, now stands, is arguably the most valuable piece of real estate on the globe. It is currently a point of intense conflict between the Jewish state of Israel and the Arab/Muslim world. The Temple plays a central role in the spiritual life of Judaism, prompting every serious Orthodox Jew to pray daily that the *Beit Hamikdash* (Hebrew for "the Holy Temple" in Jerusalem) "be speedily rebuilt within our lifetime."

Bible prophecy has important things to say about how the Temple Mount figures prominently in the plan of God—past, present, and future. In this chapter, we will explore the various ramifications of this and how current events in the Middle East surrounding the Temple Mount are prophetically significant for the world and for the Bible believer. For the Jewish people, the Temple Mount—a small, elevated area measuring only 35.5 acres wide and 2,580 feet high—is the holiest site in all of Judaism. For three thousand years, it has served as the central place of prayer to and worship of the God of Israel.

The Temple throughout Scripture

Scripture mentions this place of divine habitation throughout all sixty-six books of the Bible—from Genesis to Revelation. The history of this holy piece of real estate goes back four thousand years to when the patriarch Abraham was planning to offer his son Isaac for sacrifice. Genesis 22:2 calls the location "the land of Moriah," where God would later choose to place His name and reveal His physical presence (2 Chron. 6:6; 7:1–3).[168] This was confirmed some thousand years later, when Solomon dedicated the First Temple to Yahweh on Mount Moriah. A generation earlier, his father, King David, had purchased the land on which to build the Temple structure (2 Sam. 24:25). When Israel had disobeyed the Lord, embraced the worship of idols, and turned the holy Temple into a center for pagan idolatry (Ezek. 8), God had brought the cruel Babylonian armies of King Nebuchadnezzar against Jerusalem, and they had destroyed the structure in 586 BC. This was the clear judgment of the Lord for the desecration of the Temple by the Jewish people of that day (see Jer. 6–7).

Seventy years later, God brought Israel back into its land to rebuild the Temple under the joint leadership of Ezra, Nehemiah, and Zerubbabel. The Second Temple project was completed in 515 BC. Almost five hundred years later, in 19 BC, King Herod the Great began a massive renovation of this Temple that was completed around AD 65. About a year later, the first Jewish revolt against the Roman occupation began, and four years after that, in AD 70, Roman General Titus led a seventy-thousand-man army comprising four legions to lay siege to Jerusalem and breach the walls of the Temple. The Roman armies eventually set the structure on fire; it burned until it was finally destroyed on the ninth day of Av in the Jewish calendar—ironically, the same day the First Temple had been destroyed by the Babylonians.[169] Josephus, a Jewish historian of that time, recounted that about 1.1 million Jewish inhabitants were killed in the Roman siege and that ninety-seven thousand were sold into slavery. When the Temple itself was burned and razed, ten thousand Jewish partisans died in their desperate defense of the holy structure. Josephus, who likely witnessed this event, wrote:

> While the holy house was on fire, everything was plundered that came to hand, and ten thousand of those that were caught were slain; nor was there a commiseration of any age, or any reverence of gravity, but children, and old men, and profane persons, and priests were all slain in the same manner; so that this war went round all sorts of men, and brought them to destruction, and as well those that made supplication for their lives, as those that defended themselves by fighting. The flame was also carried a long way, and made an echo, together with the groans of those that were slain; and because this hill was high, and the works at the Temple were very great, one would have thought the whole city had been on fire. Nor can one imagine anything either greater or more terrible than this noise; for there was at once a shout of the Roman legions, who were marching all together, and a sad clamor of the seditious, who were now surrounded with fire and sword. The people also that were left above were beaten back upon the enemy, and under a great consternation, and made sad moans at the calamity they were under; the multitude also that was in the city joined in this outcry with those that were upon the hill. And besides, many of those that were worn away by the famine, and their mouths almost closed, when they saw the fire of the holy house, they exerted their utmost strength, and brake out into groans and outcries again: Pera did also return

the echo, as well as the mountains round about [the city], and augmented the force of the entire noise. Yet was the misery itself more terrible than this disorder; for one would have thought that the hill itself, on which the Temple stood, was seething hot, as full of fire on every part of it, that the blood was larger in quantity than the fire, and those that were slain more in number than those that slew them; for the ground did no where appear visible, for the dead bodies that lay on it; but the soldiers went over heaps of those bodies, as they ran upon such as fled from them. And now it was that the multitude of the robbers were thrust out [of the inner court of the Temple by the Romans], and had much ado to get into the outward court and from thence into the city, while the remainder of the populace fled into the cloister of that outer court. As for the priests, some of them plucked up from the holy house the spikes that were upon it, with their bases, which were made of lead, and shot them at the Romans instead of darts. But then as they gained nothing by so doing, and as the fire burst out upon them, they retired to the wall that was eight cubits broad, and there they tarried; yet did two of these of eminence among them, who might have saved themselves by going over to the Romans, or have borne up with courage, and taken their fortune with the others, throw themselves into the fire, and were burnt together with the holy house; their names were Meirus the son of Belgas, and Joseph the son of Daleus. And now the Romans, judging that it was in vain to spare what was round about the holy house, burnt all those places, as also the remains of the cloisters and the gates, two excepted; the one on the east side, and the other on the south; both which, however, they burnt afterward. They also burnt down the treasury chambers, in which was an immense quantity of money, and an immense number of garments, and other precious goods there reposited; and, to speak all in a few words, there it was that the entire riches of the Jews were heaped up together, while the rich people had there built themselves chambers [to contain such furniture]. The soldiers also came to the rest of the cloisters that were in the outer [court of the] Temple, whither the women and children, and a great mixed multitude of the people, fled, in number about six thousand. But before Caesar had determined anything about these people, or given the commanders any orders relating to them, the soldiers were in such a rage, that they set that cloister on fire; by which means it came to pass that some of these were destroyed by throwing themselves down headlong, and some were burnt in the cloisters themselves. Nor did any one of them escape with his life.[170]

Forty years earlier, the Lord Jesus Christ had predicted this destruction for the nation of Israel's rejection of Him (see Matt. 23:38–24:2 and Luke 19:41–43). Indeed, as the Lord was approaching the Jewish capital for the last time, He gave specific details of the prophesied destruction of how Jerusalem and the Temple would be ransacked in AD 70.

And when He was come near, He beheld the city, and wept over it, saying, "If thou hadst known, even thou, at least in this thy day, the things which belong unto thy peace! But now they are hid from thine eyes. For the days shall come upon thee, that thine enemies shall cast a trench about thee, and compass thee round and keep thee in on every side and shall lay thee even to the ground, and thy children within thee; and they shall not leave one stone upon another; because thou knowest not the time of thy visitation." (Luke 19:41–44)

This proved to be the precise method of attack against Jerusalem and the Temple Titus and his Roman legions utilized forty years later. Titus trapped in the city thousands of Jews who were attending the feast of Passover, cutting off all supplies going into the capital. He then systematically built military embankments around the city and starved to death all the men, women, and children who had been trapped. Once Jerusalem was taken, the Roman legions dismantled the Temple stone by stone, literally not leaving any "stone upon another."[171] An excavation in the early 1990s along the southwest area of the Western Wall near the Temple Mount uncovered huge stones from the Second Temple period that had been literally thrown onto the streets by the Romans in AD 70. Once again, archaeology proved the prophecy of Jesus accurate and true.

The Second Temple was destroyed chiefly because the Jewish people did not recognize that the Messiah had come in the person of Jesus, and they rejected His offer of the Messianic Kingdom conditioned upon their national repentance. Consequently, God's judgment fell on the Jewish nation, which further led Jesus to declare that Jerusalem and its Temple location would be trampled underfoot and controlled by Gentile powers until the end of the present age: *"And Jerusalem shall be trodden down of the Gentiles until the times of the Gentiles be fulfilled"* (Luke 21:24).[172] The volatile history of this pivotal piece of sacred real estate in the last nineteen hundred years has fulfilled this prophecy to the letter! The term, "the times of the Gentiles," with reference to Jerusalem and the Temple Mount, describes a period during which the Gentile powers of the world would exercise dominance over these two places.

The duration of this Gentile supremacy stretches over a long period lasting from the Babylonian capture of Jerusalem and the destruction of the First Temple in 586 BC to the future desecration and assault by Antichrist during the seven-year Tribulation of Daniel's seventieth week (Dan. 9:27; Rev. 11:1–2). This extensive period of Gentile control—specifically over the Temple Mount—does not, however, negate the temporary rule of both the city and the Temple Mount by the Jewish people, as the Maccabean Revolt (163 BC) or the Six-Day War of June 1967 proves. Both of these events afford only temporary sovereignty for now because the prophecies of Zechariah 9–10 and Revelation 11:1–2 predict the Gentile attack of Jerusalem and the seizure and subsequent desecration of the rebuilt Third Temple by Antichrist, who will rule over Israel and the Middle East. Messianic Jewish scholar Arnold Fruchtenbaum, making the same observation, writes:

> Any Jewish takeover of the city of Jerusalem before the Second Coming must therefore be viewed as a temporary one and does not mean that the times of the Gentiles have ended. The times of the Gentiles can only end when the Gentiles can no longer tread down the city of Jerusalem.[173]

Bible prophecy is clear that two more temples will be built on the Temple Mount where the Muslim Dome of the Rock mosque currently stands. Two temples have already stood on this thirty-five-acre area: Solomon's Temple and the enlarged and renovated Temple of Herod the Great. The Third Temple will be built and present for the future Antichrist to enter and desecrate by demanding that he be worshipped as God within the Holy of Holies. Bible prophecy indicates that this will occur three and one-half years into the seven-year Tribulation Period (Dan. 9: 27; 2 Thess. 2:3–4). At the conclusion of the Tribulation, the Lord Jesus Christ will return and the Fourth Temple will be built. That is where He will personally live, and it is the place from which He will rule over the world (Ezek. 43:1–7). The prophet Ezekiel provides meticulous details of the size, configuration, and physical dimensions of this magnificent structure that Bible prophecy scholars commonly call the Millennial Temple (see Ezek. 40–47).

The Temple's Role in the Life and Ministry of Jesus

The Temple played a prominent role throughout the life and ministry of Jesus the Messiah. For example, on the eighth day of their Son's life, Joseph and Mary presented the infant Jesus before the Lord at the Temple in Jerusalem in accordance with the Law of Moses (Luke 2:21–24).

Further, when Jesus was twelve, He went to the Temple with Joseph and Mary for the celebration of the Passover. While traveling with a caravan from Jerusalem back home to Nazareth, Jesus' parents noticed their Son was missing from the group, and they hurriedly returned to Jerusalem to look for Him. Three days later, they found their precocious Child: He was sitting in the Temple with the learned doctors of the Torah, engaging in deep, theological conversation. Exasperated, Jesus' mother asked why her Son had done such a thing that had led to His parents' deep worry and long search. Jesus replied that His mother and father should have known that He could be found in His Heavenly Father's house (Luke 2:49). Although the Authorized King James Version uses the phrase, "My Father's *business*" (emphasis added), the American Standard Version and other competent English translations of the New Testament render the words as, "My Father's *house*" (emphasis added). Such phrases as this attest to Jesus' affirmation of the Temple as the house of God (*Beit 'Elohim*), a term He continued to use throughout His life (see John 2:16).

If we accept that the point of Jesus' mission in this passage is to identify with His Father's house, then this phrase not only indicates that the Temple was an acceptable place of worship and teaching for Him (and reveals His filial relationship with God), but it also underscores the fact that, as Messiah, He would one day restore its glory in His millennial kingdom (Jer. 3:17; Zech. 6:13; 14:16).[174]

Obviously, by the young age of twelve (the bar mitzvah age for every Jewish boy), Jesus already realized that the Temple was in fact the earthly house of God where He—God's only begotten Son—naturally belonged. Undoubtedly, the young Jesus knew that, as God's unique and divine Son, it was His responsibility and mission to work in and keep guard over His Father's dwelling place on earth—a mission that will resume when Christ returns to Jerusalem to rebuild and restore the Temple for the millennial kingdom at the close of the present age when the divine glory will return to the Holy City (Ezek. 43:1–5).

To continue exploring the Temple's role in Jesus' life and ministry, when He faced the three temptations imposed on Him by the devil during His forty days in the Judean desert, the Temple was the site of one of those temptations. Satan was permitted to take Jesus to the "pinnacle of the Temple" (Matt. 4:5; Luke 4:9)—the highest point of the structure, probably located at the southeastern corner of the Temple proper at a point some 450 feet high and overlooking the Kidron Valley.[175] This area, literally called "the wing of the Temple," was characterized by wing-shaped protrusions designed to prevent pigeons and other birds from roosting there and defiling the building's façade.

The "wing of the Temple" is prophetically significant because the same phrase, possibly denoting the same place, is also mentioned in the prophecy of Daniel 9:27 with regard to the abomination of desolation committed by the Antichrist in the Third Temple yet to be rebuilt. The phrase in the Daniel passage literally reads from the Hebrew: "upon the wing of abominations." This, in all likelihood, refers to "the pinnacle of the Temple which has become so desecrated that it no longer serves as the Temple of the Lord, but as an idol temple."[176]

During Satan's temptation of Jesus, the devil wanted Jesus to force God's hand by daring Him to supernaturally intervene if Jesus chose to act on the insidious and presumptuous suggestion that He throw Himself from the dizzying heights of the Temple's summit. This was Satan's attempt to misuse the place where God's presence was manifested and, in effect, to desecrate it by trying to persuade the Son to act independently from the Father—an utter impossibility (see John 5:17–21; 6:38).

Satan has continually attempted to usurp the place and authority of God and naturally desires to be worshipped in this role (Isa. 14:12–14; Luke 4:5–7), so the rebuilt Temple will serve that blasphemous purpose in the future. During the Tribulation Period, the devil will accomplish this through the Antichrist, who will commit the abomination of desolation by going into the Temple and demanding to be worshipped as God by Israel and the world.[177]

During His ministry in Judea and Jerusalem, the Lord Jesus spent most of His time teaching and healing the sick in and around the Temple. He zealously guarded the sanctity of this holy habitation of God when driving out the money changers who were misusing it for selfish gain. Twice He performed this bold act—once at the beginning and again at the conclusion of His public ministry. He personally defended the Temple, calling it "His Father's house," and He rebuked the crass profiteers, who were under the avaricious supervision of the priestly class, for turning the Temple into "a den of thieves" (John 2:13–16; Matt. 21:12–14).

The last words of Jesus' public ministry on earth concerned the Temple. After the nation of Israel had formally rejected Jesus as the Messiah, He proclaimed that the Temple would remain in a desolate condition until His return to Israel at the Second Coming (which would be followed by Israel's repentance of sin and acceptance of Him): "Behold, your house is left unto desolate. For I say unto you, Ye shall not see Me henceforth, till ye shall say, blessed is He that cometh in the name of the Lord" (Matt. 23:38–39). This desolation period has lasted for almost two thousand years, with a large part of it involving Muslim dominance of the Temple Mount. Muslim control of the Temple Mount has lasted over thirteen hundred years—since AD 691 with the construction of the octagonal-shaped Dome of the Rock mosque. In AD 715, Muslim Caliph Al-Walid I converted the remains of the *chanuyot* (the storehouse where the Levites kept the implements for the daily functioning of the Temple) into the al-Aqsa Mosque. The Arabic word *al-Aqsa* means "the farthest place" and refers to the assertion in the Koran that Muhammad was miraculously transported on his horse to the city of Jerusalem, cryptically alluded to as "the far away place" (Surah 17:1)—this, in spite of the fact that Jerusalem is never explicitly mentioned once by name in the Koran!

Making Way for the Third Temple

The presence of the Dome of the Rock and the al-Aqsa Mosque make Jerusalem the third holiest place in Islam next to Mecca and Medina, respectively. And so the Temple Mount has remained in a "desolate" and desecrated condition, as Jesus foretold (with shrines and mosques, unwittingly dedicated to the Mesopotamian mood god, Allah, standing in mute testimony of this fact for the last thirteen hundred years).[178] But all that potentially changed with the 1967 Six-Day War, when the army of Israel recaptured control of the Temple Mount (along with East Jerusalem and the West Bank) from Jordan, which had controlled it since 1948. With Jewish sovereignty reestablished over the Temple Mount, the Third Temple can now conceivably be built, as end-time Bible prophecy has clearly predicted.

Currently, the Temple Mount is under the stringent control and management of the Islamic Waqf authority with the permission of the Israeli government. Christians and Jews visiting the Temple Mount cannot so much as pray or crack open a prayer book or Bible while visiting this sacred site. Violators who do are accosted and physically removed. Such a precarious arrangement over the Temple Mount, however, does not erase the threats of war, terrorism, and calls for the destruction of the State of Israel from the Waqf authority. Several times a day from the al-Aqsa Mosque, the muezzin (the one chosen to lead Muslims to pray five times a day) prays to Allah over the loudspeakers of the minaret (a tall spiral structure from which the call to prayer is proclaimed from the top) for the destruction of the Jews—knowing full well that Israel allows Muslims full, unhindered control of this ancient Jewish holy site as an act of goodwill for the sake of peace! One disturbing example, from so many, of Islam's threats of war and destruction over ownership of the Temple Mount came on May 19, 2000, when a Muslim cleric, speaking on behalf of the Waqf alliance, belligerently exclaimed that Islam will never surrender the Temple Mount or the mosques built on it, but will decapitate anyone who thinks otherwise:

> This mosque will not be entered through negotiations or peace agreements. This mosque will be entered (liberated) through armies...that will "pound the earth to powder," that will behead the heads of the disbelievers and their agents. Jerusalem will return to Muslims but not through treason. It will return to Islam and Muslims. It will not be the capital of the Palestinian state, but it will be Insha'Allah, the capital of the Islamic Khilafah State...that will tread on the heads of Europe, Russia, and the U.S. This is what Islam tells us, and this is how history was. Read history if you want and you will see wars after wars between Islam and the disbelievers that will continue.[179]

Four months later, in September of 2000, Ariel Sharon, former prime minister of Israel, and a group from the Knesset were escorted by a security detail to walk through the Temple Mount area to investigate illegal construction of an underground mosque with the subsequent destruction of Jewish antiquities dating back to the time of King Solomon. In response to this basic right of every Jew to return to the Temple Mount, the Palestinian Authority rioted the next day and its leader, the late Yasser Arafat, called for a second intifada (armed uprising) against Israel that unleashed a bloody wave of Palestinian terrorism against the innocent Israeli population for the next three years. Sharon's visit to the Temple Mount served as a poor pretense for this since Arafat had already planned the second intifada well in advance—ever since his return from the Camp David II summit in

July of 2000, where he unexpectedly rejected President Bill Clinton's offer and reduced the so-called peace process with Israel to shambles again.[180] In November of 2003, the Palestinian Authority (PA) declared that any Jewish visitation to the Temple Mount was a "crime" against the Muslim world. Archaeology, history, the victories of war, and most importantly, the Word of God establish the unimpeachable fact that Jerusalem and the Temple Mount have been under Jewish control and Israeli ownership going back to the "everlasting covenant" God made with Abraham in which He gave the patriarch and his physical descendants, the Jewish people, the land of Israel for an "everlasting possession" (Gen. 17:7–8). This divine land grant most certainly includes permanent, Jewish ownership of the Temple Mount, their two Diasporas notwithstanding (see Lev. 26:40–45). This is at the heart of the "Temple Mount tempest" between Israel and the Arab/Muslim world, and it will only greatly intensify to become a key flash point in the Tribulation period leading up to the Second Coming of Jesus the Messiah.

Bible prophecy is quite clear that the Jews will build the Third Temple on the Temple Mount where the Dome of the Rock currently stands (Dan. 9:27: Matt. 24:15; 2 Thess. 2:3–4; Rev. 11:1–2). Orthodox Jewish groups such as the Temple Mount Faithful and the Temple Institute have been quietly making serious preparations for the construction. Both groups believe that at the proper time God will providentially remove the Dome of the Rock so that the Temple can be erected on the spot where the two prior Temples of Judaism stood. In the last fifteen years, the Temple Institute and its group of rabbinic leaders and followers have made many of the instruments and implements necessary for Temple worship in eager anticipation of its reconstruction. But in order to rebuild the structure as the Bible predicts, there must also be a reconstitution and restoration of the Levitical priesthood for proper sacrifice in the Temple, as the prophecy of Malachi 3:3–4 requires. This would necessitate determining with utmost genetic accuracy which Jewish males eligible for the priesthood have truly descended from the Cohanim (the priestly descendents of Levi). Such a task would seem impossible two thousand years after the Second Temple—along with the genealogical records of the descendants of the priestly tribe in Israel that were kept there—was destroyed. However, that dramatically changed when, in 1996, Dr. Karl Skorecki, Prof. Michael Hammer, and Dr. Neil Bradman conducted a study among Jewish males from Israel, North America, and England who were thought to have a Kohen or Levi in their family background. The scientific analysis amazingly revealed certain genetic markers that were distinct, unique, and only present among Jews with a Levite lineage.[181] This discovery is now called "the Levite gene" and is currently being used to restore the Levitical priesthood in time for the rebuilding of the Third Temple.

Several yeshivas and schools among the Orthodox in Israel are devoted to training the Cohanim and Levim, members of the greater and lesser priestly classes so that they will be ready to officiate in the Third Temple once it is built. One such training center in Israel is located in the town of Mitzpe Yericho, At the time of this writing, the facility was building a replica of the Temple that will serve as a school.[182] A survey taken in Israel by *Ynetnews* and the Gesher organization also revealed that 64 percent of Israelis, including half of the secular Jewish population, would like to see the Temple rebuilt![183] This is a radical shift among the Jewish population in Israel, where for years the Orthodox Jews—a small minority—were the only ones who wanted the Temple rebuilt. Now it is becoming a national groundswell that is supported by the majority of the Jewish State for the first time since its inception!

The Heart of the "Temple Mount Tempest"

The ongoing controversy between Muslims and Jews over the ownership of the Temple Mount is really a larger battle between Satan and the God of Israel. The Temple Mount was—and will be again—the central place on earth where God's sovereign rule over the world will be established and emanate from; it is the place all nations will go to serve and submit to King Messiah in the millennial kingdom (Isa. 2:1–4; Zech. 14:16–19). At the close of the coming Tribulation, the devil will use the Antichrist to gather the world's armies to lead a military invasion of Israel. The goal of Antichrist and his forces will be to destroy the tiny Jewish state for its lone resistance to and rebellion against his global rule, and for the Jews' refusal to worship him as God Almighty. Scripture tells us that sometime in eternity past, an angel named Lucifer fell after he sought to usurp the supreme authority of the Creator. Lucifer wanted to remove God from His throne and be seated there himself to reign over the angelic hosts of heaven. His intentions are described by his five "I will" statements in Isaiah 14:12–14. Note that in verse 13, the "throne" is located on a mountain in heaven on the highest point of that supernatural dimension. It is described as the "mount of the congregation on the farthest sides of the north."

The result of Lucifer's rebellious attempt to establish his throne above God's was utter defeat; God cast him out of heaven and gave him only limited access to God's presence from time to time afterwards, as in the case of Job indicates (see Job 2). And ever since his expulsion from heaven, the fallen angel—known as the devil, or Satan—has sought to establish his throne on earth. His efforts began with the temptation of man in the Garden of Eden and will continue until the conclusion of Christ's thousand-year kingdom on earth (Gen. 3:1–4; Rev. 20:7–10). Up to and during the seven-year Tribulation Period, Satan has and will again attempt to take control of the Temple Mount in Jerusalem so that through the nefarious person of the Antichrist he can finally establish his evil rule over the earth. He is intent on preventing the King of Kings and Lord of Lords from returning to reign over all the earth from an elevated Mount Zion, where His throne—located in the glorious Millennial Temple—will stand (Psalm 48:1–2; Isa. 2:1–3).

The historical struggle for control of Jerusalem's Temple Mount is a clear indication of this spiritual battle between God and Satan, between the people of God and the children of the devil, and between good and evil. It still rages in our day and will continue until the glorious return of Israel's Messiah, Jesus Christ, when He will defeat these evil forces of usurpation and foreign occupation and deliver the Jewish people to live in their God-given land. They will worship Christ as their King and Savior in a Temple that shall never be defiled or trampled underfoot again. God has stated in His prophetic Word and decreed to His Son, our Messiah, that in the end He will successfully sit enthroned on the Temple Mount, in spite of the uproar of the Gentile nations or the global alliance of the anti-Semitic nations that will side with the future Antichrist in a vain attempt to take the Temple Mount and destroy the Jewish people of Israel at the Battle of Armageddon:

> Yet I have set My King on My holy hill of Zion. I will declare the decree: "The Lord has said to Me, 'You are My Son, Today I have begotten You. Ask of Me, and I will give You the nations for Your inheritance, and the ends of the earth for Your possession. You shall break them with a rod of iron; You shall dash them to pieces like a potter's vessel. Now therefore, be wise, O kings; be instructed, you judges of the earth. Serve the LORD with fear, and rejoice with trembling. Kiss the Son, lest He be angry, and you perish from the way, when His wrath is kindled but a little. Blessed are all those who put their trust in Him.'" (Psa. 2:6–12)

When the Temple Mount is permanently restored to its greatest glory under the just and beneficent reign of Messiah Jesus, it will be a place of joyous fellowship and feasting, where death shall be abolished and tears of pain associated with it will be forever wiped away. Israel's long-awaited Messiah will bring final deliverance and salvation.

And in this mountain shall the Lord of hosts make unto all people a feast of fat things, a feast of wines on the lees, of fat things full of marrow, of wine on the lees well refined. And He will destroy in this mountain the face of the covering cast over the people, and the veil that is spread over all nations. He will swallow up death in victory; and the Lord God will wipe away tears from off all faces and the rebuke of His people shall He take away from off all the earth: for the Lord hath spoken it. And it shall be said in that day, "Lo, this is our God; we have waited for Him, we will be glad and rejoice in His salvation." (Isa. 25:6–9)

Even so, come Lord Jesus!

CHAPTER THIRTEEN

GRASPING FOR
GLOBAL GOVERNANCE

By Daymond Duck

Those thinking the world will get better and better are victims of wishful thinking and sentimental reasoning. Their whimsical visions of a rosy future are almost the exact opposite of what God's always-accurate prophets foretold in the Bible. Global governance is bearing down on the whole world like a fast-moving, killer tsunami that cannot be stopped. But many in the church—and the vast majority of those on the outside—are asleep or in total darkness.

As absurd as it sounds, some of the so-called intellectual elite (Illuminati, Bilderberg Group, Trilateral Commission, Council on Foreign Relations, Club of Rome, United Nations, and New Age Movement) are actually trying to restructure the world. Most seem to honestly believe they are doing a good thing by laying the foundation for a coming socialist utopia. Nothing could be farther from the truth.

Global governance will evolve into a global disaster that will kill billions and cause the living to envy the dead. This coming hell on earth will wax worse and worse until Jesus returns because the dangers are not seen by those who don't have a biblical worldview. Extreme havoc is coming, and it is clearly accelerating every time the big, beautiful, bright sun rises in the eastern sky.

World Government in the Book of Daniel

Daniel said, "The fourth beast shall be the fourth kingdom upon earth, which shall be diverse from all kingdoms, and shall devour the whole earth, and shall tread it down, and break it in pieces" (Dan. 7:23). "Devour" is a word that some associate with hungry, wild animals ripping apart and ravenously gulping down pieces of poor, helpless victims. "Tread it down, and break it in pieces" signifies a stomping, crushing action. This is a ghastly picture of a powerful, beastly kingdom (global governance) ripping up the whole earth and reducing it to a pile of worthless rubble.

World Government in the Book of Revelation

Concerning the Antichrist, John said, "Power was given him over all kindreds, and tongues, and nations. And all that dwell upon the earth shall worship him, whose names are not written in the book of life of the Lamb slain from the foundation of the world" (Rev. 13:7b–8). Global governance will bring subversion of the world, satanic subversion that will ultimately lead to the temporary ruin of planet earth. Its first and only leader will be a satanically inspired man who will overthrow nations and demand to be worshipped. Most will compromise their values, submit, take his mark (or name or number of his name), and wind up spending eternity in the lake of fire (Rev. 14:9–11), but the vast majority of those who don't will be persecuted and killed.

King Nebuchadnezzar's Dream

King Nebuchadnezzar summoned his pitiful collection of so-called wise men. He told them he had a dream that troubled him. He wanted them to tell him what he had dreamed and what his dream meant. They asked him to reveal the dream and promised to interpret it if he did. But this easily stressed-out man couldn't remember the dream, and his wise men couldn't tell him what it was or interpret it for him. After a few back-and-forth exchanges, the troubled king ordered all of his wise men killed, including Daniel. When soldiers went to arrest Daniel, he asked for time to come up with the interpretation. He got Shadrach, Meshach, and Abednego to join him in a prayer meeting. That night, God revealed the dream and its meaning to Daniel. The next day, Daniel appeared before the hot-headed king.

God Knows What You Dreamed

Daniel answered in the presence of the king, and said, "The secret which the king hath demanded cannot the wise men, the astrologers, the magicians, the soothsayers, show unto the king; But *there is a God in heaven that revealeth secrets,* and maketh known to the king Nebuchadnezzar *what shall be in the latter days.* Thy dream, and the visions of thy head upon thy bed, are these; As for thee, O king, thy thoughts came into thy mind upon thy bed, what should come to pass hereafter: and he that revealeth secrets maketh known to thee *what shall come to pass.* But as for me, this secret is not revealed to me for any wisdom that I have more than any living, but for their sakes that shall make known the interpretation to the king, and that thou mightest know the thoughts of thy heart." (Dan. 2:27–30, emphasis added)

Notice three important points: 1) There is a God in heaven who reveals secrets; 2) God revealed what shall be in the latter days; and 3) God revealed what shall come to pass. Nebuchadnezzar's so-called wise men couldn't do this, but there is a God in heaven who can and did.

Nebuchadnezzar Dreamed About a Great Image

[Daniel said,] "Thou, O king, sawest, and behold a great image. This great image, whose brightness was excellent, stood before thee; and the form thereof was terrible. This image's head was of fine gold, his breast and his arms of silver, his belly and his thighs of brass, His legs of iron, his feet part of iron and part of clay. Thou sawest till that a stone was cut out without hands, which smote the image upon his feet that were of iron and clay, and brake them to pieces. Then was the iron, the clay, the brass, the silver, and the gold, broken to pieces together, and became like the chaff of the summer threshingfloors; and the wind carried them away, that no place was found for them: and the stone that smote the image became a great mountain, and filled the whole earth." (Dan. 2:31–35)

See the image below:

THE GREAT IMAGE
TIMES OF THE GENTILES---LUKE 21:24

ROCK = JESUS
DEUT. 32:3-4, 15
PSA. 18:2, 31
ROM. 9:33
I COR. 10:4

#7 = GOD'S KINGDOM

#1 = GOLD = BABYLON

#2 = SILVER = MEDES & PERSIANS

#3 = BRASS = GREEKS

#4 = IRON = ROMANS

#5 = PIECES = NATIONS

#6 = IRON + CLAY = EU + OTHERS

God's Interpretation of the Great Image

[Daniel said,] "Thou, O king, art a king of kings: for the God of heaven hath given thee a kingdom [*first kingdom*], power, and strength, and glory. And wheresoever the children of men dwell, the beasts of the field and the fowls of the heaven hath he given into thine hand, and hath made thee ruler over them all. Thou art this head of gold. And after thee shall arise *another kingdom* inferior to thee, and another *third kingdom* of brass, which shall bear *rule over all the earth*. And the *fourth kingdom* shall be strong as iron: forasmuch as iron breaketh in pieces and subdueth all things: and as iron that breaketh all these, shall it *break in pieces* and bruise. And whereas thou sawest the feet and toes, part of potters' clay, and part of iron, the kingdom shall be divided; but there shall be in it of the strength of the iron, forasmuch as thou sawest the iron mixed with miry clay. And as the toes of the feet were part of iron, and part of clay, so the kingdom shall be partly strong, and partly broken. And whereas thou sawest iron mixed with miry clay, they shall mingle themselves with the seed of men: but they shall not cleave one to another, even as iron is not mixed with clay. And in the days of these kings shall the God of heaven set up a kingdom, which shall never be destroyed: and the kingdom shall not be left to other people, but it shall break in pieces and consume all these kingdoms, and it shall stand for ever. Forasmuch as thou sawest that the stone was cut out of the mountain without hands, and that it brake in pieces the iron, the brass, the clay, the silver, and the gold; the great God hath made known to the king *what shall come to pass* hereafter: and the dream is certain, and the interpretation thereof sure." (Dan. 2:37–45, emphasis added)

Notice that Daniel called King Nebuchadnezzar a "king of kings." It's because King Nebuchadnezzar ruled over other kings in a world kingdom (global governance). Note also that Daniel said the third kingdom "shall bear rule over all the earth." "Rule over all the earth" means a world kingdom (or global governance).

First, four Gentile world kingdoms will appear. Daniel said, "Thou art this head of gold" (Kingdom #1: Gold—Babylon's Gentile world kingdom). Then Daniel said, "After thee shall arise another kingdom" (Kingdom #2: Silver—the Medes' and Persians' Gentile world kingdom). Then Daniel said, "Another third kingdom of brass which shall rule over all the earth" (Kingdom #3: Brass—the Greeks' Gentile world kingdom). And then Daniel spoke of "the fourth kingdom" (Kingdom #4: Iron—the Romans' Gentile world kingdom).

Second, Daniel said, "Shall it [the fourth Gentile world kingdom] break in pieces and bruise." God revealed that the Roman Empire would break in pieces or nations: Spain, France, England, Germany, etc. After the Roman Empire breaks up, God said, the pieces or nations will "bruise," which means they will go to war with each other and with others.

Third, Daniel said the nations will come back together and join others to form the feet and toes, "part of iron and part of clay." Be very careful: Daniel didn't say the feet and toes will be iron only (the same as the past Roman Gentile world kingdom). He said the feet and toes will be a mixture of iron plus clay (the past Roman Gentile world kingdom plus others). Since the Roman Empire would break into pieces or nations before the feet and toes appear, the Roman Empire (iron) would have to reunite and join others (clay). This writer believes the clay will be a restructured United Nations.

What Other Scriptures Teach

The fifth and final Gentile world kingdom will have one central government with one powerful demonic world leader called the Antichrist.

This wicked world kingdom will be divided into ten regions or ten groups of nations with ten leaders under the bloodthirsty Antichrist. The ten leaders are called the "ten horns" or "ten kings" in other verses of Scripture (Dan. 7:24; Rev. 17:12). The flow chart below shows how this future world government will be structured. Three groups of nations are shaded on the chart because the Antichrist will overthrow three of groups of nations. Then, the other seven will surrender their power and authority to him.

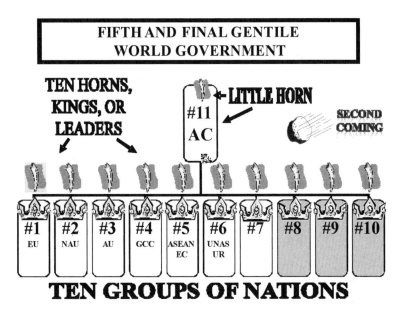

The Future

This fifth and final Gentile world government will be in existence and destroyed at the Second Coming of Jesus (the "stone" or "rock"). Daniel said this prophecy cannot be changed. Later, Peter said Bible prophecy is sure (2 Pet. 1:19–21; 2:9). This doesn't mean God will cause these sickening things to happen this way. It means that He knows they will happen this way.

A Gentile Timeline

The all-knowing God of heaven spoke through Daniel, and what Daniel said is extremely important because the strange image in Nebuchadnezzar's dream is a God-given timeline of Gentile world kingdoms. It starts at the top of the head (with Babylon) and goes down to the tip of the toes (the Second Coming of Jesus). For those who are interested, Daniel 9:24–27 is a Jewish timeline. That one starts with the command to restore and rebuild Jerusalem and ends with the reign of the Antichrist (ended by the Second Coming). So both timelines—one Gentile and the other Jewish—start at different places, but both end with the Second Coming. See the next drawing.

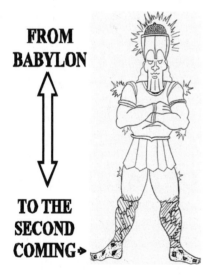

FROM BABYLON

⇕

TO THE SECOND COMING ➔

#1 = GOLD = BABYLON

#2 = SILVER = MEDES & PERSIANS

#3 = BRASS = GREEKS

#4 = IRON = ROMANS

#5 = PIECES = NATIONS

#6 = IRON + CLAY = EU + OTHERS
#7 = GOD'S KINGDOM

What Some Leaders Are Saying

People need to be aware of what some well-known leaders and writers are saying about one-world government. It's not make-believe or the ranting of prophecy kooks in the minds of these people. It's the much-desired goal of many who think they are building a better world.

Winston Churchill

The idea of a "New World Order" didn't originate with England's prime minister, Winston Churchill, but it's clear that this great leader believed the purpose of the New World Order is to establish world government. He said, "The creation of an authoritative, all-powerful *world order* is the ultimate aim towards which we must strive. Unless some effective world super-government can be set up and brought quickly into action, the prospects for peace and human progress are very doubtful."[184]

Notice that the expressions "New World Order" and "world order" are phrases that signify the coming one-world government. World leaders don't see global governance as something that will be satanic, but that's what the Bible says it will be.

Gunther K. Russbacher

Admiral Gunther K. Russbacher served with the CIA and the Office of Naval Intelligence for more than thirty years. He wrote:

> The hierarchy [Council on Foreign Relations, Club of Rome, Trilateral Commission, Bilderberger Society, and others], among other things, had called for world government to be achieved in stages through the forming of world administrative regions. This was in accordance with the UN Charter, which encourages the implementation and administration of

world government on a regional basis. [According to chapter 8, Article 52 (2–3) and 53 (1) of the Charter, under Regional Arrangements.][185]

Notice three key points:
1. World government is to be achieved in stages (three stages or phases, to be exact).
2. World government is to be achieved through the forming of world administrative regions (ten world administrative regions with a leader over each one for a total of ten leaders who will fulfill the prophecy about ten kings or ten horns).
3. The establishment of world government in stages with regions is in accordance with the UN Charter.

George Herbert Walker Bush

On September 11, 1990, exactly eleven years to the day when planes crashed into the Twin Towers of the World Trade Center, President George H. W. Bush was speaking about the Persian Gulf War before a joint session of Congress when he said, "Out of these troubled times, our *fifth objective*—a new world order—can emerge."[186]

If the New World Order is our fifth objective, one must wonder what the first four are—and whether there are others, especially since the Bible teaches that the world government will be satanic.

Zbigniew Brzezinski

In 1995, this national security advisor in former President Jimmy Carter's administration said:

I have no illusions about world government emerging in our lifetime…we cannot leap into world government through one quick step…a consensual global system is not just a matter of good wishes or good will, but it requires a process...the pre-condition for eventual and genuine *globalization is progressive regionalization.*[187]

The establishment of world government is called globalization. A precondition for world government is progressive regionalization (the formation of regions). Again, this will lead to ten regions with ten leaders the Bible calls the "ten kings" or "ten horns." According to the Bible, an eleventh leader will arise and subdue three of the ten.

He will be the first and only leader of the coming world govern-ment and is often called the Antichrist. So if Mr. Brzezinski is right, those who were alive in 1995 could see a (satanic) one-world govern-ment emerge in their lifetime.

Bill Clinton

Following a speech in Argentina on October 17, 1995, then President Bill Clinton was answering reporters' questions when he said, "What I'm trying to do is to promote a process of *reorganization of the world.*" In response to another question, he said, "If you can prove that you can *merge integrated economies and integrated democracies,* then we'll be more likely to build a global system of this kind."[188]

World government involves reorganizing the world and merging or integrating its economies and democracies. In this case, it probably involves merging the economies and governments of Canada, Mexico, and the United States, a process some call regionalization or integra-tion (Google "North American Union;" "Security and Prosperity Partnership;" "North American Leadership Summit;" etc.).

Pat Buchanan

Concerning Pat Buchanan, who was running for president of the United States in September 2000, an Associated Press article appeared in many newspapers that read, "Restarting his campaign, Reform Party contender Pat Buchanan told a Bob Jones University crowd yesterday that the United States is being drawn into a *one-world government* and should kick the *United Nations* headquarters out of the country."[189]

Third-party candidates know that one-world government and the United Nations are connected. It's in the UN Charter.

Judges on the United States Supreme Court

Judge Anthony Kennedy said, "It is proper that we acknowledge the overwhelming weight of *international opinion* against the juvenile death penalty." Judge Sandra Day O'Connor said, "In the next century, we…are going to want to draw upon judgments from *other jurisdictions.* We are going to be more inclined to look at the *decisions of the European Court of Justice.…* And perhaps use them and cite them." Judge Stephen Breyer said, "As the world grows together we are going to have to consider how our Constitution fits into the governing documents of *other nations.*"[190]

Instead of going by the Constitution of the United States, some Supreme Court judges believe they should go by international opinion, especially that of the EU, which is the chosen pattern for regional government.

Strobe Talbott

In 2006, Strobe Talbott, the assistant secretary of state under President Bill Clinton, stated, "The nation-state as we have known it will cease to exist in the twenty-first century. We will all answer to a *single global authority.*"[191]

He believes every nation will soon cease to exist and everyone will answer to a global government.

J. R. Church

In 2007, this astute prophecy teacher wrote, "The answer [to why nations are being merged into *regions* without the people getting to vote on it] lies in the United Nations' move toward one-world government. Plans are afoot to divide the world into ten economic/political *regions.* The United Europe is one region, and the North American community is another. Around the world, regions are currently being developed. Some are farther along than others, but 2010 appears to be an achievable goal for the emergence of world government."[192]

The regions are beginning as economic regions, but the goal is to turn the economic regions into ten political regions and then merge them into a world government.

Henry Kissinger

In a video interview in 2007 or 2008 (the writer has seen both dates), Henry Kissinger, former secretary of state to presidents Richard Nixon and Gerald Ford, said that *within four years,* we will see "the beginning of a new international order."[193]

If Mr. Kissinger is right, the world will have seen the beginning of world government before the end of President Obama's first term. Mr. Kissinger has suggested that one way to accomplish this is through a *regional* management system. And he is even or record as saying he hopes that President Obama will head up the New World Order.

So who will lead the world government is already being discussed.

Gordon Brown

On November 9, 2008, England's prime minister, Gordon Brown, said, "The financial crisis has given world leaders a unique *opportunity* to create a truly *global* society."[194]

In Mr. Brown's mind, the world's economic problems provide an opportunity to establish world government.

Barack Obama

In July 2008, while campaigning for the office of president of the United States, Senator Barack Obama delivered a major speech in Berlin, Germany, addressing the people of the world as a fellow citizen of the world appealing for nations to share the burdens of *global citizenship* and expressing his support for a *globalized world.*[195]

President Obama supports world government.

Ron Paul

Concerning the November 2008 G-20 meetings, Ron Paul, Texas congressman and 2008 candidate for president of the United States, said, "Obama wouldn't be there if he didn't toe the line, and when the meeting starts on November 15 for the new monetary system, this could be *the beginning of the end of what's left of our national sovereignty.*"[196]

If Congressman Paul was right, the beginning of the end of America's national sovereignty has probably already started.

Tim Geithner

On March 14, 2009, U.S. Treasury Secretary Tim Geithner spoke at the G-20 Finance Ministers and Central Bank Governors Meeting and said, "You are seeing the world move together *at a speed and on a scale without precedent* in modern times."[197]

The formation of world government has accelerated.

Pope Benedict XVI

In July 2009, the Pope released his encyclical called "Caritas in Veritate," otherwise called "Charity in Truth." In this document, the Pontiff called for the United Nations to be transformed into "*a true world political authority*" with "*real teeth.*"[198]

Daniel described the last world government as having great iron teeth (Dan. 7:7).

Other

Space does not permit, but those who are interested can Google "globalization," "globalized," "regionalization," "integration," and similar words for more information on world government. To find information on world religion, such words as "consciousness" and "spirituality" can be researched. Be aware of UN calls for global taxes to finance world government. Also, the World Economic Forum called for a global TV network to counteract criticism and promote world government. A global TV network may well be how the entire world sees the bodies of the two witnesses lying in the street of Jerusalem.

What the Bible Says about How the Last World Government Will Develop

The last Gentile world government will develop in phases or stages. Daniel was speaking about this when he said:

> The fourth beast shall be the fourth kingdom upon earth, which shall be diverse from all kingdoms, and shall *devour the whole earth*, and shall tread it down, and break it in pieces. And the ten horns out of this kingdom are *ten kings* that shall arise: and *another shall* rise after them; and he shall be diverse

from the first, and he shall *subdue three kings*. And he shall *speak great words against the most High*, and shall *wear out the saints* of the most High, and think to change times and laws: and they shall be given into his hand until a time and times and the dividing of time. But the judgment shall sit, and they shall *take away his dominion*, to consume and to destroy it unto the end. And the kingdom and dominion, and the greatness of the kingdom under the whole heaven, shall be given to the people of the saints of the most High, whose kingdom is an everlasting kingdom, and all dominions shall serve and obey him. (Dan. 7:23–27, emphasis added).

Phase 1: A kingdom will devour the whole earth. This will probably be the United Nations. That world body is not a world government now, but many are trying to transform it into a world government.

Phase 2: This world government will be divided into ten regions with one leader over each region (call it the G-10). It won't be ten regions in a revived Europe; it will be ten regions in the world. Each region will give power to a leader or king, making a total of ten leaders or ten kings.

Phase 3: After the ten regions and ten leaders appear, another leader will appear after them. This eleventh leader will be distinct from the ten; he won't be one of them. He will be the emerging Antichrist. He will come from the people who destroyed Israel in AD 70 (Dan. 9:26). Israel was destroyed by the Roman Empire in AD 70 (iron). The Antichrist will come from a revived Roman Empire or a reunited Europe.

Phase 4: The Antichrist will subdue or take away the power of three leaders.

Phase 5: The other seven leaders will surrender or give their power to the Antichrist, and he will control the whole world (Rev. 17:12–13).

Phase 6: The Antichrist will speak great words against God (be a blasphemer).

Phase 7: The Antichrist will wear out the saints (persecute and kill the Tribulation Period saints for the last three and one-half years of the seventieth week).

Phase 8: The Antichrist's dominion will be taken away from him (the "stone"—Christ—will strike him at His Second Coming).

Phase 9: God will establish the millennial kingdom at the Second Coming of Jesus.

Phase 10: God will give control of His kingdom to the saints. The church and Tribulation saints will reign with Jesus during the Millennium.

The Club of Rome Proposal

In the early 1970s, a powerful group of globalists called the Club of Rome submitted a proposal to the United Nations that called for the world to be divided into ten economic/political regions called mega-territories or kingdoms. This process of regionalization is being followed today. Below are their suggested ten regions and a map.

1. North America
2. Western Europe
3. Japan
4. Israel, South Africa, and Australia
5. Eastern Europe
6. Latin America
7. North Africa and the Middle East
8. Main Africa
9. South and Southeast Asia
10. Central Asia, including China

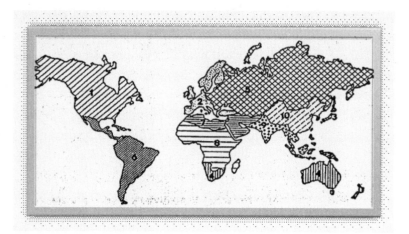

The Three-Phase Plan

The Club of Rome presented the United Nations with a three-phase plan to accomplish this process of regionalization and integration:

Phase 1: Divide the world into ten economic regions (trading blocs of nations).

Phase 2: Transform the ten economic regions into ten political regions by having each economic region adopt a regional constitution, appoint a leader, etc.

Phase 3: Integrate (or merge) the ten political regions into a one-world government.

A Progress Report

After looking at what the Bible says about how the last world government will develop and comparing it to the Club of Rome proposal, it is now time to notice how this plan is being implemented.

Phase 1: Divide the World into Ten Economic Regions.

There are now more than ten economic regions or trading blocs of nations, but the following list shows that the world is implementing the Club of Rome/UN plan. There will be changes, but it's important to know that the final world kingdom is coming on the scene right now. It's also important to know that the United Nations World Trade Organization (WTO) has decided that no nation will be allowed to trade with another nation or region unless it is a member of a region. With this rule, the WTO is forcing every nation on earth to join a region. Some of the regions are:

The European Union (EU)
The North American Leadership Summit (formerly CAFTA, NAFTA, NAU)
Japan
The Eurasian Economic Community
The Union of South American Nations
The ASEAN (Association of Southeast Nations)
    Economic Community
The Northeast Asian Nations
The African Union
The South African Development Community
The Gulf Cooperation Council

Phase 2: Transform the Ten Economic Regions into Ten Political Regions

The EU began in 1948 as an economic or trading bloc of nations. By 2009, it had been restructured many times and had grown to twenty-seven nations. It was then transformed from an economic region of nations into a political region of nations (a process called full region-alization) with the signing of the Lisbon Treaty, which established a constitution and central government that took office on January 1, 2010. This was a giant step forward because it meant that one man began to rule over twenty-seven nations.

It's important to understand that the United Nations decided to designate the EU as the first group to become a political region and to establish this political region as the political pattern for the other nine groups. This decision to establish the EU as the political pattern for the others was made so that every economic region would be structured the same way politically.

Creating regional governments takes power out of the hands of the voters and puts it into the hands of unelected bureaucrats (appointed promoters). It removes the accountability of the bureaucrats and reduces the ability of the people to stop it.

The chart below shows the target date that some of the economic regions have set for transformation into a political entity (full regionalization). Know that targets are sometimes met and sometimes missed, sometimes speeded up, and sometimes delayed.

Regional currencies are a step toward regional governments. Several of the economic regions are considering their own regional currency.

NAME	TARGET FOR FULL REGIONALIZATION	PROPOSED REGIONAL CURRENCY
EU	2009	EURO
NALS/NAU	2010	AMERO
GCC	2015	GULFO or KHALEEJI
ASEAN EC	2015	
UNASUR	2019	

Phase 3: Integrate (or merge) the ten political regions into a one-world government.

Several nations want to use the current economic crisis to speed up the formation of world government. Some, including China, Russia, India, Brazil, Iran, Libya, France, and Kazakhstan, want a one-world currency. Russian President Medvedev was photographed with a proposed world currency coin minted in Belgium and presented to world leaders at the G-8 summit in July 2009. He said, "This means they're getting ready" and called it "a good sign that we understand how interdependent we are."

More than one United Nations panel (including the UN Conference on Trade and Development and the UN Commission of Experts on International Financial Reform) has suggested that the world drop the dollar as the Federal Reserve currency in favor of a "basket of multi-currencies" or "shared reserve currencies." Their intermediate goal is a basket of ten regional or ten shared currencies, but their ultimate goal is a one-world supra-currency.

In September 2009 the G-20 nations, which control 85 percent of the world's gross domestic product, "agreed to coordinate their economic policies and programs and to submit them to the International Monetary Fund [IMF] for comment and approval."[199] When this begins in 2012, the IMF's power will be limited to supervision and moral persuasion. At a later date, the IMF will be empowered to sanction nations that don't comply.

In December 2009, President Obama attended the UN Climate Change Conference in Copenhagen. Although it was said that the main focus of the conference was to deal with climate change, there was an underlying effort to get the majority of the nations to sign a binding treaty that would establish a world government with authority. The conference was a disaster from beginning to end, and that highly sought-after, binding treaty was not signed. However, several world leaders predicted that it will be signed in the near future and possibly will have already been signed within a year of this book's writing.

Everyone needs to know that the world leaders are setting the stage for the implementation of a worldwide economic system that will be used by Antichrist to enslave the world. And if the world is close to seeing a global economic system come into existence, it is even closer to the Rapture. For several months now, world leaders, not teachers of Bible prophecy, have been openly declaring that the New

World Order is emerging. One more economic crisis, war, or terrorist attack could trigger its sudden rise. It is coming, and it may already be too late to stop it.

The United States

A region that includes the United States is now coming on the scene. It began in 1988 with the Canada-United States Free Trade Agreement (FTA). In 1994, Mexico was added and it became the North American Free Trade Agreement (NAFTA). Just before it was presented to the U.S. Congress, Henry Kissinger wrote, "What Congress will have before it is not a conventional trade agreement but the architecture of a new international system…a first step toward a new world order [world government]."[200] In the early 2000s, the heads of Canada, the United States, and Mexico started discussing the expansion of NAFTA and, for a time, they considered calling it "NAFTA-Plus." But critics started calling it the North American Union (NAU), and the name caught on. In 2005, the tri-national leaders expanded NAFTA and called it the Security and Prosperity Partnership of North America (SPPNA). In 2006, Lou Dobbs, news anchor on CNN, said the SPPNA was part of a plan to merge the United States, Canada, and Mexico into a North American Union patterned after the European Union. In 2007, Congress blocked SPPNA funding when some decided that the ultimate goal was the creation of the NAU. In 2008, President Bush suggested the SPPNA be renamed the North American Leaders Summit (NALS) to divert public attention. In 2009, President Obama got the leaders of Canada and Mexico to agree to the name change, made it official, and placed America's negotiations under White House supervision. He called on the three nations to start working on ways to "integrate and harmonize the administrative rules" for many areas of the NALS. Although many try to mask what they are doing, the ultimate goal clearly is the transformation of this economic region into another political region. In May of 2005, the Council on Foreign Relations Task Force on North America drafted a plan to "transform the current trilateral Security and Prosperity Partnership of North America into a North American union regional government" by 2010.[201] They want to establish one border around these three nations and eliminate the borders between them. Some want to create a NAU parliament of fifteen members (five from each nation) to rule over the NAU. They want to make one of the fifteen NAU parliament members the president (the Bible calls him a "leader," "horn," or "king") of the NAU. Some have suggested that the NAU parliament be given supremacy over all national governing bodies (including the U.S. Congress). And they want to establish a NAU court of justice with supremacy over the U.S. Supreme Court.[202] Other goals include:

- Allowing the unrestricted movement of people and goods between nations.
- Giving amnesty, Social Security, and health benefits to illegal aliens in the United States.
- Merging the militaries of the three nations.
- Building a superhighway called the I-69 Corridor from Mexico to Canada.

The Amero

In 2007, mention of the amero began appearing on the Internet (see below). Reports said these items were minted at the United States Mint at Denver. This triggered a big debate about what they are. An American spokesman called them "medallions." A Mexican spokesman called them "coins." And a Canadian spokesman called them "a potential reality." Some ridiculed the idea of a North American Union and the amero. They called it a myth, the product of conspiracy theorists, etc. But there's little doubt in this writer's mind that these things are fact because they involve three nations, the U.S. Council on Foreign Relations, years of negotiations, and more. Check out the following Web sites:

- http://bankling.com/2009/the-amero-currency-myths-facts-and-25-great-resources-for-further-research
- http://nationalexpositor.com/News/945.html
- http://www.globalresearch.ca/index.php?context=va&aid=7854
- http://en.wikipedia.org/wiki/Amero

The North American Union Flag

Someone connected with NAFTA developed an emblem with a flag on it. The left third of the flag is part of the American flag. The center third of the flag is part of the Mexican flag. And the right third of the flag is part of the Canadian flag. It is not shown here because it is a registered trademark of the NAFTA Secretariat, but viewers can see what it looks like on many Web sites, including the following:

- http://www.nafta-sec-alena.org/
- http://bankling.com/2009/the-amero-currency-myths-facts-and-25-great-resources-for-further-research
- http://glenngohr.wordpress.com/2007/09/01/i-pledge-allegiance-to-the-flag-of-the-north-american-union

The Loss of U.S. Sovereignty

On April 6, 2009, Jay Sekulow and the American Center for Law and Justice expressed concern about the Obama "administration's new strategy of internationalism—embracing foreign and economic policies that may very well put U.S. sovereignty at risk."[203] The next day, the Department of Homeland Security issued a report warning against the possibility of violence in the U.S. by citizens concerned about illegal immigration, increasing federal power, restrictions on firearms, abortion, the loss of U.S. sovereignty, etc. The report says end-times prophecies could motivate extremist individuals and groups to stockpile food, ammunition, and weapons.[204]

Following President Obama's August 2009 attendance at the North American Leader's Summit in Guadalajara, Mexico:

> Sources in the State Department confirmed that the more than twenty trilateral working groups will continue under the North American Leader's Summit, with bureaucrats from the three nations assigned from different agencies within each government. The groups will work on a North American agenda "integrating and harmonizing" administrative rules across a broad range of policy areas ranging from transportation to border security, health, e-commerce, movement of goods, environment, energy and financial services.[205]

The fact that the three nations are working to "integrate" and "harmonize" their administrative rules in all of these areas clearly indicates that their ultimate goal is the merger of the three nations. Reports are even being circulated that President Obama plans to use the Amnesty Bill to give top priority to fast tracking the Security and Prosperity Partnership/North American Union.[206]

How Close Is It?

The last world government will begin when the Antichrist subdues three of the ten leaders and will end with the Second Coming of Jesus. At most, it will last seven years. When prophecy teachers speak of this, someone invariably says, "But that could be thousands of years from now." No! It is coming on the scene right now, and it could be just months, not years, away.

Nebuchadnezzar's dream statue is a timeline beginning with the Babylonian capture of Judah and ending with the Second Coming. The world has moved from the top of the statue's head on this timeline down into the feet. The EU is the big toe. It has now become a political entity. The other toes are forming. It took twenty-six hundred years to go from the top of the head to the beginning of the feet. It will take many fewer years than that to get to the tip of the toes. And since the Rapture will occur at least seven years before the tip of the toes (to allow for the seven-year Tribulation Period), it is very close.

CHAPTER FOURTEEN

ECONOMIC ENGINEERING FOR NEW WORLD ORDER

By Wilfred J. Hahn

The Bible tells us that a time will come when commerce—the act of buying and selling—can be controlled worldwide. This facility will actually be invoked at some point during the Great Tribulation period by an evil personage:

> And he causeth all, both small and great, rich and poor, free and bond, to receive a mark in their right hand, or in their foreheads: And that no man might buy or sell, save he that had the mark, or the name of the beast, or the number of his name. (Rev. 13:16–17)

This is an oft-referenced verse, infamously misquoted and misinterpreted by Christians and unbelievers alike. It is the source of countless speculations about the identity of the "mark" and the "number." The most critical error in the verse's interpretation concerns the identity of who actually brings in these controls. It is not the first beast with seven heads, which is of the lineage that gives rise to the physical Antichrist. Rather, it is the second beast, which emerges from earth and has two horns like a lamb, that brings in these commercial controls. This latter beast is commonly linked with the False Prophet mentioned in Revelation 16:13.

I have always thought it a telling alert that it will be a religious figure who ends up being the world's last "economic minister." A strange coincidence? No. Seen together, macroeconomics and globalization today are the world's largest religion. The beliefs embedded in these bosom ideologies are the prevailing hope of humanity. As such, it is only fitting that a deceiving religious figure would preach such a final "prosperity gospel" to the entire world. Indeed, the value proposition the False Prophet will make at that time may sound like this: "Take the number that is being endorsed by the office of this religious official and you will have prosperity." At that time, there will be such a crisis that people will likely respond as they did to Joseph in the third year of the famine: "Wherefore shall we die before thine eyes, both we and our land? Buy us and our land for bread, and we and our land will be servants unto Pharaoh" (Gen. 47:19).

However, the intent of this chapter is to show just how ripe the world has already become for this scenario, having already prepared the very control systems that will be given over to the False Prophet and the evil purposes of the Antichrist.

Why Global Systems Are Needed

Money, the use of which is assuredly one factor that sets humans apart from animals, is the designated bargaining medium of mammon—the word used in the Bible to portray wealth as a false god. Its strategic significance in the cosmology of mankind is more than just serving as the chief temptation that qualifies "the love of money [as being] the root of all evil" (1 Tim. 6:10). Crucially, "money systems" also play a crucial eschatological role as no other form of earthly or spiritual rule. Since Satan and his hierarchy of fallen angels are not omnipresent, as is God, they must improvise a global presence. Therefore, an inventive tactic is needed to effect worldwide control. Here, a global commercial system offers the next most potent platform for omnipresence. No other medium is more conducive to world control than money. The supporting technology and the organizational structure are nearly complete...the concentration of financial command nodes is far advanced. Only one thing remains: the imperative to pull it all together—the final prescription of policy.

Concentration of Financial Control

Just how advanced is the final global financial architecture? Outlining a few trends will provide some anecdotal evidence of how rapidly global financial systems are converging and centralizing. We could cite countless more examples; however, here we point to just four telltale signs.

1. **Concentrated Owners.** For the U.S. (still the world's largest economy—and the wealthiest financially), consider that latest available year-end 2006 data shows total institutional investors—defined as pension funds, investment companies, insurance companies, banks, and foundations—controlled assets totalling $27.1 trillion. According to the Conference Board, this level represents a tenfold increase from $2.7 trillion in 1980. The equity market value of total institutional equity holdings increased from or 37.2 percent of total U.S. equity markets in 1980 to 66.3 percent in 2006. This represents a historic, all-time high and most certainly documents the rapidity of the trend of centralization. The same trend is witnessed around the globe, as the next example makes clear.

2. **More Evidence of Concentrated Holdings.** A pair of physicists at the Swiss Federal Institute of Technology in Zurich published

preliminary findings of their network analysis of the world financial economy as it looked in early 2007. Stefano Battiston and James Glattfelder extracted the information for 24,877 stocks and 106,141 shareholding entities in forty-eight countries. It revealed what they called the "backbone" of each country's financial market. These back-bones represented the owners of 80 percent of a country's market capital, yet consisted of a remarkably small number of shareholders. The most pared-down backbones exist in Anglo-Saxon countries, including the U.S., Australia, and the U.K. Paradoxically, these same countries are considered by economists to have the most widely held stocks in the world, with ownership of companies tending to be spread out among many investors. But while each American company may link to many owners, Glattfelder and Battiston's analysis found that the owners varied little from stock to stock, meaning that comparatively few hands are holding the reins of the entire market.[207]

3. Financial Institutions Become More Concentrated. Perversely, financial institutions continue to become larger, despite the clear "moral hazards" of being "too big to fail." Quoting Simon Johnson of the Peterson Institute, who is an astute observer of global financial systems:

> The largest six banks in the U.S. economy now have total assets in excess of 63 percent of GDP [Gross Domestic Product]. This is a significant increase from even 2006, when the same banks' assets were around 55 percent of GDP, and a complete transformation compared with the situation in the United States just fifteen years ago, when the six largest banks had combined assets of only around 17 percent of GDP.[208]

The same trend is evident at the global level. For example, at the end of 2008, the top fifty financial companies in the world accounted for greater than $25 trillion in assets.[209] That amount of assets is equivalent to greater than 40 percent of the entire world's net economic output. To be sure, this business sector will have become even more concentrated since this latest statistic was tabulated, as the global financial crisis triggered many takeovers and corporate consolidations.

4. Organization of the Global Financial System. This most visible evidence of a fast-centralizing global financial system is not recognized by most people. What we mean here is that the present generation of society is already so accustomed to an interconnected, homogeneous financial system that it no longer sees how advanced and recent this phenomenon is. For example, virtually every country today has a central bank. This would only be natural, most people will think. Yet, as recent as the year 1900, there were only eighteen central banks in the world. Today, there are more than 170 such banks or equivalent institutions across the globe, most working their policies with the same methodological alchemy…steering the big economic and financial ships with the small rudder of a fractional-reserve system.[210] Today, fifty-six of the world's central banks are members of the Bank of International Settlements. This institution, popularly called "the bank of central banks," serves as a policy-making forum as well as voluntary regulatory regime—and it is also active in extending reserves. Every two weeks, leaders of the major central banks around the world discuss policy and try to coordinate responses of the various participating countries. It is an influential club.

A number of other organizations have grown to wield global clout—for example, the International Monetary Fund. Founded in the late 1940s and currently comprising 186 member countries, its role today is to monitor and stabilize the world's financial markets and exchange accounts. This institution may very well be the author of the world's future unified currency. Its invention, the Special Depositary Receipt—better known as the SDR—is ideally suited to serve as a central currency for the developing, multi-polar world. Actually, the SDR already facilitates this function in some ways, although not yet

in a major capacity. A number of other global transnational organizations could be mentioned that play a role in interconnecting the
world's financial systems.

Suffice it to conclude that a one-world financial system already
exists, though perhaps not in name. Everywhere one looks, the forces
of centralization can be identified, whether in North America or globally. Today, perhaps less than ten thousand people control the world's
money flows. Some have estimated a far smaller number…as low as
six hundred. The signs of centralization are everywhere.

System Hurtled Forward by Global Financial Crisis

According to a recently released study by two well-known international economists, Carmen Reinhart and Kenneth Rogoff, the impact
of the global financial crisis upon global debt levels has been catastrophic. In their research report, they document that government
debt levels have risen 75 percent over the last two years for the top
five crisis countries (U.S., UK, Ireland, Iceland, and Spain).[211] Stop
to consider this statistic for a moment. Astoundingly, in the short
time span of only two years, government debt levels for these Western
nations have risen by more than two-thirds. This is not a statistic that
applies to a single, "banana republic" nation, but rather to leading,
developed nations.

While anyone following global financial affairs during the last few
years will not have been surprised by this development, it is nonetheless alarming. Many secular observers would agree. However, here we
wish to focus upon the world's prophetic timeline, and therefore upon
an entirely different line of inquiry: Just why the rapidity? How does
this trend correlate with the Bible? Does government debt have an
end-time role?

Taken together with several other trends and a literal scriptural
perspective, this leads to an irrefutable diagnosis, in our view. These
developments do align with end-time Bible prophecy. Though, of

course, we cannot draw any near-term, specific predictions, we would be negligent not to conclude that the world is indeed on the fast track to great troubles "such as never was" (Dan. 12:1).

Just what threat to the entire earth would cause policy makers around the globe to plunge into such lunacy? Of what great significance is this development?

How Three End-Time Conditions Interconnect

We must now return to the topic of government debt, which plays a vital end-time role. Just how does it figure into last-day developments? Isn't it strange that government indebtedness plays a role? Isn't it indebted and trapped individuals who come under the "economic" influence of the False Prophet and the Antichrist? If, as the Proverbs writer says, that "the rich ruleth over the poor, and the borrower is servant to the lender" (22:7), just how can indebted governments collaborate to rule the world?

Actually, with respect to the "money" aspects of last-days events, conditions are somewhat more complex, according to the Bible. At least three major "money" impulses can be identified from Bible prophecy, including that of an indebted world rulership. To explain how these conditions interweave, allow us to describe each of these three roles.

1. A Protracted Wealth Skew. What is meant by a wealth skew? It is the extreme distribution between the wealthy and the poor—with the wealthy becoming richer and fewer and the relatively poor more so. But is such a condition prophesied? Yes, James specifically prophesied that an amassing of riches plays a role in the end times. He said, "Go to now, ye rich men, weep and howl.... Ye have heaped treasure together for the last days" (James 5:1, 3b). Here, we understand that not only may wealth have increased overall, but it is also "heaped" or "amassed," as is implied by the Greek word *thesaurizo*. This is an important distinction, as it gives evidence of a wealth skew. Wealth cannot be heaped and concentrated without deprivation of someone else's wealth.

However, is it reasonable to deduce this end-time condition of an extreme wealth skew from only one verse? Not only is this verse clear, but many other Bible references foreshadow circumstances that align with this assumption as well. Both Old Testament and New Testament prophets outlined times of extreme commercialism and financial oppression in the last days. Isaiah and Zechariah, among other Old Testament prophets, pointed to extreme commercialism. And in the New Testament, the apostle Peter warned of "perilous times [that] shall come" that will be evidenced by covetousness (2 Tim. 3:1–2). John prophesied about the Laodicean church that says, "I am rich, and increased with goods, and have need of nothing" (Rev. 3:17). This seventh and last church admonished is commonly believed to represent the last-days church.

In December 2006, a groundbreaking report entitled *The World Distribution of Household Wealth* (World Institute for Development Economics Research, UN University—UNU-Wider) was released. The results were much more pronounced than previously indicated by other studies that surveyed income. Wealth and income, though surely related, are quite different. Income is generally defined as the annual flow of earnings and incomes, while wealth is the accumulation of income and hoarded assets. According to the authors' research, the top 10 percent of adults in the world own 85 percent of global household wealth (2005). The average member of this wealthy group therefore has 8.5 times the holdings of the global average. Furthermore, the top 2 percent and 1 percent of the world's population are estimated to own 51 percent and 40 percent of world household wealth, respectively. This is a more extreme distribution than estimated by surveying global incomes in previous studies.

2. Indebtedness as a Necessary Device. As already pointed out, for someone to become relatively rich, someone else must become steeply indebted—either involuntarily or willingly. Here, as we see, indebted governments play a role of transferring wealth from the masses to the rich. But, does the Bible support the idea that the "Antichrist system" will be an indebted entity? Actually, our understanding of this question first came from reading the prophecies of Habakkuk. Carefully consider these verses:

> For the vision is yet for an appointed time, but at the end it shall speak, and not lie: though it tarry, wait for it; because it will surely come, it will not tarry. Behold, his soul which is lifted up is not upright in him: but the just shall live by his faith. Yea also, because he transgresseth by wine, he is a proud man, neither keepeth at home, who enlargeth his desire as hell, and is as death, and cannot be satisfied, but gathereth unto him all nations, and heapeth unto him all people: Shall not all these take up a parable against him, and a taunting proverb against him, and say, "Woe to him that increaseth that which is not his! How long? And to him that ladeth himself with thick clay!" Shall they not rise up suddenly that shall bite thee, and awake that shall vex thee, and thou shalt be for booties unto them? Because thou hast spoiled many nations, all the remnant of the people shall spoil thee; because of men's blood, and for the violence of the land, of the city, and of all that dwell therein. (Hab. 2:3–8)

Here, the prophet Habakkuk sheds some light on our questions. Although his prophecies were probably first directed to the Babylon of his day, they clearly also had an end-time application. The Lord answered him, "For the vision is yet for an appointed time, but at the end it shall speak, and not lie" (Hab. 2:3). Habakkuk's prophecies could not provide a more accurate description of the world's emerging ruling structure of our times and perhaps of the future. It is built upon greed, oppression, and extortion, taking the world captive through a financial and economic trap, as well as by other means. But there is one additional insight that Habakkuk provides: The end-time ruling order is an indebted one and verse 6 reflects the condition of the "wicked foe's" indebtedness, saying, "Woe to him that increaseth that which is not his!"

3. Emergence of Rich Elites. Now that we have documented the conditions of a "wealth skew" and an "indebted world order," we come to the question of the identity of the rich elites. The prophet Daniel spoke of them in the verse that also refers to the Antichrist: "Thus shall he do in the most strongholds with a strange god, whom he shall acknowledge and increase with glory: and he shall cause them to rule over many, and shall divide the land for gain" (Dan. 11:39).

Who are "them" that will "increase with glory," "rule over many," and play a role in the dividing of land "for gain"? The answer: those who acknowledge the Antichrist (which we can also take to mean the Antichrist system of world rule). Virtually all English Bible translations use the word "acknowledge" here, which means that certain people who recognize Antichrist and accept his authority will receive a reward—land. It should be noted that the original Aramaic word used for "land" in this verse can also convey the idea of property or economic domain as well as geographic area. After all, in ancient times, land was the foundation of wealth and economy.

It only follows that these elites, whoever they are, must be a small group of people who likely will be influential in their own right. Why? They will be made rulers over many. As not everyone can be made a ruler over many, their number will be few. Not only is this logical, but the Bible also specifically tells us what the reward will be for everybody else…in other words, *all* the rest of the masses that acknowledge and worship the Antichrist. They will not be killed (a negative reward), and they will be allowed to "buy or sell." The Antichrist causes "all, both small and great, rich and poor, free and bond, to receive a mark in their right hand, or in their foreheads: And that no man might buy or sell, save he that had the mark, or the name of the beast, or the number of his name" (Rev. 13:16–17).

The elites, on the other hand, will be paid off for their loyalty with further reward—power or economic domain, we reason. It is the same or similar deal that Satan offered Christ when He was being tested in the wilderness. Satan promised that "all this power will I give thee, and the glory of them: for that is delivered unto me; and to whomsoever I will I give it. If thou therefore wilt worship me, all shall be thine" (Luke 4:6–7). The elites selected for reward must have something to barter in return—likely, their fame or endorsement. We are given at least a few criteria with which to identify these individuals at that future date. First, they must be humans. Also, they must be capable of being rulers, already likely possessing some measure of power and authority. And, they must be willing worldly conspirators.

Although these events play out during the future Tribulation period *(and therefore really do not concern us),* is it possible today to discern the power structures that these elites might command? Of course, we can only speculate as to who these persons may be that the prophet Daniel mentions. One possibility is that these could be powerful heads of large, multi-national corporations. After all, some of these companies are already larger than many individual nations in terms of their commercial influence and economic footprint.

Multi-national firms today, as a group, are probably the most influential economic force in the world. And, because "money is power" in this age, they may also be the most powerful, viewed as a group. Though these companies may have established their roots a few hundred years ago, their global muscle has only really developed over the past half-century or so. Today, of the top one hundred economic entities in the world, roughly half is made up of countries and the other half by multi-national corporations. The heads of these companies, though they answer to boards of directors, nevertheless are very influential. These firms can employ hundreds of thousands of people—more than the population of many countries. Some secular analysts foresee the day when a small group of such commercial giants will indeed dominate the world economy.

Or, could the elites mentioned by Daniel simply be ultra-rich individuals who control much wealth—perhaps entire industries and many multi-national corporations? It is in their self-interest to support the regime of the Antichrist. In their materialist worldview, preservation of their wealth must be the primary objective. They could not have reached their ultra-wealthy status without governments having also facilitated such enormous wealth transfer, either through economic policy or increasing indebtedness. These governments are in cahoots with the ultra-wealthy "princes," much in the same way as foreshadowed by the corrupt relationships today even in America—for example, between the Washington DC Beltway and Wall Street.

We cannot conclusively identify the elites Daniel mentions. This shouldn't be disappointing. The only wise and sure conclusion is that we must keep our options open—keeping ourselves oriented to the Scriptures and watching and waiting for our Lord's return so we will not be distracted or caught "sleeping." This causes us to keep watching, to not be taken unaware, and to remain open to new information. The world's power structures do keep shifting. Though "we have also a more sure word of prophecy; whereunto ye do well that ye take heed" (2 Pet. 1:19), at the same time we must also realize that our enemy is cunning and a supreme master of deception.

A Calculated Conspiracy against God

The Bible essentially identifies three main sets of players in the "mammon-controlled" financial saga of the last-days world. There is a world government that at one point takes the form of ten nations, later to be headed by the Antichrist himself (the Beast). These are the "ten horns" mentioned in Revelation 17:12. The preferred interpretation of this author is that these will be key nations—most likely heavily indebted (as many leading countries today already are)—that band together to aggregate sufficient power to establish world rule.

These nations have (must have) the complicity of the rich elites. For nations to be heavily indebted, there must also be corresponding lenders and cronies. And, given that the Bible also tells us of a great "heaping of wealth," we can know that relatively few people will be the ultra-rich who underpin the indebtedness of the nations with their claims upon wealth. We see all of these tendencies already at work today.

Biblical Perspective on World Conditions Today

Of literally hundreds of opinions by so-called economists on the causes of and remedies for the current economic troubles this writer has read in response to the global financial crisis, not one can be recalled that in any way alludes to the unbridled, basic nature of man as being the problem. This is the "human condition" of a fallen world. While the God-appointed facility of civil government during this dispensation is surely charged to pursue beneficial and wise policies (Gen. 9:6), temporal solutions must not ignore what is right in the eyes of God, in favor of what is right in their own eyes (Isa. 5:21).

The Bible says the heart of man is the issue: "The heart is deceitful above all things, and desperately wicked: who can know it?" (Jer. 17:9). Mankind is innately sinful. How then can future financial crises be entirely avoided? Not until the vices of greed and the love of money are eradicated. Until then, "They search out iniquities; they accomplish a diligent search: both the inward thought of every one of them, and the heart, is deep" (Psa. 64:6).

There was a time "that the wickedness of man was great in the earth, and that every imagination of the thoughts of his heart was only evil continually" (Gen. 6:5). God saw no other way but to intervene and end it. Today, the world is quickly approaching a similar state. Bible prophecy clearly outlines that God will again intervene in the affairs of mankind in wrath.

In another vein, the times today are similar to those during the construction of the Tower of Babel. The world's late state of globalism mirrors the sentiment of those ancient days when "they said, 'Go to, let us build us a city and a tower, whose top may reach unto heaven; and let us make us a name, lest we be scattered abroad upon the face of the whole earth'" (Gen. 11:4). Globalism is counter to the will of God, as evidenced by His supernatural intervention at Babel when He caused people to disperse and confounded their efforts by instituting different languages.

But haven't we all heard these end-time admonitions countless times before? Have not the processes identified here been underway for a long time? Yes, but with some key differences that should immediately quell the scoffer's spirit. First, we are the generation that would "see all these things," as Christ said (Matt. 24:33). The fig tree (Israel) has begun to blossom. "When her branch is yet tender, and putteth forth leaves, ye know that summer is near" (Mark 13:28). This season can be identified, and it is here. And, there will be no false starts of this prophesied event; it is a process that, once begun, will not be aborted. The Holy Spirit said through Isaiah:

> Before she travailed, she brought forth; before her pain came, she was delivered of a man-child. "Who hath heard such a thing? Who hath seen such things? Shall a land be born in one day? Shall a nation be brought forth at once? For as soon as Zion travailed, she brought forth her children. Shall I bring to the birth, and not cause to bring forth?" saith Jehovah. "Shall I that cause to bring forth shut the womb?" saith thy God. (Isa. 66:7–9)

The last season of the "last days" has indeed begun and is already far advanced. Today, all prophesied conditions are global in scale rather than applying to just one or a few nations. These conditions can all be shown to be accelerating.

Final Orientation for Christians Living in the Financial System

We live in an era of global convergence in values. The world has agreed to endorse humanist materialism. Fractional reserve banking, wealth in the form of debt, and the notion that human progress is defined by growth in gross domestic product make up the unholy trinity of toppling idols that must be propped up and nailed down at any cost. "They deck it with silver and with gold; they fasten it with nails and with hammers, that it move not" (Jer. 10:4).

Franklin D. Roosevelt is believed to have said, "The money-changers have fled from their high seats in the temple our civilization. We may now restore that temple to the ancient truths." He made this rather optimistic statement during his first inaugural address, in 1933. At that time, America was in the depths of the Great Depression. Wall Street had been chastened, and thousands of banks were closing their doors. Unfortunately, Roosevelt was wrong. He could not have imagined that the business of money would become many, many times larger relative to human life than during his day.

It surely did, and it likely will remain so. The "love of money" reigns rampant today in its advanced state, there being fewer and fewer restrainers in the world against this force. Corruption runs deep in high places, the world having committed to a materialistic "heaven on earth" (denying God), and much of religion has found a comfortable coexistence with this state of affairs. That this is the road to an eventual holocaust for mankind is supported by Christ's words: "Man shall not live by bread alone, but by every word that proceedeth out of the mouth of God" (Matt. 4:4). This statement in itself essentially condemns the modern world's slavish fixation on every nuance and statistic of the fabricated notion of gross domestic product.

The day is very near when it will be possible for a global authority to completely control global commerce. Already, it is technically impossible to live without money or a bank account. People who have attempted this must still rely on the charity and handouts of those who do have monetary income and bank accounts.

While the technology and global systems stand prepared for this eventuality, the global "political" power structure is not yet in place. Such large organizations as the Bank of International Settlements, the World Bank, etc., have not yet given their levers of power to a central authority. That development awaits the emergence of the final ten kings. These events will happen very suddenly...once their time has arrived.

Christians, as everyone, are already entrapped in a global financial system. While we enjoy its conveniences, we also suffer under the many materialistic temptations that the spirit behind these worldly systems incessantly proposes. Someday, these systems will be turned against the Tribulation saints.

Today, pre-Rapture saints are implored to enter a different kind of transaction:

> Counsel thee to buy of me gold tried in the fire, that thou mayest be rich; and white raiment, that thou mayest be clothed, and that the shame of thy nakedness do not appear; and anoint thine eyes with eye salve, that thou mayest see. (Rev. 3:18)

Those are the words of Christ to the seventh and last church, which exists even now just prior to His return. It is not an impulse purchase, an approach so widely promoted in our culture today. The gratification is not instant, but eternal. The apostles knew the cost of "gold refined by fire."

> But in all things approving ourselves as the ministers of God, in much patience, in afflictions, in necessities, in distresses, in stripes, in imprisonments, in tumults, in labours, in watchings, in fastings; by pureness, by knowledge, by longsuffering, by

kindness, by the Holy Ghost, by love unfeigned, by the word of truth, by the power of God, by the armour of righteousness on the right hand and on the left, by honour and dishonour, by evil report and good report: as deceivers, and yet true; as unknown, and yet well known; as dying, and, behold, we live; as chastened, and not killed; as sorrowful, yet always[s] rejoicing; as poor, yet making many rich; as having nothing, and yet possessing all things. (2 Cor. 6:4–10)

CHAPTER FIFTEEN

GOD'S GROANING CREATION

By Al Gist

The apostle Paul warned his young associate Timothy, "This know also, that in the last days perilous times shall come" (2 Tim. 3:1). With the "wars and rumors of wars" (Matt. 24:6), terrorism, environmental degeneration, and political and economic upheaval, it certainly appears that we are in the midst of those perilous last days.

Adults around the world are faced with the ever-increasing challenges of providing protection, education, and the basic necessities of food, clothing, and shelter for their families. Often, this requires both parents to work long hours at multiple jobs, all the while performing a delicate balancing act to ensure the "quality time" a family needs. The demands of life seem to be getting harder and harder, with no relief in sight. There are constant worries about finances, taxes, crime, the direction that our nation/society is heading, and myriad other concerns. The stress can be overwhelming!

Add to this the apparent increase in mega natural disasters and the struggle for the "good life" seems almost completely out of reach!

Hurricanes, tornadoes, volcanoes, earthquakes, tsunamis, forest fires, floods, and droughts destroy untold millions of lives annually. As Jerry Lee Lewis sang many years ago, there really is "a whole lotta shakin' goin' on"!

We may wonder: "Is our modern society really getting better, or are the complexities and pace of modern life robbing us of that simpler, more routine, quiet, and peaceful lifestyle we remember from previous generations? Are real peace and security myths? What is happening to our world?"

Where do we find answers to these probing questions about life, liberty, and the pursuit of happiness? Only one source of information is completely correct and 100-percent reliable, without any mixture of error or slanting from personal opinion. God's Word gives us the information to understand why our world is plagued by these ever-increasing troubles. From the time of man's original fall in the Garden of Eden, sin not only infected the hearts of men, but it affected all of creation as well: "The whole creation groaneth and travaileth in pain together until now" (Rom. 8:22). The resulting degradation of the planet has continued unabated and, if left to its own course, will eventually result in complete destruction. Only by the intervention of God, the one who created it, can that course be altered (and reversed) to produce a utopian society and peaceful planet. And, praise God, that intervention *is* going to happen! Jesus will one day come back to the earth to set all things straight and restore the planet to its beautiful, Edenic conditions. Unfortunately, that will not happen until *after* the most turbulent period of pain, heartache, and bloodshed humanity will ever experience.

Jesus said many signs would precede that day of tribulation and His return, letting us know that we are getting close to it. He said, "When ye shall see all these things, *know* that it is near, even at the doors" (Matt. 24:33, emphasis added). Obviously, our Lord expects us to *know* when we are nearing that momentous time.

He also said, "And when these things *begin* to come to pass, then look up, and lift up your heads; for your redemption draweth nigh" (Luke 21:28, emphasis added). Many of the signs pointing to our Lord's coming will find their ultimate fulfillment during the Tribulation, after the church has already been raptured. When we see these signs *beginning* to come to pass— that is, when they are *starting* to happen, when we can see the stage being set for their fulfillment— then we should look up, knowing that our redemption (in Him) is getting very close.

Most of the signs of the last days will develop over a period of time. They are not instantaneous events, but are *processes* building up and increasing until they culminate just before Jesus comes.

For example, in the battle of Gog of Magog (Ezek. 38–39), the Bible tells about a war that will be fought around the time of the Tribulation. Today, we are already witnessing the development of international ties that will form the coalition of nations uniting to fight this war against Israel. In other words, the international stage is being set now for that war to happen; the *process* that will lead to its actual fulfillment has begun!

Here's another example: The Bible clearly states that there will be a Third Temple in Jerusalem during the Tribulation (Matt. 24:15, 2 Thess. 2:4, Rev. 11:1–2). But the Jews won't just suddenly wake up one day and say, "Let's start building the Temple today!" Many years of planning and preparing for the construction and operation of the Temple must take place before the first stone is ever laid. Those preparations are being made now, and this *process* will soon result in the actual construction of the Temple.

In His Olivet Discourse (Matt. 24–25), Jesus made it clear that we can expect to see a *pattern* in the signs pointing to His return. After telling His disciples about many of the signs, He said, "All these are the beginning of sorrows" (Matt. 24:8). The word translated from the Greek as "sorrows" is a reference to the labor pains of a woman just before she gives birth. In other words, just as a woman knows for months that she is pregnant, and she even has a due date for the birth, suddenly one day the birth labor pains will begin. At that point, the woman knows the time of her delivery is very close, although it may yet be hours away. As the labor process continues and the pains become steadily stronger and more frequent, she understands that the birth of her child is only moments away.

Likewise, many of the events that will happen just before Jesus comes will be commonplace for years. But suddenly one day, they will begin to increase in strength and frequency. The "labor pains" of the last days of the age will have begun, telling us that we are getting very close to His arrival!

This "birth-pains" pattern is especially true when we are looking at certain signs. When His disciples asked, "What shall be the sign of thy coming, and of the end of the world?" (Matt. 24:3), Jesus began His dissertation by stating two things they should be wary of. First, He warned the disciples to be careful of the many people who would try to deceive them: "Take heed that no man deceive you" (Matt. 24:4b). In this context, we must understand that Jesus was warning His followers not to be deceived by the many charlatans who would come pointing to various *erroneous* signs of His return—or who actually would come claiming to be Christ. "Don't be deceived by them!" He instructed.

Second, Jesus said certain events to come would be so disastrous that they might lead some to think the end of the world had arrived. Specifically, He mentioned "wars and rumors of wars" (Matt. 24:6). Certainly in times of war, the pain, death, and destruction are so devastating that one might think it is the end of the world. But Jesus said it's not so. He said, "All of these things must come to pass, but the end is not yet" (Matt. 24:6).

Our Lord explained that wars would be a way of life throughout the age and their existence should not be seen as an indicator of the end of the age. Then, He added to that list three other calamities: "famines, and pestilences, and earthquakes" (Matt. 24:7, Mark 13:8, Luke 21:11). These disastrous events will happen throughout the present age, and in and of themselves they are not signs of the end of the world. However, He added the intriguing statement that all of these things would also be "the beginning of sorrows"—i.e., the beginning of labor pains. These signs, though commonplace for many centuries, will suddenly increase in intensity and frequency—and *that* will be a sign that we are nearing the end of the age and the time of His return.

The last-days signs can be categorized into several groups. For example, there are signs that deal with politics. There are also signs that deal with society, religion, the economy, the nation of Israel, and the events taking place in the Middle East. But perhaps the most recognizable signs to the average person are those that deal with *nature.* Either directly or indirectly, all three of the Matthew 24:7 signs (famines, pestilences, and earthquakes) are associated with nature.

We will do a quick study of these signs (in reverse order of their appearance in the Scripture) to determine whether we are now living in the final days of "labor" just before Jesus returns.

Earthquakes

Even though there have always been earthquakes, storms, etc., are we now living in a time that is witness to a sudden increase in their intensity and frequency? Is the earth now in the "labor pains" Jesus said would herald His return? The violent earthquakes in the first few months of 2010 could certainly cause some to wonder whether the "labor pains" have indeed begun.

On January 12, 2010, a magnitude 7.0 MMS (Moment Magnitude Scale) earthquake struck the Caribbean nation of Haiti, with fifty-three aftershocks of 4.5 or greater. In total, the quake killed more than two hundred thousand people and injured more than three hundred thousand. The devastation to buildings and property was mind-boggling.

Just over a month later, on February 27, another very powerful earthquake hit just off the coast of Chile. It measured 8.8 MMS. Because the MMS is a logarithmic scale, a measurement of 8.0 MMS would be about ten times more powerful than a 7.0 MMS. That means the Chile quake was almost one hundred times stronger than the one in Haiti.[212]

Shortly after the earthquake in Chile, a 7.0 MMS struck Japan, followed by a 6.4 MMS in Taiwan and a 6.5 MMS in the Indonesian island of Sumatra. In the first week of March, eighty-five earthquakes between 5.0 and 6.6 MMS were measured around the world (some of these were aftershocks of the huge Chile quake).[213]

On April 4 of the same year, a 7.2 MMS earthquake hit Baja California, Mexico.[214]

The U.S. Geological Survey Web site features a page titled "Global Earthquake Search,"[215] where data can be accessed for earthquakes around the globe going back hundreds of years. The page allows one to enter search criteria to find all the earthquakes that match that description. So, here's what I entered:

- I asked for all earthquakes around the planet from the year 1700 to the year 2010.
- I asked that the list include only those quakes that measured at least 6.0 MMS, thinking that such quakes would be easily recorded, even when detection instruments were not as sensitive as they are today.

The search produced 2,233 earthquakes. So, I counted the number of these major earthquakes in each decade to see if they appeared to be on the increase. The results were astounding! I plotted the decade counts in the graph on the next page.

The dark black line shows the trend. It doesn't take a rocket scientist to see that since about the 1890s, there has been a strong upward trend in the number of major earthquakes in the world.

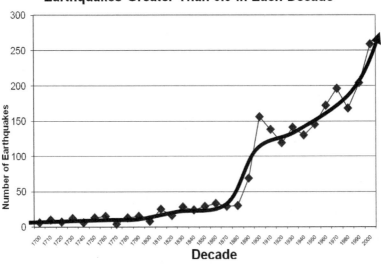

The frequency of major earthquakes worldwide is definitely increasing, but what about the intensity? Remember, the *pattern* of birth pains is a steady increase in both frequency and intensity. Plotting the top twenty-five strongest recorded earthquakes seems to indicate their intensity is also on the increase:

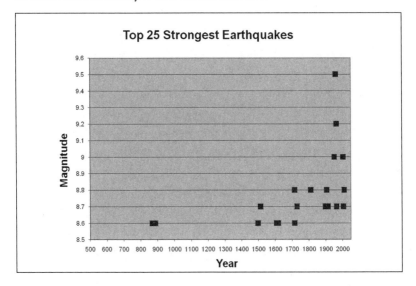

The Bible tells us that the greatest of all earthquakes is still to come! John said in Revelation that at the time of the glorious Second Coming of Jesus: "Lo, there was a great earthquake...and every mountain and island were moved out of their places" (Rev. 6:12b, 14b).

In chapter 16, more details are given describing this final earthquake as the mother of all earthquakes:

> And there were voices, and thunders, and lightnings; and there was a great earthquake, such as was not since men were upon the earth, so mighty an earthquake, and so great.... And every island fled away, and the mountains were not found. (Rev. 16:18, 20)

The prophet Isaiah seems to indicate that this great earthquake will be so strong it will even cause the planet to move on its axis of rotation: "Therefore I will shake the heavens, and *the earth shall remove out of her place,* in the wrath of the Lord of hosts, and in the day of His fierce anger" (Isa. 13:13, emphasis added).

According to an article by Gary Stearman entitled "Earthquakes! Are They Increasing?" in reference to this year's earthquake in Chile, "Seismologists who measured it...calculated a change in the earth's axis of rotation, which they say moved by eight centimeters (3.25 inches)!"[216]

Could this be the means God uses to reset the earth's weather back to its Edenic conditions that will follow in the millennial kingdom? One thing is sure: Just as the final pain of childbearing is the most horrific, the final earthquake also will be. But just as the overwhelming joy of having a new baby overshadows the pain of delivery, the overwhelming joy of King Jesus taking His rightful place as the King of kings on earth will also overshadow the horrors of the Tribulation.

Pestilence

Where I live in southwestern Louisiana, every year we have an atrocious outbreak of "lovebugs" (actually, *Plecia nearctica*)—small, black, flying insects that hatch out by the millions to live for just a few weeks, mate, and then die. Fortunately, they don't sting or cause damage by eating, but they're terrible pests. Automobiles get covered with their splattered remains, which some people claim even takes off the paint. These tiny bugs are constantly in your face and down your collar, and are just generally all over you when you're outdoors. Oh my! What a pestilence they are!

Maybe because of our annual lovebug infestation, when I think of a pestilence I envision a massive swarm of insects like locusts sweeping through the countryside, leaving devastation of every plant in its path. Or, I think of some other freak of nature that produces a gazillion insects that inflict untold damage on humanity, crops, or plant life—like a sudden outbreak of mosquitoes, flies, grasshoppers, or locusts.

But the word "pestilence" in Matthew 24:7 actually has nothing to do with insects. It is a translation of the Greek word *loimos* and means a "plague or disease," just as the Merriam-Webster online dictionary defines "pestilence" as "a contagious or infectious epidemic disease that is virulent and devastating."

Even though an epidemic disease may not be considered a sign of nature, such outbreaks are often caused by some component of nature. For instance, the infecting bacteria of the bubonic plague pandemic of the fourteenth century were carried by fleas transported on rats. Or, a common disease that can reach epidemic proportions is malaria, carried by mosquitoes. Of course, some diseases are transferred as airborne contagions, by physical contact, or by means other than rodents or insects. Nevertheless, pestilences are usually a result of some environmental facilitation.

Historically, many epidemic diseases have reached the pandemic state. The following are epidemics that spread across several continents:[217]

165-180:	Antonine plague (perhaps smallpox)
251-266:	Plague of Cyprian
541:	Plague of Justinian
1300s:	Black Death
1501-1587:	Typhus
1732-1733:	Influenza
1775-1776:	Influenza
1816-1826:	Cholera
1829-1851:	Cholera
1847-1848:	Influenza
1852-1860:	Cholera
1855-1950s:	Bubonic plague (third pandemic)
1857-1859:	Influenza
1863-1875:	Cholera
1889-1892:	Influenza
1899-1923:	Cholera
1918-1920:	Influenza (Spanish flu)[218]
1957-1958:	Influenza (Asian flu)
1968-1969:	Influenza (Hong Kong flu)
1960s:	Cholera (called El Tor)
1980s-present:	HIV
2009:	Influenza (2009 swine flu pandemic)

Even though modern science has completely or almost completely eradicated many epidemic diseases through vaccinations, it appears that we are now living in a time when the diversity of the world's cultures and the overcrowding in population centers are causing harmful mutations to develop from what were once considered *controlled* diseases. Today, deadly diseases that were once considered controlled are making a devastating comeback. These new, mutated strains are even more resistant to medical cures than the predecessors from which they came. And it is believed that the widespread use of antibiotics against these diseases is what causes them to mutate into even more deadly strains. An example of a highly resistant, constantly mutating disease is commonly referred to as a staph infection. According to an article posted by the Scitable online science library:

> Most staph infections in humans are caused by methicillin-resistant *Staphylococcus aureus*, or MRSA.... According to the U.S. Centers for Disease Control (CDC), in 2004, 63 percent of all reported staph infections in the United States were caused by MRSA (CDC, 2007). That figure represents a remarkable 300 percent increase in just ten years' time.... The irony is that methicillin, a chemically modified version of penicillin, was developed in the 1950s as an alternative treatment for the growing proportion of staph infections already resistant to penicillin. At that time, about 60 percent of all staph infections were resistant to penicillin.... Scientists estimate that about nineteen thousand people in the United States die every year from MRSA (Klevens *et al.*, 2007)— that's more than the number of U.S. residents and citizens [who] die from HIV/AIDS (about seventeen thousand every year).[219]

The Web site www.eMRSAfacts.com gives a brief history of the battle against the deadly mutation process of staph:

> Methicillin-resistant Staphylococcus aureus (MRSA) has a pretty recent history. Alexander Fleming discovered penicillin in 1928 and the antibiotic began to be deployed on a large scale to fight all types of bacterial infections in the 1940s.

However as is the trend, drug resistance became a problem with penicillin and its related family in the late 1950s. Other antibiotics like erythromycin, streptomycin, and tetracycline also failed to treat staph infections in those years.

Methicillin was introduced in 1959 and initially it was successful in treating penicillin-resistant Staphylococcus aureus infections. However in 1961, the dreaded nightmare happened. Methicillin resistance was acquired by Staphylococcus aureus with the first cases being reported in the United Kingdom.

Hospitals in eastern Australia were the first to report MRSA outbreaks in the 1970s. In the next decade MRSA had acquired nightmarish proportions in hospitals and many European facilities were struggling to deal with staph infections.

The jump of MRSA from hospital settings to community settings is not so well documented although recent cases of sporadic outbreaks in prison inmates means that healthcare workers will now be hard-pressed to understand the dynamics of the superbug.[220]

The mutation process of many diseases makes it very difficult for scientists to continue finding new medicines that will effectively treat them. Among such diseases that are constantly changing are influenza (bird flu, H1N1, swine flu, chicken flu, etc.), SARS, and HIV/AIDS.

An article titled "Infectious Diseases Mutating at Alarming Rate" in the *Miami Herald's* online *Health* magazine states:

Forty years ago, the world thought it had conquered TB and any number of other diseases through the new wonder drugs: Antibiotics. U.S. Surgeon General William H. Stewart announced it was "time to close the book on infectious diseases and declare the war against pestilence won."

Today, all the leading killer infectious diseases on the planet—TB, malaria, and HIV among them—are mutating at an alarming rate, hitchhiking their way in and out of countries. The reason: Overuse and misuse of the very drugs that were supposed to save us.

Just as the drugs were a manmade solution to dangerous illness, the problem with them is also manmade. It is fueled worldwide by everything from counterfeit drugmakers to the unintended consequences of giving drugs to the poor without properly monitoring their treatment. Here's what the AP found:

- In Cambodia, scientists have confirmed the emergence of a new drug-resistant form of malaria, threatening the only treatment left to fight a disease that already kills 1 million people a year.

- In Africa, new and harder-to-treat strains of HIV are being detected in about 5 percent of new patients. HIV drug resistance rates have shot up to as high as 30 percent worldwide.

- In the U.S., drug-resistant infections killed more than sixty-five thousand people last year—more than prostate and breast cancer combined. More than nineteen thousand people died from a staph infection alone that has been eliminated in Norway, where antibiotics are stringently limited.[221]

Nature seems to have a way of outsmarting even our smartest scientists. New diseases are appearing on the world health scene faster than cures can be found. So, it certainly appears that pestilences are not a thing of the past, but rather are on the increase!

Famine

Another sign Jesus said will follow the pattern of birth pains and can also be associated with nature is the "famines" sign. Of course, not all famines are weather-related. Some are caused by war, government oppression, and just general poverty. But in this modern day of agricultural productivity, is famine getting worse?

> Approximately 40 percent of the world's agricultural land is seriously degraded. In Africa, if current trends of soil degradation continue, the continent might be able to feed just 25 percent of its population by 2025, according to UNU's Ghana-based Institute for Natural Resources in Africa. As of late 2007, increased farming for use in biofuels, along with world oil prices at nearly $100 a barrel, has pushed up the price of grain used to feed poultry and dairy cows and other cattle, causing higher prices of wheat (up 58 percent), soybean (up 32 percent), and maize (up 11 percent) over the year. Food riots have recently taken place in many countries across the world.[222]

Additionally, the epidemic spread of wheat-killing fungi is presently devastating grain crops:

> An epidemic of stem rust on wheat caused by race Ug99 is currently spreading across Africa, Asia, and most recently into [the] Middle East and is causing major concern due to the large numbers of people dependent on wheat for sustenance. The strain was named after the country where it was identified (Uganda) and the year of its discovery (1999). It spread to Kenya, then Ethiopia, Sudan, and Yemen, and is becoming more virulent as it spreads.[223]

Adding to the insecurity of already-strained world food supplies, controversy rages over the future effects of changing food grains over to the production of biofuels. With the ever-increasing demand for energy and the gradual decline in the planet's hydrocarbon resources, farmers are finding more profits by diverting to crops for biofuel production. "In order for the United States to meet the biofuel target introduced in the Energy Independence and Security Act, 40 percent of the land that is currently devoted to corn production would have to be converted to biofuel feedstock production."[224] Will this lead to food shortages? The World Bank's president, Robert Zoellick, stated that "while many worry about filling their gas tanks, many others around the world are struggling to fill their stomachs. And it's getting more and more difficult every day."[225]

Some interesting facts about hunger and starvation are given on the "Think Quest" Web site:

- Every year, 15 million children die of hunger.
- The World Health Organization estimates that one-third of the world is well-fed, one-third is underfed, and one-third is starving.
- Every 3.6 seconds, someone dies of hunger.[226]

So, in spite of man's advancements in technology and agricultural productivity, the age-old scourge of starvation still stalks the planet. But secular forecasts of the future food supplies and distribution seem to be evenly divided between the positive and the negative, some claiming man's technology and the world's resources have not been exhausted and will ultimately triumph, and others pointing to those same elements and claiming that they will be the very causes for future mass starvation.

It is difficult to say whether we are currently experiencing a rise in famine, but the Bread for the World Web site paints a sad picture of today's world hunger, poverty, and starvation with these statements:

- The world is facing a hunger crisis unlike anything it has seen in more than fifty years.

- 1.02 billion people are hungry.
- Every day, almost sixteen thousand children die from hunger-related causes. That's one child every five seconds.
- There were 1.4 billion people in extreme poverty in 2005. The World Bank estimates that the spike in global food prices in 2008, followed by the global economic recession in 2009 and 2010, has pushed between 100–150 million people into poverty.[227]

Revelation 6 gives an overview of events that will transpire in the seven-year Tribulation through the symbolism of what some have called "the four horsemen of the Apocolypse." In a gruesome progression, each provides the impetus for the next:

- First is the WHITE HORSE rider, symbolic of the Antichrist, who goes "forth conquering, and to conquer" (Rev. 6:2). His conquests bring on...
- ...the second rider on a RED HORSE, symbolic of bloodshed through warfare. War always produces famine and starvation as farms are destroyed and nations' agricultural assets are redirected to weaponry and militaries, causing food shortages. Thus, the next rider on the scene is...
- ...the BLACK HORSE rider, symbolic of that famine and starvation. Along with malnutrition and the destruction of warfare comes the aftermath of disease and widespread death, symbolized by the fourth horseman on a sickly, yellowish-green...
- ...PALE HORSE. "And his name that sat on him was Death, and Hell [the grave] followed with him. And power was given unto them over the fourth part of the earth, to kill with sword, and with hunger, and with death, and with the beasts of the earth" (Rev. 6:8b).

So again, just as with earthquakes, the Bible tells us that the worst famine and starvation that man will ever experience will be in the

Great Tribulation, just before Jesus returns. It will be the day of "climaxes." And even though some may report that man's ability to feed the masses is improving, destructive weather, warfare, and politics are working to move us ever closer to those dark days of tribulation just ahead.

Even though it is difficult to quantify famines statistically and state emphatically that starvation is on the rise, one thing is certain: In all of man's advances in science, technology, and agronomy, the ever-growing tide of famine has not been halted. And even with great scientific strides toward high-yield food production, even with new methods of efficiency to gain the most food from the least resources, and even with the many varied programs around the world to equalize and stabilize the food/population equation, the one major contributing aspect that cannot be controlled and is the most common cause of famine is destructive weather.

Destructive Weather

In addition to earthquakes, Luke records that Jesus also said that "great signs shall there be from heaven." The word translated from the Greek as "heaven" means the sky—so, in other words, there would be upheaval and disturbances in the atmosphere: great storms, floods, droughts, etc. Luke 21:26 says these cataclysmic events will result in "men's hearts failing them for fear, and for looking after those things which are coming on the earth: for the powers of heaven shall be shaken."

Are destructive weather patterns becoming ever more prevalent in our day? Are we witnessing more hurricanes, tornadoes, floods, droughts, and thunderstorms than ever before?

An in-depth study of the historical destructiveness of storms globally is not feasible here. But we must ask ourselves, "Are there more floods, droughts, hurricanes, thunderstorms, and tornadoes today than in the past? And, are the numbers of these disturbances expected to increase in the future?" Readers will have to come to their own conclusion. However, some scientists believe that an increase in greenhouse gases in our upper atmosphere is producing a gradual climb in earth temperatures. This "global warming" is affecting the atmospheric conditions that establish our weather patterns. To date, the debate continues on the existence and extent of global warming and what effect, if any, it will have on our future weather.

According to an Environmental Protection Agency Web site, a major contributing factor to greenhouse gases and global warming is man's use of fossil fuels (gasoline, coal, etc.), which is expected to increase:

> Estimates of future emissions and removals depend in part on assumptions about changes in underlying human activities. For example, the demand for fossil fuels such as gasoline and coal is expected to increase greatly with the predicted growth of the U.S. and global economies.[228]

If man's use of fossil fuels does have a negative impact on earth's weather patterns, it can probably be assumed that future weather systems will be affected since only the future depletion of those resources will produce a real reduction in their use.

In an unscientific straw poll, I have asked members of church congregations their opinion on this subject. I've asked, "Does it appear to you that in your lifetime, destructive weather patterns (hurricanes, tornadoes, floods, and droughts) are increasing?" A conservative estimate on the response is that at least 70–80 percent of the people I've asked believe our weather is getting more destructive. Again, this is just an unscientific survey of personal observations about our weather. But it certainly looks like most people feel that destructive weather is increasing. And earth's human activity appears to be only aggravating the situation.

Conclusion

Although it is difficult to say with statistical certainty that we are now experiencing a sharp increase in the strength and frequency of all these signs of nature (earthquakes, famines, pestilences, and storms), one can clearly recognize that we are definitely not experiencing a decline in any of them. Even with man's advancements in technology and productivity, these calamities continue to plague us. And as it has been shown, our new technologies often even contribute to these destructive events (the use of antibodies against disease leading to new, more resistant mutations, the expansion of industry and the use of biofuels jeopardizing food sources, greenhouse gas emissions affecting the weather, etc.). A significant positive change in any of these contributing factors does not appear to be in sight.

The one area in which human activity is not a contributing factor is in the occurrence of earthquakes. It is as though our planet is reeling under the pains of labor, the surface of the planet surging and recoiling with increasing consistency. All these signs studied together make for a compelling argument that nature is shouting, "Get ready! The end of the age and the coming of Messiah are approaching!"

Jesus said concerning these events, "And when these things *begin* to come to pass, then look up, and lift up your heads; for your redemption draweth nigh" (Luke 21:28, emphasis added).

CHAPTER SIXTEEN

ISRAEL'S END-TIMES ZECHARIAH EFFECT

And this shall be the plague wherewith the LORD will smite
all the people that have fought against Jerusalem:
Their flesh shall consume away while they stand upon their feet,
and their eyes shall consume away in their mouth.

ZECH. 14:12

By Jim Fletcher

T he coolness of the courtyard made a nice companion for the foliage and flowers. The American Colony Hotel is one of Jerusalem's best features. I looked around and imagined some of the more famous guests of the hotel sipping coffee here: Marc Chagall, T. E. Lawrence…even Joan Baez.

A former sultan's palace and later home to a group of American transplants, the Colony is now an exclusive "Arab" hotel, just down the street from the fabled Old City. The Garden Tomb—"Gordon's

Calvary"—is close by, as well. Foreign journalists, diplomats, UN personnel and World Bank types congregate here.

I watched water trickle down a Turkish fountain as I waited for a friend. Originally the opulent home of a pasha, the American Colony today is a meeting place, but it is not the first place most American tourists on a pilgrimage to the Holy Land would settle; during the Second Intifada, Hamas posters graced walls just down the street, and the whole area is located in "Arab East Jerusalem."

Still, I waited with anticipation. My friend is a retired officer in the Israel Defense Forces, and I won't name him. Suffice it to say he is an expert on weaponry, geopolitics, and the Arab mindset.

Presently, he entered and strode toward my table. A young, handsome Palestinian waiter poured more of the heavy, black liquid that passes for coffee in the Middle East.

My friend was here to share with me some of his research, some of the writings about Arab threats to Israel's existence. In a macabre sort of way, I couldn't wait to dig into the material. With Palestinian terrorists becoming more sophisticated and aggressive in developing and using weapons, I was anxious to understand. Just a day before, in the same courtyard, I had slapped open a copy of the *Jerusalem Post*, and just as I took the first bite of a traditional Middle East breakfast (eggs, olives, cheeses, fruit, etc.), my fork froze in midair; eleven Israeli soldiers' pictures stared back. The day before, they had been ambushed by terrorists in Hebron. All had been killed.

Since this was 2002 and Yasser Arafat was, tragically, still alive and directing the guerilla war/serial killing he'd been famous for since the sixties, I knew my friend could provide important insights. Much of his research informs this chapter on the amazing prophecies of Zechariah, the prophet.

The one thing that remains forever in my memory from that morning discussion with my friend is his remark about the Bible.

Israelis are famous for their reticence when discussing faith. Yet often, they will talk at length about God and the Bible. After too many cups of coffee that morning, and after we had discussed various aspects of life in the Middle East (war is a constant threat), I digressed into an area I really hadn't intended to explore. The discussion of missiles and missile defense systems got me thinking. I turned the cup over in my hand.

"You know, there's a question I have that, for me, is relevant. You know that I'm religious, that I'm an evangelical Christian."

He nodded.

"So I wonder what you personally think of biblical passages such as Zechariah 14:12, in light of the nuclear threats?"

And this shall be the plague wherewith the LORD will smite all the people that have fought against Jerusalem; Their flesh shall consume away while they stand on their feet, and their eyes shall consume away in their holes, and their tongue shall consume away in their mouth.

He looked at me, expressionless. I pressed ahead. "It seems to me that this passage is describing a nuclear exchange. Do you think it's describing such a scenario?"

He looked away for a moment, then looked at me again with those cool blue eyes.

"It is describing a nuclear exchange…if one believes the Bible is true."

I slowly leaned back in my seat, not taking my eyes off my friend. I could scarcely believe he'd just answered as he had.

You see, the comment "if one believes the Bible is true" is so profound it impacts a whole host of issues, including how people understand Israel and the Jews. Of course, there are also existential issues such as the arms race, the current Iranian threat, and whether diplomacy or military preparedness is the greater priority.

Zechariah: Fact or Fantasy?

One of this generation's greatest Bible prophecy teachers is David Reagan of Lamb and Lion Ministries. Dave relates that when he was growing up in a particular denomination, he asked his pastor about Zechariah 14:4.

The passage is a straightforward prediction that in the "last days" the Messiah will physically appear on the Mount of Olives; His feet will "touch down," as it were.

Not so, according to Dave's pastor: "Well, this Scripture reference is actually symbolic of Jesus 'coming down' into a new believer's heart."

Dave blinked and tried to process this interpretation. Fortunately, his analytical mind and recognition that the Bible is a supernatural communication that is meant to be *actually understood* by all people alerted him to the fact that this pastor was torturing the plain-sense text.

Zechariah 14:4 tells us that one day in the future, the Messiah will physically appear on the Mount of Olives in Jerusalem. His feet will come to rest on the mountain itself.

In effect, the Zechariah passage is a news story, recording facts that will take place. It isn't a dreamy, symbolic plot element in an ancient Hebrew novel. This is an important point.

If, like me, you need to see tangible things, the following might help.

On a trip to Israel in 2005, I spent an afternoon walking through the Old City of Jerusalem. Near the end of the day, I sat on a retaining wall near the famed Eastern Gate (more about that later). I sat there for the longest time, gazing at the Mount of Olives.

As with most sites in the Holy Land, I was initially surprised at the close proximity of one site to another. For example, the Garden Tomb is only a few yards from Golgotha, the "Place of the Skull"— the traditional site of the crucifixion. So it was with the walls of the

Old City and the Mount of Olives. In the rural area where I live in the U.S., it's still common for people to refer to a small valley as "a holler." I thought of this as the sun began to dim while I studied the Mount of Olives.

Only a few hundred yards from where I sat was the pinnacle of the Mount. At the base are various religious shrines, tombs, and the fabled Garden of Gethsemane.

In those moments, with the blare of car horns, the smell of earth (you really can smell the Holy Land!), and chirping birds (all my senses were heightened), Zechariah 14:4 came vividly into focus for me. The green mountain, forested in the last century (another fulfillment of prophecy; numerous Old Testament passages predict the land will be reclaimed from its desert-like status in the last days), the Mount of Olives is a real place.

I once listened to a lecture from the radical Christian scholar John Shelby Spong. He openly mocked the idea of Christ's return (or, presumably, the Jewish belief that this will be the Messiah's "first" visit to earth). Spong laughingly mentioned the numerous laws of physics that would have to be broken for a being from another dimension to break through into earth's atmosphere.

But, having read Spong's writings—and especially his autobiography, *Here I Stand*—I am certain that he is simply biased against Scripture. I am biased *for* Scripture; everyone is biased about everything.

What If It's True?

It matters what we think about words. Words mean something. In their most extreme form, words alert us to critical information.

For many people in our world today, believers and skeptics alike, the Bible is an interesting book, but one filled with myth, endless metaphor, and outright mistakes. In other words, the collection of ancient writings is a human product.

But what if it is in fact what Scripture itself indicates, and what millions of Bible-believers rest upon: The Bible is a supernatural communication between the Creator and humans?

In this light, the Bible is in large part a warning. It warns of a future apocalypse...a dramatic conclusion of history.

Several years ago, *USA Today* reporter Jack Kelley wrote that many people are familiar with the term "Armageddon." But they are familiar with it in what I'd call a "Hollywood way"—through movies that strain the bounds of credulity. In this context, most people have at least a vague understanding that the very word "Armageddon" signals a catastrophic end of the world, centered on a legendary battle between good and evil.

Kelley went on to state that when he mentions the fact, most people are stunned to learn that "Armageddon" really exists. In northern Israel, the Valley of Megiddo is the site of countless ancient battles. Napoleon called it the greatest natural battlefield he'd ever seen.

Har Megiddo—"the Hill of Megiddo" in Hebrew—is a mountain rising from the plains. One can visit it today.

The Bible records in Revelation that this will be the site of a confrontation between the forces of the last-days Antichrist and the true Messiah. In fact, there are more messianic prophecies in the book of Zechariah than in any of the other books of the so-called "minor prophets."

Who Was Zechariah?

A prophet of Israel during the post-exhilic period in the fifth century BC, Zechariah was a prime catalyst for the Jews to rebuild the Temple in Jerusalem upon their return from captivity in Babylon.

A prophet from a family of prophets (his grandfather, Iddo, was also a prophet), Zechariah was also a priest. His very name, meaning "Jehovah remembers," calls to mind the office of prophet. He is mentioned twice in the book of Ezra.

The book of Zechariah opens with Darius the Mede, ruler over the Persian Empire, having allowed the exiled Jews to return to their Holy City. The Lord reminds Zechariah that his forefathers had been spiritual harlots—a recurring theme in Scripture—and in an almost chilling warning/exhortation, He sets a path before Zechariah: "Follow Me, or else."

A series of visions are given to Zechariah involving myrtle trees, angels, a golden candlestick, and a flying roll, among others; the Lord is reminding him of the captivity in Babylon, yet the Jews will be delivered and allowed to return. This, by the way, is a historical fact, as the Jews did in fact return after seventy years in captivity. These passages are also heavily concerned with Messianic visions, setting up the final chapters of the book of Zechariah to deal with a time far into the future.

One of the lesser-known facts about the recorded prophecies in the book of Zechariah is found in the reference to a place called "Hadrach" in Zechariah 9:1. The bit of history is important when we consider that the Bible is often attacked by critics as being mythological.

For the longest, proponents of the myth theory said that Hadrach had never existed. However, in the late nineteenth century, references to it began to appear in the archaeological records. Hadrach had in fact been a Syrian city, along with Damascus and Hamath.

The destruction of the city of Tyre (also seen more dramatically in the book of Ezekiel) is also predicted by the Lord in the ninth chapter of Zechariah. The port city, powerful and rich through the end of the Persian Empire, was destroyed by Alexander the Great in the fourth century BC, thus strengthening the prophetic claims recorded by Zechariah.

But it is the latter chapters of Zechariah that are most relevant for us today.

Throughout, God has made it plain that He loves both the Jews and their capital city of Jerusalem. It is the place He has reserved for His physical presence on earth, manifested most dramatically in the future Temple, in the inner area of the Temple known as the Holy of Holies.

The second half of the book of Zechariah shifts in terms of time. There is almost, if we can use the analogy, a Greek tragedy quality to the story, as we see the nations (what we would now refer to as the international community) grow more mad in their hatred of the Jews.

God clearly intends to judge those nations, for they have hunted and harassed the Jews for many thousands of years. And so we find a final scene of human history in which the nations become more and more obsessed with "the Jewish question." As they determine to confront, attack, and annihilate Israel in the latter days, God Himself intervenes, as He did in the days of old.

Indeed, the relevance of Bible prophecy is perhaps nowhere more pronounced than in these final chapters of the book of Zechariah.

Remember, the Bible's critics (and the criticism grows louder) have painted the biblical characters as primitive, evolving humans who are only just emerging from the mists of the past.

In fact, the charge is not only false, but as we will see, it is dramatically false.

Zechariah (like other prophets, among them, Job—see Job 19:25) is allowed to see visions of a time far into the future. He is told that the Messiah, the Savior of mankind, will emerge in the end and, as noted earlier, stand on the Mount of Olives.

Zechariah also sees a terrifying confrontation during a climactic battle for the city of Jerusalem. In the end, God tells us that Jerusalem will not be attacked by a couple of surrounding Arab countries. No, "all the people of the earth [will] be gathered together against it."

We then learn of a catastrophic battle that will employ weapons not known in Zechariah's time:

And this shall be the plague wherewith the LORD will smite all the people that have fought against Jerusalem: Their flesh shall consume away while they stand upon their feet, and their eyes shall consume away in their mouth. (Zech. 14:12)

I submit to you: What does that sound like? It seems logical that a nuclear strike is being described.

In modern Israel, the vast majority of the nation's population is clustered in a three-square-mile area around Tel Aviv, Israel's modern city on the Mediterranean coast. The sweeping coastal plain, scene of great agriculture and also a powerhouse high-tech industry, is obviously important. This also is not lost on the Arabs; at one time, Saddam Hussein's Iraq had two thousand ballistic missiles aimed at this region.

Yet it is Jerusalem that is dominant in the end-times vision of Israel's ancient prophets. Right at this moment, the status of Jerusalem is literally an overriding obsession of the United Nations. Dave Hunt (the great apologist who heads Berean Call Ministries) has often issued a bulletproof challenge, asking critics to explain the world's overwhelming obsession with the status of Jerusalem, apart from the Bible. It is the perfect question, and we see today with each passing week that the intense negotiations over the Holy City are intensifying.

Birth Pangs

Israel declared Jerusalem as its undivided capital in 1980 and ever since, the Palestinians have understood the political value in also demanding Jerusalem as the capital of a proposed Palestinian state. Complicating matters is the fact that, today, Palestinian neighborhoods are almost on top of Jewish neighborhoods in Jerusalem. The two peoples are locked in a death struggle, geographically and demographically. Literally between the two peoples is the fabled Old City of Jerusalem. The gleaming, scrubbed Jewish neighborhoods of west Jerusalem are inches from the Old City walls; conversely, on the other side, the Palestinian rage against the Jews festers. The whole area feels like a pile of dead wood in summer, awaiting a match.

In numerous biblical passages, we are told repeatedly how history will "go down": The Lord will actually gather the nations to do battle against Jerusalem. This will be their Waterloo. As in the famous "Gog-Magog" war of Ezekiel 38 and 39, it appears that God will almost force the nations to turn their attention suddenly to Israel and Jerusalem, and attack. This setting of the scene is intended to set the stage for God's judgment on the nations.

There have, of course, been almost countless battles for Jerusalem throughout history, the most recent being in 1967, after Israel had been established. Ferocious fighting, much of it hand-to-hand, characterized Israel's War of Independence nineteen years before, and failing to capture the Old City of Jerusalem had been a bitter pill for the Israelis in 1948.

The dramatic Six-Day War of June 1967 returned the city to sovereign Jewish hands for the first time in two thousand years and suddenly, the visions of Zechariah came sharply into focus.

Jerusalem had become once again a flashpoint for global powers.

Sounding the Alarm

For decades, Bible commentators like Hal Lindsey have been explaining that the Bible describes a series of apocalyptic wars in the last days. Blunting the effectiveness of this message (although many did "get it") was a succession of liberal clergy, social commentators, and entertainment figures, who all laughingly dismissed Lindsey's ideas.

No one is laughing now.

Once the Soviet Union crumbled and morphed into a new entity (the Russian Federation, along with newly formed nations), the nuclear arms race shifted from the USSR and the U.S. to an even more dangerous proposition. Besides Western powers like France and Great Britain, other nations now have nuclear arsenals: India, Pakistan, and now, it seems likely, Iran.

Iran changes the game dramatically.

At the same time, American President Barack Obama has inexplicably pledged that the U.S. will not automatically respond with nukes, should the nation be attacked by biological or chemical weapons. Obama has also telegraphed weakness in myriad ways to terrorist enemies, from "toning down" language used to describe the fight the world is engaged in to demanding that al-Qaida and other terrorists are tried in civilian courts, as if 9/11 were a matter for the New York Police Department.

It is, however, the issue of nuclear weapons that has thrust Zechariah into the forefront of Bible prophecy at this time in history. Obama's pledge could have become the catalyst for setting a dangerous series of events in motion.

Syndicated column Charles Krauthammer, writing from Washington in the spring of 2010, understands the implications perfectly, and he isn't afraid to call it like he sees it. After describing Obama's "standing-down" posture on nukes, Krauthammer said, "This is quite insane." Further, he presents the chilling ramifications:

> Apart from being morally bizarre, the Obama policy is strategically loopy. Does anyone believe that North Korea or Iran will be more persuaded to abjure nuclear weapons because they could then carry out a biological or chemical attack on the U.S. without fear of nuclear retaliation?
>
> The naiveté is stunning. Similarly the Obama pledge to forswear development of any nuclear warheads, indeed, to permit no replacement of aging nuclear components without the authorization of the president himself. This under the theory that our moral example will move other countries to eschew nukes.[229]

This is all supremely relevant for Israel, because at the same time Obama has been appeasing nuclear-equipped enemies, he has been treating Israel with contempt.

For decades, Israel has possessed what some have referred to as the "Samson Option," meaning that the Israelis would meet an existential threat by using nuclear weapons. Based at Dimona, in the southern part of the country, Israel's nuclear arsenal is not even publicly acknowledged, but the program was started under the watchful eye of Zionist icon David Ben Gurion, who saw far enough ahead to know that what had begun in Japan at the end of World War II would one day have a global reach.

Israel's nuclear deterrent has long been a point of consternation for the surrounding Arab nations. The nuclear option has done its work: it has certainly deterred the Arabs and, in an earlier time, their Soviet benefactors.

Obama's bi-level plan—to marginalize Israel through diplomatic pressures while appeasing the Arabs with soft rhetoric and sidelining American arms—has suddenly brought Zechariah 14 into sharp focus.

China, India, Pakistan, and North Korea are all "kings of the east" who possess both the capacity to use nuclear weapons and the latent anti-Semitism to use them against Israel. By squeezing Israel, Obama is setting up the perfect storm to make the conditions ripe for the nuclear confrontation clearly discussed in Zechariah. No longer is the subject laughable. If Zechariah is historically true, both past and future, then a scenario in which humans die while standing on their feet, their tongues and eyes melting…is most definitely plausible.

For years, Muslim states like Iraq, Syria, and Egypt have aimed ballistic missiles at Israel. Conventional missiles were bad enough; a nightmare scenario of nuclear-tipped missiles is the delivery system longed for by the enemies of the Jewish state.

Further, in an almost uncanny way, international developments are pushing Jerusalem into its climactic end-times role. Consider the strategic importance of the ancient city to modern nations:

> Plainly, where Palestinian Arabs might be able to block troop and supply movements because of the Israeli necessity of moving them through PA [Palestinian Authority]-held territory, by prior agreement, these Palestinians would almost

certainly be tempted to do so. Especially if, in the face of foreign reporters and journalists, PA spokesmen (or Hanan Ashrawi) feigned some kind of breakdown in the PA's capacity to control its "forces on the ground" while it characteristically, if surreptitiously, egged them on and assisted them militarily, nonetheless, Israel would have a serious problem on its hands. In strategic terms, its options are indeed limited. "The only lateral axis from the coast to the Jordan Valley which is populated by Jews in great numbers and therefore more defensible is via Jerusalem. The only area along the crest of the mountains at the center of the Land of Israel, which is heavily populated by Jews, is Jerusalem and its surroundings." This argument is not dissimilar to the one which can be used to show the critical importance of communities settled on the hilltops of Judea and Samaria and within the Gaza Strip.[230]

Well! The above-quoted material is fascinating when one considers the geopolitical and military implications in today's world. It pulsates with both biblical and current political tensions.

In past days, as has been mentioned, proponents of biblical prophecy have been ridiculed for suggesting that Zechariah is future history. Most specifically, dispensationalists have argued that the confluence of events in the great prophetic book—from the intense conflict over Jerusalem to the appearance of the Messiah—will be part of the great rapturing away of believers. It is one thing for a John Spong to make a career out of dismissing the idea out of hand to a perfect storm of events shaping it as completely plausible. It is a matter of simple logic: If Zechariah's prophecies come into focus one by one, why would not all of them be fulfilled? If Jerusalem has indeed become that "cup of trembling" (and it has in dramatic fashion), then we can have confidence that the Messiah is preparing to reenter history and appear bodily in Jerusalem. This is the great hope of the saints, and Paul's thrilling exhortations to watch for it are about to find their fulfillment.

Back to geopolitical implications.

I had the very great pleasure of interviewing legendary Israeli General Ariel Sharon. My friend—famed prophecy teacher David Lewis—and I sat with Sharon for an hour at his office in Tel Aviv. At the time, the wily old general was sitting in the first government of Benjamin Netanyahu. Sharon told me that one cannot conquer the land of Israel without controlling the territory. In particular, since the Holy City is in the middle of the country, one sees very steep hills all around. Conventional armies in modern times have not been able to wrest the area from the Jews; in fact, the city was famously reunified under Jewish sovereignty in June, 1967. All this has pushed Zechariah's prophecies, so unreal and implausible earlier, to reality.

There have been several "dry runs" in recent decades as well. Consider the famous Israeli raid on Saddam's nuclear facility in 1981:

> In June 1981, a daring Israeli Air Force raid destroyed the Iraqi nuclear reactor at Osirak. Israeli intelligence maintained that the reactor was about to be loaded with highly enriched uranium, and that radioactive fallout of any later raid might have decimated Baghdad. International condemnation was fast and furious [sadly, even from the Reagan Administration], and an emergency session was convened of the United Nations Security Council. A decade later as the Gulf War began, and a decade after that as America engineered a regime change in Iraq, the strike at Osirak was hailed as masterful military foresight.[231]

Jewish settlement of the land began in earnest around the time of the Osirak raid, and today, about three hundred thousand live in communities, including those mentioned in and around Jerusalem.

The fact that we now have the ideal conditions for a truly international military effort against Jewish-controlled Jerusalem is an astonishing proof that the Bible is true. We can see clearly that a multi-nation nuclear attack can happen by something as mundane as routine Israeli troop movements in or near PA-controlled territory. No wonder one sees dozens of white vehicles with black, block-lettered "UN" designations tooling all around Jerusalem.

The world is watching.

It is not inconceivable that the very trigger for a nuclear exchange is not a first strike of nukes from Arab nations, but an Israeli response to biological and chemical weapons. Such an attack is just as deadly to the Jewish state as a pure nuke strike.

While Jimmy Carter might be surprised, Egypt has for many years been developing biological agents that can wipe out entire populations:

> Indeed, Egypt's relatively advanced biotechnological abilities allowed it to deal with these two agents [plague-producing agents]. The production and storage of the first one—the pestilence bacterium—are not at all simple, while the second one—Rift Valley Fever virus, is even more complicated to handle. To this, one has to add Egypt's development of botulinum toxin and a virus that causes encephalitis as further biological warfare agents.[232]

Before he was wonderfully removed from planet earth, Saddam Hussein had also developed quite a program of chemical and biological weapons, with the following delivery systems: "artillery shells, aerial bombs, aerial spraying devices, various rockets, mobile spray units, airborne units, and various warheads."[233]

To Cease to Be

And Syria could be setting herself up for the fulfillment of Isaiah 17:1 by stockpiling, at various times, chemical warfare agents like sarin,

VX, and cyanide. In fact, the arsenal was "tried out on" eighteen thousand Sunni Syrians by the order of the (gratefully) late Hafez Assad. Sadly, his successor son, Bashar, has shown the same sinister demeanor and is now working closely with the Iranians to export terror to Israel proper.

It is also chilling to note that in the last several years, we have learned that not only do the nations immediately surrounding Israel possess ballistic missiles, but also the following Muslim nations: Saudi Arabia (CSS-2 and Astros II); United Arab Emirates (Scud B); Yemen (Scud B; SS-21; Frog-7); Algeria (Frog-4/7); Sudan (Scud B/Al-Husayn); Afghanistan (Scud B; Frog-7). Said countries have in the neighborhood of four hundred launchers.[234]

And while Jerusalem will soon be the focal point of the nuclear exchange predicted by Zechariah, the greater Tel Aviv/Dan area of Israel is in peril, since Egypt and Syria, for twenty years, have possessed a number of Scud missiles that can have apocalyptic consequences. ("A lethal hit on this target means the effective annihilation of the Jewish State."[235])

Of further relevance to all this is the fact that if 70 percent of Israel's population lives in the Dan area, then so does 70 percent of its reserve troops! No wonder Israeli premiers from Ben Gurion to Benjamin Netanyahu are white-headed.

It could be said that Netanyahu, in his second go-around as prime minister, spoke prophetically at the 2009 Feast of Tabernacles celebration in Jerusalem:

Well, we say to you today, the people of Israel are with you. We're together. And we're together in a great, great adventure that stretches back thousands of years. The dreams and prayers of the Jewish people to come back to this land. To reestablish our life here in a free, independent Jewish state with a united Jerusalem as our capital. I know you share this vision. I know the strength of your faith. And, God willing, with our common efforts and our great friendship we shall explain and make clear to all of mankind, even to the United Nations, that we're here to stay.[236]

Truly, Jerusalem is coming into focus prophetically, politically, militarily...as it never has before in all of world history. Netanyahu declares—with Scripture—that Israel will remain in control of the Holy City. The world hates that reality, and with the Americans now officially distancing themselves from the Jewish state, the stage is set.

We are all standing at the edge of history, awaiting the end of history. May the Lord be glorified in what is about to happen!

CHAPTER SEVENTEEN

THE INTERNET AND THE MARK OF THE BEAST

By Todd Strandberg

Out of all of mankind's technological accomplishments, nothing matches what we have done with computers and the Internet. Web technology has advanced so much since my youth that the days of green-screen computers and 1200-baud modems seem like they were during the Stone Age. The microwave oven has also improved over the years, but we didn't go from taking an hour to warm up a cup of coffee to cooking a twenty-pound turkey in thirty seconds.

People used to talk about the miracle of the jet age. In 1903, Orville and Wilbur Wright made their first controlled flight, at about seven miles per hour. It took another twenty years before anyone could travel over two hundred miles per hour. In 1947, Chuck Yeager broke the sound barrier with a speed of 670 miles per hour. In the 1960s, planes reached twice the speed of sound at twelve hundred miles per hour, and the speed race came to an end in 1976 with the SR71—an advanced, long-range, Mach 3 strategic reconnaissance aircraft—reaching 2,194 miles per hour. Since then, we have actually gone backwards; the SR71 has been decommissioned without a replacement.

The exponential growth curve in the computer world shows no signs of ending. In 1971, the central processing unit (CPU) for a computer had twenty-three hundred transistors. Today, the same CPU has more than 2 trillion transistors. When I launched the Rapture Ready Web site—www.raptureready.com—in 1987, our monthly bandwidth limit was twenty-five megabytes. Today, we have a monthly limit of around 40 trillion bytes of data.

The growth in the number of Web domains and users has also undergone a sharp growth spike. In fact, the number of Web users is growing so fast that it's likely that the majority of earth's population will be using the Internet in the next few years. The only limitation is people's ability to afford access to the global online community. In 1991, hardly any Web sites were in operation on the Internet. But by 2009, more than 200 million sites had been established. As late as 2001, only 360 million people were using the Internet, but by September 2009, more than 1.7 billion people were regularly going online to conduct business, do some shopping, play games, keep in touch with friends, do research, and more.

A Sea of Garbage

The Internet might be considered the modern equivalent of the printing press: Because of the worldwide network of information exchange, virtually everyone now has the ability to become a publisher and share his or her voice with a global audience. However, just as junk mail has become the bane of the printed world, junk information has been filling the Web all too quickly.

When the Worldwide Web was first established, it was much easier to find specific resource material on various subjects. But today, users have to wade through a sea of garbage to find useful information. The Web is clogged with ads, broken links, and self-serving pages. There is such a clutter of useless sites that I routinely turn to trusted bookmarks for many of my inquiries.

One of the key factors that has transformed the Net into a garbage dump is self-interest. Site operators, for the most part, are either trying to sell something or they just want to ramble on about themselves. Millions of Web sites are part of "hit farms"—their only purpose is to coax people into clicking on their links, which are ads made to look like useful information.

Even well-meaning Christians can add to the trash pile. I recently found a blog by a woman suffering from multiple sclerosis. She had started the online journal to benefit others. But rather than sharing her testimony about the sustaining power of God in trials, she instead posted collections of her random, trivial thoughts on things like the weather, shopping, and food. She only referred to the Bible once. Because few people were interested in reading the blog, it was discontinued after a few months—and it left behind an Internet path to a dead end.

At a conference I once attended in Dallas, an author of a book about prophecy asked me if I would add his Web site to Rapture Ready's "links" page. When I checked his site out later, I was shocked to find its sole focus was to promote the book. It was one of the most egregious examples of self-promotion I had ever seen. Just like the blog example, the Gospel message was nowhere to be found.

I think we need a "Smokey the Bear"-type of mascot to ask people not to pollute the Web. We don't throw litter out of our car windows because we know it will degrade the environment; why should people be allowed to throw electronic trash into cyberspace?

The Core Problem with Christian Web Ministry

Because of this tendency to feature too much trash and not enough substance, the Internet is lacking a good Christian witness. There are many reasons the Internet is lacking a good Christian witness. I was going to list several of them, but decided to focus on what I think is the key problem at hand. The reason we lack an effective approach is that the Internet has reduced the value of information. Little monetary or personal reward comes from doing the Lord's work online.

This factor has had a similar impact on the accessibility of the Bible. At one time in history, the vast majority of people did not own a copy of God's Word. Until the invention of the printing press, each copy of the Bible had to be transcribed by hand. Today, I have dozens of Bibles around the house. You can go to a discount store and find piles of Bibles that were mass produced in China. For a buck, you can also buy a digital copy of the Good Book.

Its amazes me to think that an electronic file of the Bible only takes three seconds to transmit to someone with a cable modem. During the Middle Ages, it would have taken three years to produce the same text—and that would have only been for those wealthy enough to afford one.

Unfortunately, the accessibility of the Bible has not improved the average Christian's understanding of the Holy Word. In fact, many Christians today have far less understanding of Scripture than people who only know the Bible from what they hear in church.

In the early church age, some Christians would invest their whole lives in efforts to send copies of the Bible and messages about the gospel to people living in various nations. Today, any one person can reach more than 140 nations in a single month through a simple Web connection. Yet most congregations would rather build new day-care centers than spend a few bucks on better Web sites for their churches.

Any large Christian organization could be the one-stop source of

Christian information if its members wanted to spend a few million dollars of their budget. Thousands of ministries have an annual income of over $50 million, yet the vast majority of those high-budget ministries spends less than five thousand dollars a year on their Internet ministry.

When the Yahoo Internet search engine was launched in 1994, it had a directory-based format that listed similar domains together. Rapture Ready was listed under the heading "Bible prophecy" with several other end-times sites. I saved that list, and was surprised to discover that after checking the links in 1997, 90 percent of the sites no longer existed. The owners had apparently lost interest and closed up shop.

When the Internet was brand new, everyone was thrilled by the idea that hundreds of people were visiting their message boards. Many sites would list all the countries represented by people who registered on their traffic counters. Today, the web is so pervasive that nothing is special about the fact that someone from China, for example, might pass through one's domain.

The good thing about the lack of personal or financial reward from using the Web is that it separates the devoted Christians from those who don't really care. Whenever I want to measure the dedication of a certain ministry, one area I always check is how well it maintains its Web site.

Putting All This Power to Good Use

One reason Rapture Ready has been successful as a prophecy site is that our focus has always been to use the Web as a vehicle to offer Bible-based information to as many people as possible. We target questions that people might pose when they come to the Net looking for answers.

Whenever I get ready to write an article about a given subject for the site, I always do a search first to see if any other sites have covered the topic. Most of the time, I don't find anything that comes close to what I plan to write. I realize that I do have a unique way of approaching some subjects, but I believe the bigger dynamic at work is that most people only care about content that suits their personal interests. For example, millions of online articles tell visitors what's wrong with the world, but only a handful of articles offer advice on how to fix the problems.

What makes the Internet such a wonderful tool for reaching the lost with the gospel message is that fact that the information is offered to the public at almost zero cost. In the world of books, DVDs, and CDs, production costs are rarely, if ever, lower than a dollar per unit. And once a book's sales have dropped below a certain level, the publisher removes it from its catalog listing. The *Left Behind* novels written by Tim LaHaye and Jerry B. Jenkins were part of one of the most successful series in the history of Christian media. In the publishing world, however, all good things must eventually come to an end: One day I saw tapes for some of the popular books for sale in a dollar store.

However, there is no bargain bin for Web sites—and a Web page can remain active for an indefinite amount of time. Some articles on Rapture Ready have been around for nearly two decades. Each month, they continue to receive visits by several thousand people.

Adding Your Witness to the Net

A fundamental duty of every Christian is to share his or her faith with the lost: "But sanctify the Lord God in your hearts: and be ready always to give an answer to every man that asketh you a reason of the hope that is in you with meekness and fear" (1 Pet. 3:15). I firmly believe the Internet is one of the best ways to fulfill this obligation. If the 80 million professing Christians in the U.S. added one page of biblical content or messages about their faith to the Net, nonbelievers would be repeatedly exposed to the truth.

I would be happy if one-tenth of that number did something productive. Unbelievably, the vast majority of Christians never do anything in the way of service to the Lord or ministry to others. We are told to pray for others, but most of us don't even bother to pray for our own needs. I would estimate that fewer than two hundred individuals are responsible for producing 90 percent of the prophetic content on the Net.

There is little interest in God's business because most Christians don't see the rewards in it. Most are more worried about making money here on earth than they are about adding to their heavenly bank account.

The wonderful thing about doing something is that once you invest the time to do it, you put yourself ahead of a long line of people who do nothing. With a little effort, you can become the two-hundred-and-first person to share the claim to the 90-percent portion of the end-time pie.

Rapture Ready has long had an open policy for posting the works of other authors. Those with a testimony to share or a message to get out don't have to create a whole Web site; they can simply spend all the time they need writing a single article and then send it to us for posting. Those who have shared their witness on the Web can have the satisfaction of knowing that, every month, hundreds of people are reading the material and being guided to the truth: "For thou shalt be his witness unto all men of what thou hast seen and heard" (Acts 22:15).

The Master Plan

I'm sure you have seen one of those infomercials that offers a bonus amount on some type of cheap product. After describing the wonders of a set of plastic storage containers, for example, the announcer then says, "But wait! Act now and we will double your order."

Well, I'm about to double, triple, quadruple, quintuple, sextuple, septuple, and octuple your potential reward. Actually, the windfall is so great that I have no idea how high it even reaches.

A few years ago, I wrote an article called "The Master Plan" detailing what will happen when billions of people realize they have been left behind and turn to the Web for answers. During a short period of time, an article that may have previously been read only a few hundred times could receive hits that number into the millions.

When the Lord Jesus comes to earth to remove the church, I strongly believe the Rapture will generate one of the greatest panics in human history. The intense need for information will cause millions of people to turn to the Internet for answers.

It's not that I have a bias for Internet resources versus books. I think both are good outlets, but the Net has one huge advantage over the printed page: When this book is published, the most we can hope for is selling from ten thousand to twenty-five thousand copies.

I recently spoke to one of the top-selling authors in biblical prophecy. He told me that the last four books he wrote have averaged twenty-five thousand copies per book. If all these sales are local in the U.S., that would mean an average of one person out of every twelve thousand bought his book.

Finding a prophecy book after the Rapture will be like locating buried treasure. Suddenly, millions of people will be looking for any resource material they can find on the end times, and almost none will be found. The few books that might be at Christian bookstores, on eBay, or at secondhand stores will instantly be snatched up. The Bible says that during the last days, it will be very difficult to hear the Word of God: "Behold, the days come, saith the Lord GOD, that I will send a famine in the land, not a famine of bread, nor a thirst for water, but of hearing the words of the LORD" (Amos 8:11).

It is a blessed thing for you to read this book before the Rapture. It marks you as likely being a believer who has an interest in looking for the Lord Jesus' soon return. If you are one of the few people who have come into possession of this book after the Rapture, the situation is not as rosy, but a great blessing awaits you nonetheless.

Currently, only about 0.00115 percent of global Internet users visit the site Terry James and I maintain. When the Rapture takes place, millions of people will try to access the domain that is ranked number one for this subject. I would not be surprised if a sizable portion of the post-Rapture population eventually reads an article from www.raptureready.com.

It will only be a few days or even hours after the Rapture before all the leading sites on prophecy will crash or exceed their monthly bandwidth limit. To help reach people with the end-time truth, we have created dozens of sites that mirror the content from Rapture Ready. In fact, more than thirty sites have regularly changing names and locations. Here are seven domain names that will not change:

www.RR-Rapture.com
www.Raptureme.com
www.Tribulation.us
www.Tribulation.ws
www.Anti-antichrist.com
www.Help-help.org
www.Secretpath.us

It is never too late to become actively involved in the master plan. As I said earlier, we are always open to receiving articles from the public. I have an article on the site that was submitted to me more than fifteen years ago. Since that time, it has been featured by several media outlets and has been read by more than a million people.

What allows me to make this offer is the understanding that few people will take me up on it. Experience has taught me that it is an impossibility that all twelve thousand of our visitors will ask to have a piece of the action. Even when people do volunteer to submit material, it is unlikely that even as many as 20 percent will fulfill their pledges.

Of course, I don't need large numbers of people. I may not even need your help, but we all sure have a requirement to be involved in the Lord's work. The day will come when Jesus asks every believer what things he or she did in His name: "For we must all appear before the judgment seat of Christ; that every one may receive the things done in his body, according to that he hath done, whether it be good or bad" (2 Cor. 5:10).

Even if you're ninety years old, you still have time to make up for lost time. To share in the wonderful opportunity the Internet offers, you need to act. I started Rapture Ready more than twenty years ago by asking myself a very basic question, one we would all do well to ask ourselves: "Until the Lord comes, what should I be doing?"

One of my earliest memories of Bible prophecy was seeing images of people with the number 666 or bar codes on their hands. I saw them in little cartoon tracts that described what the world would be like under the mark-of-the-Beast system. One thing that struck me as odd was how casual everyone was about having these gaudy tattoos on their hands.

As we fast forward thirty years, a great deal has changed. There is no need for a visible mark. Microchip implants are now seen as the most logical tool the Antichrist would use to control the world's financial system. People's perception of technology has also evolved. Most people don't see a global network of computers as spooky as they once did. In fact, people have met "Big Brother" and seem to have found him to be a rather nice guy. I have kept track of privacy issues for several decades, and have noticed a steady decline in opposition to the components that will someday make up the mark-of-the-Beast system.

One of the greatest misconceptions about the U. S. Constitution is the belief that it contains an express right to privacy. The Bill of Rights offers some protection for specific aspects of privacy, such as the privacy of beliefs, privacy of the home against it being used to house soldiers, privacy against unreasonable searches, and privacy against self-incrimination. Someone who says his or her constitutional right to privacy is being violated is claiming something that doesn't exist.

Several laws protect sensitive or personal information. The Privacy Act of 1974 bars the unauthorized disclosure of personal information held by the federal government. The Fair Credit Reporting Act protects information gathered by credit reporting agencies. These legislative acts can be changed by Congress at any time.

Celebrities are constantly claiming the need for privacy. One of the most famous cases was Barbra Streisand's futile privacy lawsuit against a photographer who dared to take an aerial snapshot of the California coast that included her property. Streisand's desire to declare her Malibu beach home as a new Area 51 ran into conflict with the First Amendment's guarantee of freedom of the press.

The award-winning singer and actress lost the suit and was mocked repeatedly in the press for being a diva. The photographer posted the check she had to cough up to cover his portion of the legal fees, and he also posted a cartoon that showed her lawyer standing in front of a judge with an image of planet earth, promising to also sue NASA for taking satellite photos of Streisand's estate.

The actress Lindsay Lohan is currently suing E*Trade Financial Corp. for $100 million. She claims a "milkaholic" baby girl who appeared in a commercial was modeled after her. Lohan's attorney argues that the online brokerage's use of the girl, also named Lindsay, in the ad improperly invoked her "likeness, name, characterization, and personality" without permission, violating her right of privacy. Lohan was ordered in 2007 to serve one day in jail, undergo an alcohol education program, and spend three years on probation after admitting to drunk driving and cocaine possession.

The problem here is that you can't claim privacy while living the life of an exhibitionist.

The judge who ruled in the Streisand cased noted that she granted reporters interviews in her home, permitted national magazines to publish photos of the home's interior and its grounds, and opened her home to guests.

Lohan is an exhibitionist of the worst kind. She could do wonders to fix her privacy concerns by putting on some underwear. Several photos of her private areas have been taken at public venues. In one incident, she gave a crowd of pre-teen kids a view of her backside at a Nickelodeon awards show when a breeze lifted up her dress.

The Internet has turned a large portion of the general population into exhibitionists. Millions of people have personal Web pages that share vast amounts of information about their daily lives. Because everyone is on equal ground with everyone else, Internet users have grown accustomed to informational exhibitionism.

The Internet Is Leading to the Mark of the Beast

We live in an age when it is common to share our personal information with strangers. It's all done in the name of convenience. Whenever I call to order a pizza, the person taking my order always asks for my phone number. When I share my phone number, the order-takers instantly know my address so they will know where to deliver the pizza. They can also know what I want (based on my previous orders), and they have my credit card information for payment for the pizza. Most people couldn't care less if a database somewhere knows he or she likes to order a large hamburger pizza once or twice a month.

What has allowed people to become so free in sharing personal information is the lack of concern about government control. There are still a few totalitarian governments left, but the most infamous ones from the twentieth century have largely faded from memory. During the height of the Cold War, as much as 10 percent of the citizens of Soviet bloc nations were employed by the government as spy against their comrades. The Soviet secret police would have a blast with all the information available today. They could track people without even leaving their offices.

People don't fear the power of the Internet because it has never been used against them. It is also so pervasive in nature that I doubt anyone will curse it when the Antichrist uses it to control the world. It would be like people blaming the internal combustion engine for helping Hitler come to power in Europe.

The Internet may be a friendly tool now, but someday it will be a key factor in allowing the Antichrist to come to power. We have never had a global dictator. The logistical requirements have always been too great to span the globe. Now that the vast majority of the world is wired together, it will be very easy for someone to establish a political and economic system that reaches every nation.

The Bible predicts that someday everyone will be required to take a mark that will allow him or her to be part of a financial network. Without this ID, no one will be able to buy or sell. Someone might have a million dollars in the bank, but without the mark, he or she won't be able to spend a penny of it.

> And he had power to give life unto the image of the beast, that the image of the beast should both speak, and cause that as many as would not worship the image of the beast should be killed. And he causeth all, both small and great, rich and poor, free and bond, to receive a mark in their right hand, or in their foreheads: And that no man might buy or sell, save he that had the mark, or the name of the beast, or the number of his name. (Rev. 13:15–17)

I believe the Rapture will be the key factor in the Beast's rise to power. The White House chief of staff, Rahm Emanuel, once said, "You never want a serious crisis to go to waste—and what I mean by that is an opportunity to do things that you didn't think you could do before." The departure—the Rapture of the church—will, I have no doubt, create the greatest crisis in history.

CHAPTER EIGHTEEN

BIG BROTHER IS WATCHING

By Alan Franklin

If you want to be a film star, come to Britain. We're all on camera. All you have to do is walk through any town or drive down any road and you are watched, filmed, and monitored. When my wife, Pat, and I tour America, we feel neglected because the roadside cameras are no longer ever-present—*not yet.*

As the world moves towards a "Big Brother" society beyond the nightmares of author George Orwell, who predicted a world in which the state watched everyone in his 1948 classic novel, *1984,* it is like we are inmates of a high-tech prison. Big Brother really is watching us in Europe. The rest of the world is not far behind: Those who drive using global positioning satellite (GPS) navigation systems realize that their GPS devices know where they are and where they are going. Cell phones can track our whereabouts long after we have moved on, as can most mobile communications devices. That's why criminals buy throwaway, anonymous mobile phones!

Every minute, someone somewhere is keeping track of what we do, what we spend, and where we go and is following the pattern of our lives—from our library book borrowing to our hotel stays. All this information is logged into vast databases, electronic storehouses of our lives and our times. If we buy and sell using credit or debit cards (cash is frowned on and checks will be obsolete soon), we leave a data trail as distinctive as our fingerprints.

We don't need to leave home to be spied on, because Big Brother also patrols the Internet, where tiny bugs called "cookies" are left on our computers to track what we look at. Most firms keep a record of all employee emails. And in newspapers, as I know from personal experience, all stories are logged and the time spent writing them is recorded, as is the subject matter. Suppose, for example, you want to see all stories a particular reporter has written. It would only take a few clicks to list all his or her output; I could do this when I was an editor. It is easy to see how this facility could be used against people. Then there is Echelon, an electronic eavesdropping system that monitors all emails, mobile phone calls, and international phone calls for key words of interest. It's all to protect us, of course…

To illustrate the reality of life in the European Union (EU) super-state (the revived Roman Empire predicted by the prophet Daniel twenty-five hundred years ago), I have a picture taken from the living room of our former home in southeast England. Looming up over the fence and facing into our windows is a tall pole, atop which are three cameras that operate twenty-four hours a day. Should they wish, the watchers could see who comes and goes into and out of our home. Good-bye, privacy!

It gets worse. Another slide I have always gets a laugh: I am pictured searching through our trash bin—we call them "wheelie bins"—for any microchip that might be found in it. All over Britain, councils are inserting chips to check our trash. Put the wrong rubbish in the wrong receptacle and you are in serious trouble, with a fine to follow. How many bins have been fitted with chips is hard to say, but the number has already reached many hundreds of thousands, if not millions. The *Southport Visitor* online news source in the north of England, quotes a Sefton Council representative as saying: "Yes, each wheeled bin will have an electronic code. This will assist retrieval of 'lost' bins and allow performance and participation to be measured. Removal of the chip is a criminal offence and may result in the bin not being emptied."[237]

The site, checked on February 12, 2010, gives news of a heartening fight back against "rubbish spies":

> An enormous mutiny against wheelie-bin spy bugs is sweeping Britain, with thousands of rebellious households removing the electronic devices and either throwing them away or even posting them "back" to their local councils. Protesters are ignoring threats of prosecution for criminal damage in their resentment at having their rubbish surreptitiously monitored by council chiefs. In the Wiltshire village of Winterbourne Monkton, a "Ban the Bug" campaign is being led by retired policeman Martin Meeks. Mr. Meeks, a former Chief Inspector with Special Branch, said: "From my time in Special Branch, I know all about the permissions that have to be sought to keep tabs on someone, and here no one had told the residents what was going on. Kennet Council has covertly installed this device on my property, and in my book that is an intrusion into my private life."

Radio frequency identification (RFID) technology now tracks livestock and pets in Europe, where every dog and cat not only has his day, but has his pet passport as well—a microchip under the skin! The same technology that monitors travelers at toll roads is used to check the medical history of every animal brought into Britain. These microchip tags are inserted in a few seconds; I have filmed vets fitting them and noted how easy and painless it is. *Shades of things to come!*

My new passport has a microchip with many details on it. I wave it at a computer whenever I travel and enter America. The computer also does an eye scan on entry. Many countries are building database systems involving the establishment of national ID cards under the banner of "saving you from terrorism," when in fact organizations like the Department of Homeland Security pose an even greater threat to our freedom. Our privacy and freedom are quickly vanishing as a computer-linked global society is created, with any crisis used to justify further freedom curbs. Remember, the one who controls the world's giant databases controls the world!

When you shop for clothes—or anything else—RFID chipping of most items bought and sold, coupled with transaction records on your credit cards, combine with all the other ID and surveillance methods to build a means of control over people that would have astounded the Nazis, who thought *they* had total power! Years ago, I viewed the giant computers based in Brussels, Belgium—headquarters of the European Union and future base of Antichrist. Even in the 1980s, the computer system was known jokingly as "the Beast." It's no longer a joke. Big Brother now bestrides the globe.

This spying on citizens has reached such a level where I live that it astounds visiting Americans. I just drove to my hometown of Guildford, Surrey, a prosperous place eighteen miles from London. Going down the hill leading into town, I noted that drivers had better slow down, for a camera was standing in the middle of the road waiting to catch anyone going above thirty miles per hour. Drivers who did would get a souvenir picture of themselves they'd rather not keep—but one that the courts will.

A few yards away, I saw a police camera van parked, filming motorists trying to go about their business. Then, as if this weren't overkill, within a hundred yards I spotted a police mobile surveillance unit. Add to this scenario the scores of spy cameras mounted on poles and buildings dotted all over Guildford, and you'll get a picture of super-surveillance. Many towns also have camera cars with sinister-looking camera logos on their sides, constantly on the move to see if they can film anyone breaking the law. In 1999, our son, who was then a media student and who now works for an international TV news network, went out to make a film with me focusing on the subject of surveillance. We filmed one spy camera on a pole in a small Hampshire village and had the surreal experience of the camera swivelling around to film *us* filming *it!*

In my job as a newspaper editor, I visited a number of surveillance control rooms where watchers monitor closed-circuit television (CCTV) twenty-four hours a day. I experienced how thorough this close control is one day in our city center office. A man with a grievance against our newspaper came in and started behaving oddly. He grabbed some furniture and tried to drag it out of the room. When I was called, I found him sitting on a desk, refusing to move. My colleagues and I knew we could not frogmarch him out, as this would undoubtedly have resulted in his pressing charges of assault against us! So we called the police, who arrived after the man left. "He's gone," I told them. "We know," they replied. "We watched him on camera as he left your office, then tracked him 'round the town."

Remember, these are the last days. My wife, Pat, wrote this in the first chapter of our book, *Goodbye America, Goodbye Britain:*

Modern communication.

Technology exists to communicate with everyone on earth, a prerequisite for the Antichrist kingdom foretold in the book of Revelation.

The mark.

Technology exists to mark everyone on earth. "And he causeth all, both small and great, rich and poor, free and bond, to receive a mark in their right hand, or in their foreheads:

and that no man might buy or sell, save he that had the mark, or the name of the beast, or the number of his name" (Rev. 13:16).

The watchers.

Technology exists to watch and control everyone on earth, which Antichrist will certainly do (Rev. 13). None of this was possible before, but God knew all about technology long before the first computer chip was invented. Now, every can of beans you buy is electronically recorded if you use a card. Every book you check out of the library, every email you send is information filed somewhere electronically.[238]

In the future, we may not just be watched; our minds could be invaded! Will Antichrist be able to know our thoughts? I personally doubt this, as God places limits on the adversary. However, machines are being developed to monitor our brain's reactions. Here's part of a report entitled "Mind-Reading Systems Could Change Air Security" from Fox News:

> The aim of one company that blends high technology and behavioral psychology is hinted at in its name, WeCU—as in "We See You."
>
> "The system that Israeli-based WeCU Technologies has devised and is testing in Israel projects images on to airport screens, such as symbols associated with a certain terrorist group or some other image only a would-be terrorist would recognize," company CEO Ehud Givon said.
>
> "The reaction could be a darting of the eyes, an increased heartbeat, a nervous twitch or faster breathing," he said.
>
> The WeCU system would use humans to do some of the observing, but would rely mostly on hidden cameras or sensors that can detect a slight rise in body temperature and heart rate.

Far more sensitive devices under development that can take such measurements from a distance would be incorporated later.

Some critics have expressed horror at the approach, calling it Orwellian and akin to "brain fingerprinting."[239]

For now, we have the sky spies. In case my reservations about spy cameras are thought unreasonable, let me quote from a report in *The Times* of London, March 7, 2009. The story was headlined "Every Step You Take, We'll Be Watching You," and the subheading was: "Are we monitored constantly by CCTV? *The Times* has set out to investigate the extent of Britain's surveillance society." The reporter, Kaya Burgess, wrote:

> I followed an average London commuter's journey from Angel, Islington, to *The Times'* offices in Wapping, taking note of the cameras along the way. No fewer than nine CCTV [closed-captioned television] cameras in and around the concourse of the Angel underground station captured me setting out as I turned into the heart of residential Islington.
>
> From the top of a tall pole, higher than any lamppost, a council-run camera watched me as I made my way down City Road, past a nest of four traffic cameras observing the crossroads. Never before had I noticed the small cameras discreetly placed above dozens of doorways along the street as I passed from the view of one camera to the next along the length of the road.
>
> Across the 3.1 mile stretch of my route—through Old Street and Aldgate and down past Tower Bridge into Wapping—there were a total of 283 CCTV cameras watching me on my way to work. This is an average of one camera every eighteen metres....
>
> On my journey into the city, dozens more cameras loomed over the streets, some obvious, some hidden within tinted bulbs embedded on street corners.[240]

The latest wheeze is talking cameras. If you are hard up for company, go and chat to a camera in our country. In at least twenty cities across Britain, street cameras are being fitted with listening devices and microphones so "they" can listen for trouble or lecture you if you are naughty.[241] This is something police discourage parents from doing, by the way. In Hampshire, where we live, a mother who scolded her children for misbehaving at a supermarket was spotted by an off-duty policeman. The man was on watch, though—"politically correct" watch, which says parents cannot correct their children lest their "rights" be infringed. This policeman followed the mother home, scaring the life out of her, and then reported her to the local authority as a potential child abuser! But the cameras are allowed to give you a good "talking to."

I always assumed America was too vast for camera surveillance to work, but this is no longer true. When I was speaking at the East Coast Prophecy Conference in Pennsylvania, a man who worked as a forest ranger told me that cameras had been installed in forests he patrolled. Watching for forest fires may be their present purpose. Then I saw a report from the Environment News Service entitled "Forest Service Buys Eyes in the Sky for Surveillance":

> The U.S. Forest Service has bought pilot-less aircraft to provide day and night photo reconnaissance for its law enforcement program, according to agency records released by Public Employees for Environmental Responsibility, PEER. The two "unmanned aerial vehicles," or drones, may lead to wider conversion of military robotic technology for civilian uses.[242]

If you watch old films about the Rapture, they often feature groups of people who become followers of the Lord Jesus after our departure. These folks are often pictured as hiding out in the woods. No hiding out in the woods now; a drone could swoop in and film them!

America's size does make it more difficult to track people with cameras, so the FBI has plans for a massive new database that serves the same purpose. You may be on it!

In February 2008, CNN reported that the FBI is planning to create a massive computer database of people's physical characteristics. Those pesky terrorists are the reason, of course. But we'll all be in the dragnet. The report said the agency will use eye scans combined with other data to pick out "suspects." That's a wide definition, and throughout history it has meant people who disagree with the powers that be. It is estimated that it will take a decade and $1 billion to build the database full of biometric information, including eye scans and palm prints.

"It's the beginning of the surveillance society where you can be tracked anywhere, any time, and all your movements, and eventually all your activities, will be tracked and noted and correlated," said Barry Steinhardt, director of the American Civil Liberties Union's (ACLU) Technology and Liberty Project.[243]

The FBI is collecting mug shots and pictures of scars and tattoos, images that are being stored as the technology is perfected. The FBI also wants to start comparing people's eyes— specifically the iris, or the colored part of an eye, in its new biometrics program called Next Generation Identification.[244]

The public relations story will be about nailing criminals or terrorists, but more than 55 percent of the investigations the FBI runs involves criminal background checks for people applying for government jobs or working with children and the elderly, according to the FBI. Much information can be used to enforce political correctness or criminalize the "wrong" opinions, as has happened in Britain. In the *Daily Mail*, London, on November 25, 2002, Melanie Phillips reported a poster she saw on the subway—the London Underground rail system. She wrote:

I was startled to learn…that Commander Cressida Dick, head of the Metropolitan Police's "Diversity Directorate" (yes, really) was urging us all to report to the police anyone whose views we found hateful.

If anyone had committed a thought crime—abusing people because of their faith, race, religion, or disability or because they were lesbian, gay, bisexual, or transsexual—Commander Dick wants us to provide the police with a "name, an address, or even a description of offenders."[245]

Iris technology and fingerprints are the most accurate identifiers to date, but even the way people walk is another possible way of picking out "suspects." The ACLU's Mr. Steinhardt said that while the original idea was to track or identify criminals, this has moved on to include large groups of ordinary people. He added ominously: "Eventually, it's going to be everybody."[246]

Although our countries are reluctant to profile those most likely to be terrorists—i.e., Islamic males aged 18 to 40—and pretend that grandmas visiting their families are as likely as people named Mohammed to have liquid explosives in their hair gel, governments are much readier to target the truly dangerous: committed Christians.

Our own Web site, www.thefreepressonline.co.uk, contains this report—"America's Top Law Enforcement Agency Demonizes All the Sane Citizens!"—from Pastor Chuck Baldwin, originally posted on April 18, 2009:

The Department of Homeland Security (DHS) has just released an "assessment" report entitled "Rightwing Extremism: Current Economic and Political Climate Fueling Resurgence in Radicalization and Recruitment." With virtually no references, documentation, or annotations, the report, which was released to all branches of American law enforcement, demonizes a host of citizens as having the capacity to become violent "right-wing extremists."

The DHS report warns law enforcement to be on guard against anyone who opposes illegal immigration, same-sex marriage, "free trade agreements," gun control, the "New World Order," "One World Government," the outsourcing of American jobs, the "perceived" threat to U.S. sovereignty by foreign powers, abortion, "declarations of martial law," "the creation of citizen detention camps," "suspension of the U.S. Constitution," or the abridgement of State authority. Also branded are people who believe in "end-times" prophecies, and who "stockpile" food, ammunition, or firearms.

I dare say that at least 75 percent (or more) of the American people have beliefs that fall into one or more categories of the above list. If you are one of them, DHS suspects you of being a "rightwing extremist."

Chuck had reported on March 17, 2009:

Watch out, liberty lovers. Police now class us as terrorists!

Thanks to a concerned Missouri state policeman, a nationally syndicated radio talk show host stated that he was alerted last week to a secret Missouri state police report that categorized supporters of Congressman Ron Paul, Bob Barr, and myself as "militia influenced terrorists." The report, he said, "instructs the Missouri police to be on the lookout for supporters displaying bumper stickers and other paraphernalia associated with the Constitutional, Campaign for Liberty, and Libertarian parties."

So the cameras know what to swivel in on now—your fender stickers!

This is a foretaste of what is in store. For more than three and a half years, Antichrist will extend his hold over earth. Media and communications will come under his direct control. I find it particularly interesting that many of the mega mergers going on in big business involve telecommunications, broadcasting, and food production. I knew the head of Britain's major cable company and asked him how easy it would be to monitor conversations. "Very easy," he replied. "But why would I want to, Alan?" I have no doubt he would not.

The technology that allows increased electronic surveillance into every home is getting "smarter" all the time. For example, when I decided to take Sky Television's new digital satellite service (a sister network to Fox in the USA), I had to sign an acknowledgment that my family's TV viewing would be monitored. A cable was installed linking our satellite hook-up with our telephone line. Every day, details of our viewing go to a central computer, which uses the information to build a pattern of what we like to watch. The purpose is purely commercial, but it is another link in the electronic chain with which we are being bound, ready for the ultimate control freak. Within a year or two of signing a seven-year peace treaty with Israel, Antichrist will have total control of the world. Nobody will be able to buy or sell unless he or she takes, on the forehead or right hand, the computer mark of the Beast—which will almost certainly be a tiny microchip.

In my first book, *EU: Final World Empire,* I wrote the following in chapter twelve, entitled "Introducing Antichrist":

> I have spoken to the first man in the world to have a computer chip inserted under his skin, Professor Kevin Warwick of Reading University in Berkshire. Kevin used a tiny $6 chip for his experiment, during which he opened doors, turned on his office computer, and adjusted his central heating system without lifting a finger.
>
> Professor Warwick, head of cybernetics at Reading University, was the first human guinea pig to have an under-the-skin "smart card." He appeared on TV with *X-Files* actress Gillian Anderson, who called him: "Britain's leading prophet

of the robot age." Newspapers were full of the wonders of Kevin's experiment, majoring on the good news that we will soon be able to throw away our plastic credit cards. Cards can be lost, stolen, copied, or damaged. They are a constant headache. We lose them, we worry about them. You can see how easy it will be to persuade an unthinking population how superior a chip implant will be. You can't steal an implant, unless you chop someone's hand or head off! The latter is what will happen to those who refuse the mark—the Tribulation saints.

Kevin Warwick told the press: "With the implant in me it creates a high-speed link from my body and my unique identity to a range of computers. It is already far quicker than using a conventional smart card for these basic operations. This is just the beginning of how this could work. The potential of this technology is enormous. We will be able to communicate directly with computers. For example, it is quite possible for an implant to replace an Access, Visa, or bankers' card. There is very little danger in losing an implant or having it stolen. An implant could also carry huge amounts of data such as National Insurance number and blood types."

But Kevin, who is not part of some evil conspiracy, but a dedicated scientist with a good mind, gave a warning: "I know all this smacks of Big Brother. With an implant, a machine will know where anyone is at all times. Individuals could be clocked in and out of their offices automatically. It would be known at all times exactly where an individual was within a building and whom they were with. An individual might not even be able to pay a visit to the toilet without a machine knowing about it." In fact, this is already happening. I know of companies where every employee has swipe cards with them at all times, to gain access to different areas of their headquarters building. A log is kept of their movements. It is already possible to track every keystroke on a computer and relay the findings to the boss's room. Because of this device, costing only $99, several Americans have already lost their jobs.

Professor Warwick's secretary said that one advantage of his chip implant was that she could trace him at all times. "Since the implant we always know where he is," she said. Professor Warwick advocates that students should be fitted with chips to check their attendance at lectures. "It is a desirable technical advance, but we have to decide on the moral and ethical issues of twenty-four hour surveillance of everyone fitted with a chip," he said. He believes the ultimate application will be to tap into the brain's thought processes, currently a mystery to scientists.

The professor seems to think that man is in charge of his destiny, which is an ever onward, ever upward forward progression. Yet progress is only possible within the rule of law. In much of the West today, the spirit of lawlessness grows fiercer as Antichrist's time draws near.[247]

Because Christianity has been largely removed from the classrooms, many people are wilder and out of control, and in Britain we have numerous "problem families." Instead of getting them saved and reformed, our government resorts to "control freakery." Here's an excerpt from an article entitled "Britain to Put CCTV Cameras Inside Private Homes," posted by Charlie Sorrel on the Wired Web site:

> As an ex-Brit, I'm well aware of the authorities' love of surveillance and snooping, but even I, a pessimistic cynic, am amazed by the government's latest plan: to install Orwell's telescreens in twenty thousand homes.
>
> Some £400 million ($668 million) will be spent on installing and monitoring CCTV cameras in the homes of private citizens. Why? To make sure the kids are doing their home-

work, going to bed early, and eating their vegetables. The scheme has, astonishingly, already been running in two thousand family homes. The government's "children's secretary" Ed Balls is behind the plan, which is aimed at problem, antisocial families. The idea is that, if a child has a more stable home life, he or she will be less likely to stray into crime and drugs.[248]

The surveillance state is fast covering everybody in all twenty-seven formerly independent nations of Europe, nations that were subsumed into the European Union (EU) state as of December 1, 2009. Here is how Stephen Booth of *Open Europe* described it in Britain's *Guardian* newspaper:

> While the UK government pushes ahead with new ways to stockpile our personal data and watch us at every street corner, the European Union is quietly getting on with establishing its very own Europe-wide version of the surveillance state.
>
> Once [the] Lisbon [Treaty] is finally ratified, [which it is as of December 1, 2009—A. F.] it will be full steam ahead. Plans are already underway for a fledgling EU "Home Office," which has been dubbed the "committee on internal security." It will decide how national police, border, immigration, and criminal justice authorities should deal with cross-border issues throughout the EU.

From the opposite political spectrum, the right-wing *Daily Telegraph* of London ran this headline on December 6, 2009: "EU Security Proposals Are 'Dangerously Authoritarian.'" The subheading stated: "The European Union is stepping up efforts to build an enhanced pan-European system of security and surveillance which critics have described as 'dangerously authoritarian.'"

Bruno Waterfield, writing from the "belly of the beast" in Brussels, reported that civil liberties groups say the proposals would create an

EU ID card register, Internet surveillance systems, satellite surveillance, automated exit-entry border systems operated by machines reading biometrics, and risk-profiling systems.

Europe's justice ministers plan to bring in the "domestic security policy" and surveillance network proposals, known in Brussels circles as the "Stockholm programme"—the EU's first-ever internal security policy—as the newly united superstate gets under way this year—2010.

Jacques Barrot, the European justice and security commissioner, said the aim was to "develop a domestic security strategy for the EU," once regarded as a strictly national "home affairs" area of policy. "National frontiers should no longer restrict our activities," he said.[249] *Shades of the coming world government!*

Creating a new "information system architecture" of Europe-wide police and security databases will create a "surveillance state," according to critics. The *Telegraph* report added that Tony Bunyan, of the European Civil Liberties Network (ECLN), believes EU security officials will harness a "digital tsunami" of new information technology without asking "political and moral questions first."

"An increasingly sophisticated internal and external security apparatus is developing under the auspices of the EU," he said. "In five or ten years time when we have the surveillance and database state, people will look back and ask, 'What were you doing in 2009 to stop this happening?'" [250]

Civil liberties groups are particularly concerned over these "convergence" proposals to herald standardized European police surveillance techniques and to create "tool-pools" of common data gathering systems to be operated at the EU level.

One of the great campaigners against the EU superstate is my friend Derek Bennett, editor of *The Euro Realist* (linked to our website, www.thefreepressonline.co.uk). This is part of his comment from the December 2009 edition:

In 2010 the invisible rulers of the EU finally get their hands on great chunks of power and we will begin to see some drastic changes, sadly none for the better…the EU will bring in more and more Big Brother-style surveillance. The EU plans to put a black box in every car, to spy on us every time we travel. One of the main reasons for the EU's enthusiasm to bleed all motorists of their fast-dwindling finances is to justify its disastrous space odyssey, i.e., the Galileo GPS satellite, which is way over budget and behind schedule. [The satellite system would link to the black boxes to see where we all go, all the time!—A. F.]

Because of this, the EU wants every car to be fitted with black boxes at a cost of £500 each to enable it to monitor all movements, and to charge drivers for each mile driven. These boxes, which smack of "Big Brother," would also monitor how people drive.

That's not all. It's fast forward on identity cards, which will have every detail of our lives permanently imprinted on their microchips. A group fighting this, called NO2ID, says proposed UK ID cards are not simple identity documents, but involve a complicated and oppressive permanent surveillance. They say that in fact Home Office plans (from 2011) to make people register on a database for life when they renew their passport will put many people off traveling altogether.

I believe this has long been the plan, fast being extended worldwide as the car is demonized and we are told to curb our travel to "save the planet." Only one person will save the planet. His name is Jesus and He will be here shortly! Meanwhile, every kind of restriction is being placed on private travel, for a car driver is a free person, able to go where he or she wishes at a time of his or her choosing. From driving up motoring costs by bringing in ridiculous rules to curb

CO_2 emissions—at a time when the world is demonstrably getting cooler, not warmer—to putting taxes on gasoline so high that travel is kept to a minimum, watch our rulers curb everyone's movement but their own. The ultimate travel deterrent, the electric car, has just been launched as I write. It's GM's Volt, which depends on a huge battery to get it moving. If you think U.S. motorists will go for that, you have spent too long in the Beltway in Washington DC, whose inhabitants have long since lost touch with reality. As my wife, Pat, said when she saw the new "batterymobile": "Only dolts will buy Volts."

Britain has long had plans to track and log every vehicle journey. Steve Connor, science editor of the *Independent* newspaper, wrote the following on December 22, 2005:

> Britain is to become the first country in the world where the movements of all vehicles on the roads are recorded. A new national surveillance system will hold the records for at least two years.
>
> Using a network of cameras that can automatically read every passing number plate, the plan is to build a huge database of vehicle movements so that the police and security services can analyze any journey a driver has made over several years.[251]

Britain has almost five million closed-circuit TV cameras—one for every twelve men, women, and children in the country—and many of these are being converted to read number plates automatically night and day to provide ceaseless coverage of all motorways (highways) and main roads, as well as towns, cities, ports, and gas-station forecourts.

The in formation goes to a central database at the Police National Computer Center in Hendon, north London, which will store the details of thirty-five million number-plate "reads" every day. The time, date, and precise location, with camera sites monitored by global positioning satellites, will be on record, and this could be for up to five years as plans for a database extension progress. Plus, if many thousands more cameras are linked in to do their bit for Big Brother, details of up to one hundred million number plates can be fed each day into the central databank.

The cameras are impartial: The good, the bad, and the lost will all be filmed so the movements of millions of ordinary people will be routinely recorded and kept on a central computer database for years. The chief police officers and more than fifty leading local councils have signed agreements to convert many thousands of existing cameras to read number plates. They say it's to solve and prevent crime, but is this really true?

I was a courts and crime reporter for years, working with many law enforcement officers and prosecutors. They will tell you, for example, that only a really stupid criminal would do a drug deal under the gaze of a camera. They will go around to the back of the building and do the transaction there. All cameras usually catch is Mr. and Mrs. Joe Public trying to get on with their lives.

Here's another excerpt from the *Independent* report:

"Every time you make a car journey already, you'll be on CCTV somewhere. The difference is that, in future, the car's index plates will be read as well," said Frank Whiteley, Chief Constable of Hertfordshire and chairman of the Association of Chief Police Officers' steering committee on automatic number plate recognition (ANPR).

"What the data centre should be able to tell you is where a vehicle was in the past and where it is now, whether it was or wasn't at a particular location, and the routes taken to and from those crime scenes. Particularly important are associated vehicles," Mr. Whiteley said.

Mr. Whiteley said Britain's secret service MI5 will also use the database. "Clearly there are values for this in counter-terrorism," he said.[252]

The secret service already has access to all our emails and much else, and there is now no detail of our lives that is safe from the sky spies of big government. "Combating terrorism and crime" is the usual excuse for this intrusion into what used to be our private lives. But who is a terrorist suspect? This kind of watch could easily be used against, for example, home schoolers, who are regarded with suspicion in the socialist superstate of Europe.

If you wish to escape the all-seeing surveillance state, the watchers will know about your travel plans. The UK Border Agency aims to track 95 percent of journeys out of Britain by the end of 2010.[253] Whether you come and go by sea, by air, or through the Channel Tunnel, your trip is recorded and stored on a database for a decade. Detailed information such as credit card information, exact itineraries, and home and email addresses will go with your passport—complete with its own microchip—to make up a full picture of your life. All these journeys have to be registered in advance. Swimming the English Channel won't allow you to escape scrutiny: All swimmers and their support teams will be subject to the rules!

By 2014, Britain's dwindling number of fishermen will be further persecuted by having to use the Internet to record their details every time they sail out of British waters. Yachtsmen and pilots of small planes will be included, with a fine of up to £500 if they don't.

How long will we be free to expose this sinister supervision? Bernard Connolly is a former top EU official who was so appalled at how the superstate was heading that he wrote a book called *The Rotten Heart of Europe*. He was sacked for his pains and "put on trial" by his masters. In a letter to the *Daily Telegraph* published on March 9, 2001, Mr. Connolly said the following:

The court recognized that one of the points at issue was that of free speech. It paid lip service to the notion but made clear that free speech is not a value that can be allowed to get in the way of "Europe." The court ruled that anything "liable to prejudice the interests of the Community" is "such as to justify restricting freedom of expression." Moreover, overruling the House of Lords [previously Britain's highest court of appeal—A. F.], it defined a new offence of seditious libel in EU law as conduct "that seriously prejudiced the Community's interests and damaged the institution's image and reputation."[254]

Mr. Connolly instances a claim from a Labor politician that even the *Telegraph's* Brussels reporter "can ply his trade in complete safety." His response is:

For how long? Article 52 of the EU Charter of Fundamental Rights declares that all freedoms and rights can be restricted to "meet objectives of general interest recognized by the Union." The rights that can be thus restricted include not only free speech and the right to life, but also the right not to be punished by retroactive legislation, the right to a fair trial, the presumption of innocence and the absence of double jeopardy.[A. F. adds: This means you could be tried twice for the same offence!][255]

So where is our hope in all of this? The answer is that we have the Blessed Hope—the soon return of the Lord Jesus. This should give us urgency and wake us from our spiritual slumbers. As the world shrinks and we are all watched and monitored, Christianity is cracked down upon, and evil flourishes, remember that all this was prophesied in Matthew chapter 24 and many other books of the Bible.

Here's how my wife, Pat, concluded her chapter, titled "These Are the Last Days," from *Goodbye America, Goodbye Britain:*

A small world.

Last but certainly not least, transport and technology exist to reach the entire earth with the gospel.

There are more signs one could point to, but those are the main ones. We are living in the end times; there is no doubt about it whatsoever. Previous generations have thought their day was the time, but world conditions were not right. Israel was not back in the land; the Roman Empire had not re-emerged; and technology did not exist for worldwide persecution or control. World conditions now leave no room for doubt. It is as though the curtain has gone up for the last act, and all the props and all the actors are either already in place or just waiting in the wings to step out. There is a breathless hush, and the last act commences.

Should we be frightened by all this? Once you begin to understand what is really happening in the world, the news behind the news, it can seem overwhelmingly bleak, until you remind yourself of the end of the Book. There is the happiest of endings, dear friends. It is all leading up to the coming of the Lord Jesus—first coming *for* us to take us home to heaven with Him and later coming *with* us back to this earth for the destruction of Israel's enemies and the setting up of the Lord's glorious millennial kingdom—with its capital at Jerusalem! Praise the Lord.

It will look for a time like the powers of evil are winning, but our Lord will have His way. All will come to pass, just as the Bible says. The last act has been written. Those who acknowledge Jesus' Name now will rejoice when He acknowledges them before His angels! Those who work for Him now will certainly receive a reward from His dear hands. Those who love Him will reign with Him. And those who are glad at His appearing will receive a special crown![256] I don't deserve one single thing, but I want that crown, don't you? I would rather have that crown than all the crown jewels of Britain. I don't want to be found doing anything that would make me ashamed when my Lord suddenly appears and calls His people out of these end times.

IN THE TWINKLING

By Terry James

A monumental event is about to occur! The change will be stupendous and will make a severe impact on every person in every nation on earth. The repercussions will shake the planet far beyond anything to this point in recorded history.

Yet the apostle Paul, who prophesied the happening nearly two thousand years ago, used a gentle metaphor to describe the catastrophic occurrence in an almost hushed tone in his letter to the Thessalonians:

> Behold, I shew you a mystery; We shall not all sleep, but we shall all be changed, In a moment, in the twinkling of an eye, at the last trump: for the trumpet shall sound, and the dead shall be raised incorruptible, and we shall be changed. (1 Cor. 15:51–52)

This astonishing change Paul predicts in revealing "a mystery" was first foretold by Jesus Christ Himself. He said to His disciples who were present and to all of His disciples that would follow until the moment of the great event:

> Let not your heart be troubled: ye believe in God, believe also in Me. In My Father's house are many mansions: if it were not so, I would have told you. I go to prepare a place for you. And if I go and prepare a place for you, I will come again, and receive you unto Myself; that where I am, there ye may be also. (John 14:1–3)

Supernatural Stopwatch Needed

No humanly designed stopwatch could record how fast this change will take place. But God's Word, through Paul, uses a Greek expression that gives the slightest inkling of just how swift the departure will take place: *atomos,* which describes the "twinkling-of-an-eye" measurement given in the King James Version. The meaning is a quantity of time that can't be divided; in fact, calculating the increment of time that will elapse is like trying to witness with the naked eye the splitting of an atom. It cannot be done. Some have suggested *atomos* indicates a period faster than the time it takes light to enter the eye and strike the retina. At approximately one hundred eighty-six thousand miles per second, that would be fast indeed!

But even that description fails to accurately embrace the concept God, through Paul, conveys to the believer. The speed of the Rapture is likely an infinite matter that the finite mind can't possibly grasp.

Paul prophesied that every Christian—all born-again believers who have died or are alive when the Rapture happens—will be instantaneously face to face with Christ. We know it will be a glorious, personal meeting with Jesus because Paul said, "Beloved, now are we the sons of God, and it doth not yet appear what we shall be: but we know that, when He shall appear, we shall be like Him; for we shall see Him as He is" (1 John 3:2).

The Departure Described

Bible prophecy doesn't give the time of the snatching-up of the church age (age of grace) saints, even though it gives an inkling of just how quickly it will happen. As a matter of fact, Jesus told His followers that we will not know the exact time of the departure in advance: "But of that day and hour knoweth no man, no, not the angels of heaven, but My Father only" (Matt. 24:36).

We can, however, know with comforting assurance that the Rapture will take place before certain extremely troubling, prophetically scheduled things happen. All believers of the church age will meet in the air with Jesus Christ before the time He describes as follows: "For then shall be great tribulation, such as was not since the beginning of the world to this time, no, nor ever shall be" (Matt. 24:21).

Jesus was prophesying about the Tribulation. Specifically, He was talking about the last three and one-half years of the seven-year period of God's wrath and judgment falling upon the rebellious people living upon planet earth. However, the entire seven years of Tribulation will be God's judgment—a time of testing to "try," in the judicial sense, the sinful people left behind following the Rapture.

Christ's calling all believers (His church) to be with Him (John 14:1–3; 1 Cor. 15:51–52; 1 Thess. 4:16–17) will be to keep them from the Tribulation hour, as Jesus in His ascended majesty prompted John to write: "Because thou hast kept the word of My patience, I also will keep thee from the hour of temptation, which shall come upon all the world, to try them that dwell upon the earth" (Rev. 3:10).

Paul gave God's word of assurance in this regard through his first letter to the Thessalonians:

For God hath not appointed us to wrath, but to obtain salvation
by our Lord Jesus Christ, who died for us, that, whether we
wake or sleep, we should live together with Him. Wherefore
comfort yourselves together, and edify one another, even as
also ye do. (1 Thess. 5:9–11)

The New Testament is written in the Greek language, which provides more precise definition and more microscopic focus than the
English affords. It is with this reality in view that this book's title was
employed.

Departure Defined

"The departure" is the most precise term with which to define the
Greek word used in a very key scriptural treatment of what has
become known as "the Rapture." Dr. Thomas Ice, a top scholar and
writer on biblical eschatology, presents well-researched thought on the
term "departure" and what the 2 Thessalonians 2 prophetic portion of
Scripture has to say about the Rapture and its timing.

Here is the scriptural reference: "Let no man deceive you by any
means: for that day shall not come, except there come a falling away
first, and that man of sin be revealed, the son of perdition" (2 Thess.
2:3). Ice dissects this profound prophetic passage as excerpted here:

> I believe there is a strong possibility that 2 Thessalonians 2:3
> is speaking of the Rapture. What do I mean? Some pretribu-
> lationists, like myself, think that the Greek noun apostasia,
> usually translated "apostasy," is a reference to the Rapture and
> should be translated "departure." Thus, this passage would
> be saying that the Day of the Lord will not come until the
> Rapture comes before it. If apostasia is a reference to a physi-
> cal departure, then 2 Thessalonians 2:3 is strong evidence for
> pretribulationism.

The Meaning of Apostasia

The Greek noun *apostasia* is used only twice in the New Testament. In addition to 2 Thessalonians 2:3, it occurs in Acts 21:21 where, speaking of Paul, it is said, "that you are teaching all the Jews who are among the Gentiles to forsake (*apostasia*) Moses." The word is a Greek compound of *apo* "from" and *istemi* "stand." Thus, it has the core meaning of "away from" or "departure." The *Liddell and Scott Greek Lexicon* defines *apostasia* first as "defection, revolt," then secondly as "departure, disappearance" [Henry George Liddell and Henry Scott, A Greek-English Lexicon, Revised with a Supplement (1968) by Sir Henry Stuart Jones and Roderick McKenzie (Oxford: Oxford University Press, 1940) 218]. Gordon Lewis explains how the verb from which the noun *apostasia* is derived supports the basic meaning of departure in the following:

> The verb may mean to remove spatially. There is little reason, then, to deny that the noun can mean such a spatial removal or departure.... The verb is used fifteen times in the New Testament. Of these fifteen, only three have anything to do with a departure from the faith (Luke 8:13; 1 Tim. 4: 1; Heb. 3:12). The word is used for departing from iniquity (2 Tim. 2:19), from ungodly men (1 Tim. 6:5), from the Temple (Luke 2:27), from the body (2 Cor. 12:8), and from persons (Acts 12: 10; Luke 4:13). [Gordon R. Lewis, "Biblical Evidence for Pretribulationism," *Bibliotheca Sacra* (vol. 125, no. 499; July 1968) 218.]

"It is with full assurance of proper exegetical study and with complete confidence in the original languages," concludes Daniel Davey, "that the word meaning of *apostasia* is defined as departure." [Daniel K. Davey, "The 'Apostesia' of 2 Thessalonians 2:3," ThM thesis, Detroit Baptist Theological Seminary, May 1982, 27.]

Paul Lee Tan adds the following:

> What precisely does Paul mean when he says that "the falling away" (2:3) must come before the Tribulation? The definite article "the" denotes that this will be a definite event, an event distinct from the appearance of the Man of Sin. The Greek word for "falling away," taken by itself, does not mean religious apostasy or defection. Neither does the word mean "to fall," as the Greeks have another word for that…. The best translation of the word is "to depart." The apostle Paul refers here to a definite event which he calls "the departure," and which will occur just before the start of the Tribulation. This is the Rapture of the church. [Paul Lee Tan, *The Interpretation of Prophecy* (Winona Lake, IN: Assurance Publishers, 1974) 341].

So the word has the core meaning of departure and it depends upon the context to determine whether it is used to mean physical departure or an abstract departure such as departure from the faith.…

The Use of the Article

It is important to note that Paul uses a definite article with the noun *apostasia*. What does this mean?

Davey notes the following:

> Since the Greek language does not need an article to make the noun definite, it becomes clear that with the usage of the article reference is being made to some-

thing in particular. In 2 Thessalonians 2:3, the word *apostasia* is prefaced by the definite article, which means that Paul is pointing to a particular type of departure clearly known to the Thessalonian church. [Davey, "Apostesia," 47.]

Dr. Lewis provides a likely answer when he notes that the definite article serves to make a word distinct and draw attention to it. In this instance he believes that its purpose is "to denote a previous reference." The departure previously referred to was "our being gathered to him" and our being "caught up" with the Lord and the raptured dead in the clouds (1 Thess. 4:17), notes Dr. Lewis. [Gordon R. Lewis and Bruce A. Demarest, *Integrative Theology*, vol. 3 (Grand Rapids, MI: Zondervan, 1996) 420.] The "departure" was something that Paul and his readers clearly had a mutual understanding about. Paul says in verse 5, "Do you not remember that while I was still with you, I was telling you these things?"

The use of the definite article would also support the notion that Paul spoke of a clear, discernable event. A physical departure like the Rapture would fit just such a notion. However, the New Testament teaches that apostasy had already arrived in the first century (cf. Acts 20:27–32, 1 Tim. 4:1–5; 2 Tim. 3:1–9; 2 Pet. 2:1–3; Jude 3–4, 17–21), and thus such a process would not denote a clear event as demanded by the language of this passage. Understanding departure as the Rapture would satisfy the nuance of this text. E. Schuyler English explains as follows:

Again, how would the Thessalonians, or Christians in any century since, be qualified to recognize the apostasy when it should come, assuming, simply for the sake of this inquiry, that the church might be on earth when it occurs? There has been apostasy from God, rebellion against Him, since time began. [E. Schuyler English, *Re-Thinking the Rapture* (Neptune, NJ: Loizeaux Brothers, 1954) 70.]

Whatever Paul is referring to in his reference to "the departure" was something that both the Thessalonian believers and he had discussed in depth previously. When we examine Paul's first letter to the Thessalonians, he never mentions the doctrine of apostasy; however, virtually every chapter in that epistle speaks of the Rapture (cf. 1:9–10; 2:19; probably 3:13; 4:13–17; 5:1–11). In these passages, Paul has used a variety of Greek terms to describe the Rapture. It should not be surprising that he uses another term to reference the Rapture in 2 Thessalonians 2:3. Dr. House tells us:

Remember, the Thessalonians had been led astray by the false teaching (2:2–3) that the Day of the Lord had already come. This was confusing because Paul offered great hope, in the first letter, of a departure to be with Christ and a rescue from God's wrath. Now a letter purporting to be from Paul seems to say that they would first have to go through the Day of the Lord. Paul then clarified his prior teaching by emphasizing that they had no need to worry. They could again be comforted because the departure he had discussed in his first letter, and in his teaching while with them, was still the truth. The departure of Christians to be with Christ, and the subsequent revelation of the lawless one, Paul argues, is proof that the Day of the Lord had not begun as they had thought. This understanding of *apostasia* makes much more sense than the view that they are to be comforted (v. 2) because a defection from the faith must precede the Day of the Lord. The entire second chapter (as well as 1 Thess. 4:18; 5:11) serves to comfort (see v. 2, 3, 17), supplied by a reassurance of Christ's coming as taught in [Paul's] first letter. [House, "Apostesia," 275–76.][257]

The Departure's Dynamic Disturbances

We have examined many signals of the coming apocalyptic storm in this volume. These forewarnings continue to mount in frequency and intensity—as Jesus said, in birth-pang fashion. The geopolitical, socioeconomic, geophysical, and religious contractions are but faint harbingers of the agony that will follow the departure of the church from this judgment-bound planet.

John the prophet, who wrote the visions he was given while exiled as an old man on the Aegean island of Patmos, presents in apocalyptic language the wrath and judgment to come upon the post-Rapture earth. The symbolic language he used in Revelation represents literal events even more horrific than therein expressed.

First, the Departure

Before God's wrath falls, in the twinkling of an eye (an *atomos* of time), millions of Christians—those born again by believing in the shed blood of Christ on the cross two millennia ago for salvation—will vanish from the earth's surface. The departure—the Rapture—will bring planet-rending disturbances to an already reeling world of non-believers.

God has been patient in allowing the world to see the Tribulation storm alerts. He has shown mercy and grace, as there is no prophecy given that must be fulfilled in order for the Rapture to happen. The departure can take place at any moment.

Getting out the warnings is the duty of spiritual meteorologists. This is a commission each author in *The Departure: God's Next Catastrophic Intervention into Earth's History* takes most seriously. We prayerfully hope many, upon reading the book, will take to heart the call of the only Lord and God of all Creation, who prompted the apostle Peter to write: "The Lord is not slack concerning His promise, as some men count slackness; but is longsuffering to us-ward, not willing that any should perish, but that all should come to repentance" (2 Pet. 3:9).

This is the only way to be saved from the sin that separates the sinner from the Heavenly Father. This is the only way to be secure from the approaching Tribulation storm.

> If thou shalt confess with thy mouth the Lord Jesus, and shalt believe in thine heart that God hath raised Him from the dead, thou shalt be saved. For with the heart man believeth unto righteousness; and with the mouth confession is made unto salvation. (Rom. 10: 9–10)

We join with the prophet John, who wrote, "He which testifieth these things saith, 'Surely I come quickly.' Amen. Even so, come, Lord Jesus" (Rev. 22:20).

ABOUT THE AUTHORS

Terry James, General Editor

Terry James is author, general editor, and co-author of numerous books on Bible prophecy—hundreds of thousands of which have been sold worldwide. Some of his most recent titles include: *The American Apocalypse: Is the United States in Bible Prophecy?*; *The Nephilim Imperatives: Dark Sentences*; *The Rapture Dialogues: Dark Dimension* (foreword by Tim LaHaye); and *Are You Rapture Ready?* (foreword by Tim LaHaye).

James is a frequent lecturer on the study of end-time phenomena, and he is interviewed often by national and international media on topics involving world issues and events as they might relate to Bible prophecy. He has appeared in major documentaries and media forums in all media formats in America, Europe, and Asia. He currently appears as an expert source in a History Channel series entitled "The Nostradamus Effect."

An active member of the Pre-Trib Research Center Study Group, James is a regular participant in the annual Tulsa Mid-America prophecy conference. He is also partner and general editor in the www.raptureready.com Web site, which is the attraction of national and international media and was recently rated as the number-one Bible prophecy site on the Internet.

Contributors

Todd Baker

Dr. Todd Baker is president of B'rit Hadashah Ministries and pastor of Shalom, Shalom Messianic Congregation in Dallas. He previously was a chaplain at Medical City Hospital, one of the largest hospitals in Dallas, and devotedly served in that capacity for almost fifteen years. With his extensive background in Jewish evangelism, he has led several gospel outreaches to Israel.

Dr. Baker is an author, speaker and a teacher who has been interviewed on radio and television. He is also currently a theological consultant and a former tour guide to Israel for Zola Levitt Ministries.

To contact Todd, write him at Brit Hadashah Ministries, P.O. Box 796127, Dallas, Texas 75379-6127; email him at todd@brit-hadashah.org; or visit his Web sites at www.Brit-Hadashah.org or www.searchthescripturesonline.org.

Joseph Chambers

Joseph Chambers is the author of six books and co-author of two, and he has written and produced numerous booklets and videos addressing various Christian topics. He has served as pastor for many years, most recently as senior pastor of Paw Creek Ministries in Charlotte, North Carolina.

He is the founder and president of Paw Creek Christian Academy, host of a one-hour weekly radio program, *Open Bible Dialogue*, and co-founder of Concerned Voice for Child Care. He is also the general overseer of the Bible Holiness Ministerial Fellowship, which was organized in November 1998 and has ministers in the U.S. and four foreign countries. Chambers is a member of the Pre-Trib Research

Center, which associates him with Grant Jeffrey, Tim LaHaye, and Dave Hunt. His ministries' Web site is www.pawcreek.org.

Daymond Duck

Daymond Duck of Dyer, Tennessee, is founder and president of Prophecy Plus Ministries and the best-selling author of numerous books dealing with prophecy and prophetic issues, including *On The Brink: Easy-to-Understand End-Time Bible Prophecy* and *The Book of Revelation: The Smart Guide to the Bible.* His commentary, *Revelation: God's Word for the Biblically-Inept,* was the second best-selling commentary on the book of Revelation in the United States for several months.

Duck has taught prophecy conferences for Southwest Radio Church in Nashville and Knoxville, Tennessee; he has been interviewed frequently on many nationwide radio programs, including *Prophecy Update Radio* and NPR's *Weekend America*; he has written articles for major Web sites such as Rapture Ready and Prophecy Update, and has made more than three hundred appearances on television. He is also a member of the Pre-Trib Study Group in Arlington, Texas.

Jim Fletcher

Jim Fletcher is a writer and editor with a degree in journalism from the College of the Ozarks. With two decades of experience in the book publishing industry, he cut his editing teeth on the books of authors like Terry James and David Allen Lewis. Fletcher has gone on to have his own titles published by Regnery and Strang Communications, and he has deep contacts in the pro-Israel community, both Jewish and Christian. He is a weekly blogger for Rapture Ready, WorldNetDaily, the American Family Association, and the *Jerusalem Post.*

Alan Franklin

Alan Franklin, a newspaper editor in Britain for twenty-one years and a journalist and author for more than forty years, runs thefreepressonline.co.uk Web site with his wife, Pat. The site features news and views for Christians and anyone interested in end-times events, with a special focus on Israel. The Franklins have co-written two books: *Goodbye America, Goodbye Britain,* and *Cults and Isms: True or False?*

Alan's first book, *E.U: Final World Empire,* led him to team up with Southwest Radio Church, for whom he does regular broadcasts on more than three hundred radio stations, and Lamb and Lion Ministries of Texas, among others. He has been featured on many radio stations and speaks on the *American Priorities* program and at prophetic conferences across America. In Britain, he is one of the speakers for the Prophetic Witness Movement International.

Al Gist

After working as an engineer and corporate manager for fifteen years, Al Gist answered God's call to serve as a pastor for the next fifteen years in three growing Southern Baptist churches, he founded Maranatha Evangelistic Ministries, and in August 2000 stepped out into full-time evangelism. Having been a student of Bible prophecy for twenty years, God soon began to direct his new ministry to proclaiming the soon return of Jesus Christ.

Today, Gist leads a full schedule of preaching at Bible prophecy revivals, teaching Bible prophecy series, and speaking at Bible prophecy conferences across the United States. He has served as president of the Louisiana Conference of Southern Baptist Evangelists for the last three years and hosts tours to Israel twice a year. Maranatha Evangelistic

Ministries produces a bi-monthly newsletter called "reMEMber," hosts the annual Louisiana Bible Prophecy Conference, and supports missionary works in El Salvador, Kenya, Mongolia, and the Ukraine.

To contact Gist, write him at Maranatha Evangelistic Ministries, 224 Al Gist Road, Longville, LA, 70652; call him at 337-725-6209; email him at al_gist @hotmail.com; or visit his Web site at www. maranathaevangelisticministries.com.

Phillip Goodman

Phillip Goodman is the founder and president of Prophecy Watch, a Bible Prophecy ministry dedicated to encouraging and strengthening faith in Jesus Christ. He is the host and teacher on the television program, *Prophecy Watch*, seen across the country on Direct TV and around the world on Internet TV at www.prophecywatch.com.

Phillip is the author of *The Assyrian Connection*, which develops the outlines of the final world empire and the origins of the Antichrist, and *The Sequence of End-Time Events*, as well as many booklets and DVD programs on Bible prophecy. He is a contributing author, sharing space with some of the world's best prophecy experts, to the books *Piercing the Future, Prophecy at Ground Zero, Revelation Hoofbeats, One World*, and *Frightening Issues*. Phillip is a regular guest on radio and television and sponsors the Mid-America Prophecy Conference. His wife, Mary, was born and raised in Bethlehem, Israel. They have four sons, and live in Tulsa, Oklahoma.

Wilfred Hahn

Wilfred Hahn is known for his analysis of global geopolitical, economic, and money trends, viewed from a biblical perspective. He brings unique insights to the end-time roles of money given his global investment industry experience spanning three decades. He has held various executive positions, from director of research for a major Wall Street firm to chairman of Canada's largest global investment group. A one-time top-ranked global analyst and strategist, he continues to write and work as a chief investment officer. The Mulberry Ministry, founded in 1995 with his wife, Joyce, publishes and distributes *Eternal Value Review* and more than forty books and booklets. For the past nine years, he has been a contributor to *Midnight Call* magazine.

Michael Hile

Michael "Mike" Hile is president of Signs of Our Times, a biblically based research ministry, and is author of *Timeline 2000*, which discusses several of God's time cycles in the Bible and shows how God has dealt with Israel down through the centuries in specific periods of time. (To order copies, call 877-421-7323 or 360-802-2907.) Mike was a contributing author for *Piercing the Future* and *Prophecy at Ground Zero*, edited by Terry James. Hile is a regular participant in the Tulsa Mid-America Prophecy Conference, he writes articles for the Rapture Ready Web site, and sends out weekly email updates on current events and Bible prophecy.

A former research and development chemist for Johnson & Johnson, petroleum chemist, and environmental scientist, Hile holds degrees in zoology and chemistry from the University of Arkansas. He served as president and chairman of the board for the Southern Weights and Measures Association, and was a member of the executive committee for the National Conference on Weights and Measures. Mike taught an adult Bible class for several years and wrote a "Signs of the Times" column for a weekly Christian publication. He and his wife, Joyce, have four children and seven grandchildren.

Thomas Horn

Thomas Horn is an internationally recognized lecturer, radio host, and best-selling author of several books, including his newest, *Apollyon Rising 2012: The Lost Symbol Found and the Final Mystery of the Great Seal Revealed*. He is a well-known columnist whose articles have been referred to by writers of the *Los Angeles Times* syndicate MSNBC, *Christianity Today*, *New Man* magazine, World Net Daily, News Max, White House correspondents, and dozens of newsmagazines and press agencies around the globe.

He has been interviewed by U.S. congressmen and senators on his findings, as well as featured repeatedly in major media including top-ten talk shows *America's Morning News* for the *Washington Times*, *The 700 Club*, *The Harvest Show*, *Coast to Coast AM*, *Prophecy in the News*, and *Southwest Radio Church*, to name a few. Horn received the highest degree honorary doctorate bestowed in 2007 from legendary professor Dr. I. D. E. Thomas for his research into ancient history, and has been endorsed by such national leaders as Dr. James Kennedy.

Jack Kinsella

Jack Kinsella has been the publisher and managing editor of the Omega Letter (www.omegaletter.com) since October 14, 2001. The Omega Letter is an online daily Christian intelligence digest analyzing current events in light of Bible prophecy. Its mission is to equip the saints to be ready to give an answer for the hope that is within them.

Jack continues to co-labor with his friend and mentor, Hal Lindsey, with whom Jack has worked continuously since 1993. Jack is also the head writer of the weekly television broadcast *The Hal Lindsey Report*, and has been a featured expert on national TV programs such as National Geographic's *Doomsday: Book of the Revelation* and Cloud

Ten Productions' *The Shadow Government*, as well as ministry programs like *This Week in Bible Prophecy, The Hal Lindsey Report, Zola
Levitt, Jewish Voice International,* and *Celebration!*

Jack has written or co-written several books, including his latest
book, *The Last Generation* (2007) and Hal Lindsey's *Vanished* (1997).
He is also a regular featured speaker on Jan Markell's *Olive Tree Views*
weekly radio show and is author of more than four dozen video documentaries. In 2009, Jack was honored to write the foreword to Terry
James' best-selling book, *The American Apocalypse.*

Don McGee

In September of 2002, Don McGee resigned his
position as a located pulpit minister and began a
new work called Crown and Sickle Ministries. Being
centered on the prophetic Word, the ministry's name
comes from Revelation 14:14 where Jesus is seen preparing to pour out
His wrath upon a world that has rejected His grace and mercy. This is
the critical message for today, both for unbelievers and for those who
are professing Christians. The Holy Spirit often uses prophetic messages in powerful ways to bring conviction to the hearts of those who
have yet to respond to Jesus' invitation. In like manner, He can also use
such messages to reawaken the sensibilities of Christians whose love of
our Lord's appearing has grown somewhat cool.

It is the work of this ministry to present the prophetic word and its
implications without sensationalism, but in such a clear and concise manner as to redraw our attention to the imminent and greatest event of modern history: the removing of the church from this planet. It is our prayer
that the thrust of this ministry is as exciting to audiences as it is to us.

To find out more information about the ministry, visit www.crown
andsickle.com. Contact Don McGee by email at dmcgee@crown
andsickle.com; by phone at 985-748-2943; or by standard mail at
60498 Floyd Rd., Amite, LA, 70422.

Chuck Missler

Chuck Missler, an author, conservative Christian Bible teacher, and former businessman, is the founder of the Koinonia House ministry based in Coeur d'Alene, Idaho. Through this organization, Missler distributes a monthly newsletter, Bible study tapes, and a radio show, and is a frequent featured speaker at prophecy conferences throughout the country.

Before founding Koinonia House in 1992, Missler, a graduate of the United States Naval Academy, spent time in the United States Air Force completing flight training before he became branch chief of the Department of Guided Missiles. Following his military service, he moved into the private sector of business and technology, holding positions with several large companies. He has also served as a senior analyst with a non-profit think-tank, where he conducted projects for the intelligence community and the Department of Defense. He holds a master's degree in engineering from the University of California at Los Angeles and a PhD from Louisiana Baptist University.

Larry Spargimino

Larry Spargimino is associate pastor and editor at Southwest Radio Ministries in Oklahoma City, Oklahoma, where he has served for twelve years. A graduate of Southwestern Baptist Theological Seminary in Fort Worth, Texas, with a PhD in New Testament and Greek, he has the strong conviction that the local church is God's primary instrument during the church age, and is committed to a solid theological education for pastors and has spent several years in teaching.

Spargimino has written numerous books, including *No Uncertain Future* (a Bible study guide on the book of Revelation), *Islam: Religion of Peace or Refuge of Terror?* (written right after 9/11), *Is Muhammad in the Bible?*, *The Anti-Prophets: The Challenge of Preterism*, and *Suddenly No More Time*. His latest book is *Digging Deeper: Questions and Answers on the Bible, the Christian Life, and the Endtimes*. He is currently working on two books: *The Ministry of the Local Church in These Last Days* and a book on the Trinity.

Todd Strandberg

Todd Strandberg is founder of www.raptureready. com, the most highly visited prophecy Web site on the Internet. He is partner in the site with Terry James. The site has been written about in practically every major news outlet in the nation and around the world.

Founded in 1987 when few Web sites existed, Rapture Ready now commands the attention of a quarter million unique visitors per month, with more than 13 million hits registered during most thirty-day periods.

Strandberg is president of Rapture Ready and co-author of *Are you Rapture Ready?*, a Penguin Group book under the E. P. Dutton imprint.

He has written hundreds of major articles for the site, which have been distributed in major publications and Web sites around the nation and world. He writes a highly read column under the site's "Nearing Midnight" section. Strandberg created "The Rapture Index"—a Dow Jones-like system of prophetic indicators—which continues to draw the attention of most major news outlets.

Dix Winston III

For the past thirty-five years, Dr. Dix Winston has been an able and articulate teacher of the Bible and defender of the Christian worldview. With a master of theology in Hebrew and Semitic studies from Dallas Theological Seminary, his doctorate in apologetics was under Dr. Norman Geisler at Southern Evangelical Seminary.

Winston has taught and defended Christianity both in the United States and abroad. He was one of the first Bible teachers to enter the former Soviet Union after the Red Curtain fell. He is comfortable with one-on-one dialogues as well as speaking before thousands. He currently teaches during the week and on Sundays at Cherry Hills Community Church in Highlands Ranch, Colorado.

NOTES

Introduction
One Giant Leap!
By Terry James

1. Robert Rhodes James, *Winston S. Churchill: His Complete Speeches 1897–1963*, vol. VII (New York and London: Chelsea House, 1943–49) 7285–7293.

2. Michael Klare, "A Global Epidemic of Violent Crime," *Salon* (Apr. 7, 2009) http://www.salon.com/news/feature/2009/04/07/crime_wave/index.html.

Chapter One
Worldwide Violence: As It Was in Noah's Day
By Chuck Missler

3. Isa. 24:19–21; Zeph. 2:3; Psa. 27:5; John 14; 1 Thess. 4:13–18; 1 Cor. 15:50–55.

4. Adapted from Dr. Peter Hammond's book, *Slavery, Terrorism and Islam: The Historical Roots and Contemporary Threat* (Cape Town, South Africa: Christian Liberty, 2005).

5. Cf. Job 1:6; 2:1; 38:7. Jesus implies the same term in Luke 20:36.

6. The book of Enoch was highly esteemed by both rabbinical and Christian authorities from about 200 BC through AD 200, yet the document was not included in the "inspired" canon. However, even though the book of Enoch was not included in the canon, the document is still very useful to authenticate lexigraphical

usages and the accepted beliefs of the period. For further reference, see R. H. Charles' study, *The Book of Enoch* (Oxford: Clarendon, 1912). Also see James H. Charlesworth's *The Old Testament Pseudepigrapha*, 2 vols. (Garden City, NY: Doubleday, 1985).

7. The term has been transliterated "giants"; however, the Greek root is a form of a word meaning "earthborn," which is a term used of the Titans, or the sons of heaven and earth, Coelus and Terra. The appellation of "giants" in the sense of size was coincidental.

8. One of the classic references on this is John Fleming's *The Fallen Angels and the Heroes of Mythology* (Dublin: Hodges, Foster, and Figgis, 1879). Also refer to John Henry Kurtz's *Die Ehen der Söhne Gottes mit den* (Berlin: Töchtern der Menschen, 1857).

9. See Exod. 12:5, 29:1; Lev. 1:3; et al. There are more than sixty references, usually referring to the fact that appropriate offerings did not have physical blemishes.

10. *Second Apology, Writings of Justin Martyr and Athenagoras*, transl. *Clark's Ante-Nicene Library*, vol. 2, 75–76.

11. *Against Heresies*, 4.36, 4.

12. *Second Apology*, vol. 2, 406–7.

13. *Homilies*, 7.12–15; 8.11–15.

14. *The Instructor* 3.2, *The Clementine Homilies and Apostolical Constitutions*, transl., *Clark's Ante-Nicene Christian Library*, vol. 17, 1870, 142–46.

15. *On the Veiling of Virgins*, 7.

16. *De Velandis Virginibus*, c. 7; *Liber De Idololat.*, c. 9; *De Hab. Muliebri*, c. 2.

17. *Divine Institut.*, lib. bk. 2, ch. 15.

18. Many fail to recognize that Gen. 6:1 and 2 are a single sentence.

19. See the *International Standard Bible Encyclopædia*, vol. 5 (Grand Rapids, MI: Eerdmans) 2835–2836.

20. Homer, *Iliad*, viii 16.

21. Although sometimes translated "preached," the Greek term

kerusso would be more accurately translated "to proclaim officially after the manner of a herald."

22. Jude is commonly recognized as one of the Lord's brothers. See Matt. 13:55; Mark 6:3; Gal. 1:9; and Jude 1.

23. See Jude 6 and 2 Cor. 5:2, both of which allude to the heavenly body with which the believer longs to be clothed.

24. See the book of Enoch, chapters 7–9, 64.

25. See Isa. 26:14. *Rephaim* is often translated "dead" (e.g., in Psa. 88:10; Prov. 2:18; 9:18; 21:16; and Isa. 14:9; 26:14). Jesus did *not* become either a Nephilim or a Rephaim, nor did He die for them.

26. *Mire,* in Hebrew, means "dust" or "dirt" to be swept away.

27. The word *Rephaim* (giants) is translated "dead" in Psa. 88:10; Prov. 2:18; 9:18; 21:16; and Isa. 14:9; 26:14.

28. Ezek. 37:10. KJV "exceeding" is actually an adverb.

29. Cf. "thy hidden ones," Psa. 83:3. Some of us suspect that God's manifest dealings with Israel will be post-church.

Chapter Two
Twenty-First Century Sodom: As It Was In the Days of Lot
By Larry Spargimino

30. James B. DeYoung, *Homosexuality: Contemporary Claims Examined in Light of the Bible and Other Ancient Literature and Law* (Grand Rapids: Kregel, 2000) 222.

31. For a thorough treatment of this, see Timothy Dailey, *The Other Side of Tolerance: How Homosexual Activism Threatens Liberty* (Washington DC: Family Research Council), http://downloads.frc.org/EF/EF06J60.pdf. Dailey documents how there is intolerance toward Christians in public schools and universities, how Christians are denied the right of peaceful protest, discrimination in the workplace, discrimination against those who oppose same-sex "marriage," and how religious organizations, such as Catholic Charities in Massachusetts, have been barred from

offering adoption services because the organization allegedly "discriminates" on the basis of sexual orientation by refusing to place children in homosexual homes.

32. William D. Watkins, *The New Absolutes* (Minneapolis: Bethany House, 1996) 207–208.

33. The full text can be viewed at http://www.ralliance.org/GayAgendaSwiftText.html. A note under the title "The Gay Manifesto" states that this manifesto is "Misrepresented by religious political activists to create a lie." The Rainbow Alliance Web site, http://www.alliance.org/GayAgenda.html, explains that this is only a "satire" and tries to prove its point by claiming that "homophobes" fail to cite the opening words: "This essay is an outre, madness, a tragic, cruel fantasy, an eruption of inner rage, on how the oppressed desperately dream of being the oppressor." Like many of the arguments of gay activism, this argument sounds compelling at first glance. The argument, however, that it is only a "satire" is invalid. "The oppressed" have indeed become "the oppressor." Swift's words are being accomplished today and not accidentally. The "inner rage" is evident everywhere in the movement. *After the Ball* delineates the same strategy.

34. President, Proclamation, "Lesbian, Gay, Bisexual, and Transgender Pride Month" (June 1, 2009) http://www.whitehouse.gov/the_press_office/Presidential-Proclamation-LGBT-Pride-Month.

35. Phyllis Schlafly, "'Social Justice': Code Word for Anti-Americanism." *Eagle Forum* (Jan. 2009), http://www.eagleforum.org/psr/2009/jan09/psrjan09.html.

36. Abraham Lincoln, "Address before the Young Men's Lyceum of Springfield, Illinois" (Jan. 27, 1838) http://www.constitution.org/lincoln/lyceum.htm.

37. Joe Dallas, *The Gay Gospel: How Pro-Gay Advocates Misread the Bible* (Eugene, OR: Harvest House, 2007) 23–24.

38. "Extra Small Condoms for 12-year old Boys Go on Sale," *Fox*

News (Mar. 4, 2010) http://foxnews.com/printer_friendly_ story/0,3566,587980,00.html.

39. Kathleen Farah, "Girl Scouts Taught How to Be 'Hot,'" *WorldNetDaily* (Mar. 16, 2010) http://www.wnd.com/index. php?fa=PAGE.view&pageId=128389.

40. Judith Levine, *Harmful to Minors: The Perils of Protecting Children from Sex* (Minneapolis, MN: University of Minnesota, 2002).

41. Debra Roffman, "Harmful to Minors (book review)," *Psychology Today* (Aug. 2, 2002) http://www.psychologytoday. com/print/23692.

42. Dallas, 84–87. This volume provides a helpful refutation of Boswell's approach to, and conclusions regarding, what the Bible teaches about this subject.

43. Al Dobras, "Oxford's New Pro-Homosexual Bible a Hit with 'Gay' Activists," *Orthodoxy Today*, http://www.orthodoxytoday. org/articles/DobrasOxfordBible.htm.

44. "How Did MCC Begin?" *Metropolitan Community Churches*, http://www.mccchurch.org/AM/Template. cfm?Section=About_Us&Template=/CM/htm.

45. Bryan Fischer, "News Just Keeps Getting Worse for Homosexuality," *American Family Association* (Mar. 18, 2010) http://action.afa.net/Blogs/BlogPost.aspx?id=2147492738. See also: "CDC: HIV Infection Rates Highest in Homosexual Population," http://lhla.org/breaking_news/?P=4313; "The CDC (Finally) Makes It Official: Gays and Other MSM Are Fifty Times Likelier to Have HIV than Women or Straight Men," http:// www.preventionjustice.org/blog/cdc-finally-makes-it-official-gays-and-other-msm; and "Homosexuality Triggering HIV Escalation," http://www.lifesitenews.com/1dn/Printerfriendly. html?articleid=05111812.

46. J. Matt Barber, "'Intolerance' Will Not Be Tolerated! The Gay Agenda vs. Family Values. *Across Ministries* (2004) http://across. co.nz/IntoleranceNotTolerated.html.

47. Andrea Kane, "CDC: Blacks, Gays at High Risk for HIV Infections," *CNN* (Sept. 12, 2008) http://www.cnn.com/2008/HEALTH/conditions/09/12/hiv.blacks.gays/index.html.

48. Sabin Russell, "Young Gays Contracting HIV at 'Explosive' Rate, CDC says," *San Francisco Chronicle* (June 1, 2001) http://articles.sfgate.com/2001-06-01/news/17603087_1_gay-men-aids-epidemic-infected.

49. James Dobson, *Bringing Up Boys: Practical Advice and Encouragement for Those Shaping the Next Generation of Men* (Wheaton, IL: Tyndale House) 115–116.

50. "Exposed: The Myth that '10 Percent Are Homosexual,'" *Traditional Values,* http://www.traditionalvalues.org/urban/two-print.html. See also "Myth and Reality About Homosexuality—Sexual Orientation Section," http://www.freerepublic.com/focus/f-news/1034938/posts.

Additional resources on the subject addressed in chapter two are as follows:

Joe Dallas, *When Homosexuality Hits Home: What To Do When a Loved One Says They're Gay* (Eugene, OR: Harvest House, 2004).

Mike Haley, *101 Frequently Asked Questions about Homosexuality* (Eugene, OR: Harvest House, 2004).

Alan Sears and Craig Osten, *The Homosexual Agenda: Exposing the Principal Threat to Religious Freedom Today* (Nashville, TN: Broadman & Holman, 2003).

Larry Spargimino, *Gay Rights Activism: Advancing Its Agenda at the Expense of Liberty* (Oklahoma City: Bible Belt, 2008).

Larry Spargimino, *Living in Sodom Today* (Oklahoma City: Bible Belt, 2003).

Mathew D. Staver, *Same-Sex Marriage: Putting Every Household at Risk* (Nashville, TN: Broadman & Holman, 2004).

Chapter Three
Nostradamus, 2012, and Other Deception
By Terry James

51. History Channel promotion sheet, "The Nostradamus Effect."

52. Margarita Troitsina, "Apocalypse Predictions Includes a Threat from the East and Fire from the Sky," *UFO Digest* (Jan. 26, 2010) http://www.ufodigest.com/news/0110/apocalypse.php.

53. Ibid.

54. John Major Jenkins, "The End of the World?" *Fox News* (Aug. 17, 2009) http://www.foxnews.com/story/0,2933,539960,00.html.

55. Charles Babington and Alan Cooperman, "The Rev. Moon Honored at Hill Reception, Lawmakers Say They Were Misled," *Washington Post* (June 23, 2004) A0, http://www.washingtonpost.com/wp-dyn/articles/A61932-2004Jun22.html.

56. "Nation: Messiah from the Midwest," *Time* (Dec. 4, 1978) http://www.time.com/time/magazine/article/0,9171,912250-3,00.html.

57. Barbara Kantrowitz, "The Messiah of Waco," *Newsweek* (Mar. 15, 1993) http://www.newsweek.com/id/111176.

58. Scott James, "In Internet Era, an Unwilling Lord for New Age Followers," *New York Times* (Feb. 4, 2010) http://www.nytimes.com/2010/02/05/us/05sfmetro.html.

59. Sam Greenhill, "I'm God, Says Renegade Spy David Shayler," *Daily Mail Online* (Aug. 2007) http://www.dailymail.co.uk/news/article-474364/Im-God-says-renegade-spy-David-Shayler.html.

60. Deborah Baker, "Bond Lowered for N.M. Sect Leader Accused of Sex Crimes," *Fox News* (May 8, 2008) http://www.foxnews.com/wires/2008May08/0,4670,ChurchChildrenSeized,00.html.

61. Email to author.

62. Nick Pope, "If the Cosmic Phone Rings...Don't Answer," *Sun* (Jan. 28, 2010) http://www.thesun.co.uk/sol/homepage/news/ufos/2828017/Should-we-be-offering-hand-of-friendship-to-ET.html.

Chapter Four
Perilous-Times Tremors: An Apostle's Departure
By Dix Winston III

63. J. Dwight Pentecost, *Things to Come* (Grand Rapids: Zondervan, 1980) 154.

64. Lewis Sperry Chafer, *Systematic Theology,* vol. IV (Dallas: Dallas Seminary, 1976) 375.

65. John R. W. Stott, *Bible Speaks Today: The Message of 2 Timothy* (Downers Grove, Ill.: InterVarsity, 1979) 84.

66. Max Anders, gen. ed., *Holman New Testament Commentary,* vol. 9 (Nashville: Holman, 2000) 298.

67. Dr. Thomas L. Constable, "Notes on 2 Timothy," *Dr. Thomas L. Constable's Expository Notes* (2007) http://www.soniclight.com/constable/notes/pdf/2timothy.pdf.

68. Donald Guthrie, gen. ed., Leon Morris, *Tyndale New Testament Commentaries,* vol. 14 (Grand Rapids, MI: Eerdman's) 175.

69. Guthrie, 176.

70. Stott, 84.

71. C. E. B. Cranfield, *International Critical Commentary: A Critical and Exegetical Commentary on the Epistle to the Romans,* 6th ed. (Edinburgh: T & T Clark, 1975, 1979).

72. Ralph Earle, "1 Timothy," *Expositor's Bible Commentary: Ephesians–Philemon,* vol. 11 (Grand Rapids, MI: Zondervan, 1978) 152.

73. Allison Smith-Square, "How Can Any Mother Abandon Her Children?" *Daily Mail Online* (Mar. 28, 2007) http://www.dailymail.co.uk/femail/article-444808/How-mother-abandon-children.html.

74. "Self-Control, and Lack of Self-Control, is Contagious," *Science Daily* (Jan. 18, 2010) http://www.sciencedaily.com/releases/2010/01/100113172359.htm.

75. Guthrie, 175.

Chapter Five
Humanism's Hubris and the Coming Collapse
By Jack Kinsella

76. "All About Entropy: The Laws of Thermodynamics and Order from Disorder" *Entropy Law*, http://www.entropylaw.com/entropyenergy.html.

77. "Humanist Manifestos I and II," *American Humanist Association*, http://www.jcn.com/manifestos.html.

78. Ibid.

79. Terri Schiavo was diagnosed in a persistent vegetative state. Her husband ordered her feeding tube disconnected despite the wishes of her parents, who insisted that she was capable of recognizing them when they visited. The ensuing court case involved the Congress, the White House, and ultimately the Supreme Court, who ordered Schiavo disconnected from life support. When she failed to die, she was disconnected from her feeding tubes to die of hunger and thirst. Her mother had to get the court's permission to wet the dying woman's lips with a damp cloth. Terri Schiavo survived for thirteen days without food or water before her death on March 31, 2005.

80. American Humanist Association.

81. "World Population Growth," *Vaughn's Summaries* (Apr. 7, 2010) http://www.vaughns-1-pagers.com/history/world-population-growth.htm.

82. "World Population Projected to Reach 7 Billion in 2011," *CNN* (Aug. 12, 2009) http://www.cnn.com/2009/TECH/science/08/12/world.population/index.html.

83. Ibid.

84. "Causality," *Wikipedia* (Apr. 28, 2010) http://en.wikipedia.org/wiki/Causality.

85. "Scientists Discover Missing Link Between Man and Apes, *London Mail Online* (Apr. 5, 2010) http://www.dailymail.

co.uk/sciencetech/article-1263488/Missing-link-evolutionary-chain-resolved-new-species-discovered-cradle-humanity.html?ITO=1490.

86. "Fossil Fish with 'Limbs' Is Missing Link, Study Says," *National Geographic* (Apr. 5, 2010) http://news.nationalgeographic.com/news/2006/04/0405_060405_fish.html.

87. Gareth Cook, "Fossil Discovery Fills a Piece of Evolutionary Puzzle," *Boston Globe* (Apr. 6, 2006) http://www.boston.com/news/science/articles/2006/04/06/fossil_discovery_fills_a_piece_of_evolutionary_puzzle/.

88. Steve Connor, "Scientists Find Missing Link to Land Vertebrates," *The Independent,* http://www.independent,co.uk./news/science/scientists-find-missing-link-to-land-vertebrates-472991.html.

89. Mark Henderson, "The Fish That Took the First Step for Mankind," *Times Online* (Apr. 5, 2006) http://www.timesonline.co.uk/tol/news/world/article702409.ece.

90. "Scientists Call Fish Fossil The 'Missing Link'," *New York Times* (Apr. 5, 2006) http://www.nytimes.com/2006/04/05/science/05cnd-fossil.html?_r=1&hp&ex=1144296000&en=fe3427d67e965e46&ei=5094&partner=homepage.

91. "Did Jesus Walk on Water? Or Ice?" *BBC* (Apr. 5, 2006) http://news.bbc.co.uk/2/hi/middle_east/4881108.stm.

92. Kevin Bonsor, "How DNA Computers Will Work," *How Stuff Works* (Nov. 17, 2000) http://www.howstuffworks.com/dna-computer.htm.

Chapter Six
The United States, the Rapture, and God's Judgment
Is the United States Mentioned in Bible Prophecy?
By Michael Hile

93. James Michael Hile, *Timeline 2000* (Mukilteo, Wash.: Winepress, 1998) 116–117. (To order copies, call 877-421-7323 or 360-802-2907.)

94. "British Empire," *Wikipedia,* http://en.wikipedia.org/w/index. php?title=British_Empire&oldid=370157564.

95. "Strength in Numbers," Global Firepower, http://www. globalfirepower.com/.

96. Charles H. Spurgeon, *The Second Coming of Christ* (Chicago: Revell, Moody, 1896) 117–118, quoted in Hile, *Timeline 2000.*

Chapter Seven
Abortion: Blood Sacrifice to the "Gods" of Planet Earth"
By Joseph Chambers

97. This subject is of such an emotionally charged, serious, and inherently graphic nature that this material might be disturbing to some readers. I promise you that I have sobbed before God in heartrending grief every time I have reviewed the manuscript. What you are reading has been bathed with tears.

98. "Considering Abortion? Learn About Abortion Procedures and Abortion Risks," Option Line (http://www.pregnancycenters. org/abortion.html.).

99. Ibid.

100. Ibid.

101. "Intact Dilation and Extraction," *Wikipedia* http://en.wikipedia.org/w/index. php?title=Intact_dilation_and_extraction&oldid=362555048.

102. "Surgical Abortion Procedures," *American Pregnancy Association* (http://www.americanpregnancy.org/unplannedpregnancy/ surgicalabortions.html.)

103. "Intact Dilation and Extraction."

104. Dr. Francis Schaeffer, *The Great Evangelical Disaster* (Wheaton, Ill.: Crossway, 1984) 141.

105. David Benoit and Eric Barger, *Entertaining Spirits Unaware* (Oklahoma City, OK: Hearthstone, 2006) 26.

Chapter Eight
End-of-Days Demons in High Places
By Thomas Horn

106. Gary Stearman, "The Extraterrestrial Question," *Prophecy in the News* (Mar. 2010) 10.

107. Jane Picken, "Medical Marvels," *The Evening Chronicle* (Apr. 13, 2007).

108. Joseph Infranco, "President Barack Obama Warped and Twisted Science with Embryonic Stem Cell Order," *LifeNews* (Apr. 13, 2009) http://www.LifeNews.com.

109. Wikipedia contributors, "Transhumanism," *Wikipedia* http://en.wikipedia.org/w/indexphp?title=Transhumanism&oldid =346807522.

110. William Grassie, "What Does it Mean to Be Human?" John Templeton Foundation Research Lecture Query (2006).

111. Doug Wolens, "Singularity 101 with Vernor Vinge," *H+ Magazine,* http://hplusmagazine.com/articles/ai/singularity -101-vernor-vinge.

112. Case Western Reserve University, "Case Law School Receives $773,000 NIH Grant to Develop Guidelines for Genetic Enhancement Research: Professor Max Mehlman to Lead Team of Law Professors, Physicians, and Bioethicists in Two-Year Project" (Apr. 28, 2006).

113. Nick Bostrom, "Transhumanist Values," *Nick Bostrom,* http://www.nickbostrom.com/ethics/values.html.

114. "Facing the Challenges of Transhumanism: Religion, Science, Technology," http://transhumanism.asu.edu/.

115. The University of Arizona, "The Sophia Project," http://lach.web.arizona.edu/Sophia/.

116. Leon R. Kass, *Life, Liberty, and the Defense of Dignity: The Challenge for Bioethics* (New York: Encounter, 2002).

117.. Rick Weiss, "Of Mice, Men, and In-Between," *MSNBC* (Nov. 20, 2004) http://www.msnbc.msn.com/id/6534243/.

118. Mark Stencel, "Futurist: Genes Without Borders," *Congressional Quarterly* (Mar. 15, 2009) http://news.yahoo. com/s/cq/20090315/pl_cq_politics/politics3075228.

119. George Annas, Lori Andrews, and Rosario Isasi, "Protecting the Endangered Human: Toward an International Treaty Prohibiting Cloning and Inheritable Alterations," *American Journal of Law and Medicine* 28, nos. 2 and 3 (2002) 162.

120. Chris Floyd, "Monsters, Inc.: The Pentagon Plan to Create Mutant 'Super-Soldiers'," *CounterPunch* (Jan. 13, 2003) http:// www.counterpunch.org/floyd01132003.html.

121. Katie Drummond, "Darpa's News Plans: Crowdsource Intel, Edit DNA," *Wired* (Feb. 2, 2010) http://www.wired.com/ dangerroom/2010/02/darpas-new-plans-crowdsource-intel-immunize-nets-edit-dna/.

122. Katie Drummond, "Pentagon Looks to Breed Immortal 'Synthetic Organisms,' Molecular Kill-Switch Included," *Wired* (Feb. 5, 2010) http://www.wired.com/dangerroom/2010/02/ pentagon-looks-to-breed-immortal-synthetic-organisms-molecular-kill-switch-included/.

123. Hendrik Poinar, "Recipe for a Resurrection," *National Geographic* (May 2009) http://ngm.nationalgeographic. com/2009/05/cloned-species/Mueller-text.

124. Chuck Missler and Mark Eastman, *Alien Encounters* (Coeur d'Alene, ID: Koinonia House, 1997), 275.

Chapter Nine
Media: Priests of Last-Days Madness
By Don McGee

125. "Opium of the People," *Wikipedia* (Mar. 19, 2010) http:// en.wikipedia.org/wiki/Opium_of_the_people.

126. "L.A. Riots of 1992: Rodney King Speaks," *You Tube* (Mar. 21, 2010) www.youtube.com/watch?v=tgiR04ey7-M.

127. "National TV Spots: Cost of Advertising on Television," *Resources for Entrepreneurs* (Mar. 19, 2010) http://www.gaebler.com/National-TV-Spot-Ad-Costs.htm.

128. *Bandit Trans Am Club* (Mar. 31, 2010) http://www.bandittransamclub.com/.

129. "Fourth Branch of Government," *Wikipedia* (Mar. 16, 2010) http://en.wikipedia.org/wiki/Fourth_branch_of_government.

130. "Joseph Goebbels," *Wikipedia* (Mar. 22, 2010) http://en.wikipedia.org/wiki/Joseph_Goebbels.

131. "Tet Offensive," *Digger History* (Mar. 21, 2010) http://www.diggerhistory.info/pages-conflicts-periods/vietnam/tet.htm.

132. "Ellen DeGeneres," *Wikipedia* (Mar. 23, 2010) http://en.wikipedia.org/wiki/Ellen_DeGeneres.

133. "Kathy Griffin," *Wikipedia* (Mar. 25, 2010) http://en.wikipedia.org/wiki/Kathy_Griffin.

134. "Humanism Unmasked—As Defined by John Dewey, the Father of Modern Education," *Wikipedia* (Mar. 24, 2010) http://www.christianparents.com/humanism.htm.

135. American Humanist Association, "About Humanism," *American Humanist* (Mar. 24, 2010) http://www.americanhumanist.org/Who_We_Are/About_Humanism/Humanist_Manifesto_I.

Chapter Ten
Turning to Fables: The Emergent, Laodicean Church
By Alan Franklin

136. "How Many Churches Are There in the U.S.?" *Answers.com/WikiAnswers,* http://wiki.answers.com/Q/How_many_churches_are_there_in_US?

137. Alan and Pat Franklin, *Goodbye America, Goodbye Britain* (Bethany, OK: Bible Belt, 2006) 7.

138. Alan and Pat Franklin, *Cults & Isms, True or False?* (St. Louis: Banner, 2009). Copies may be ordered from the authors' Web site at http://www.thefreepressonline.co.uk.

139. Roger Oakland, *Faith Undone* (Silverton, OR: Lighthouse Trails, 2007).

140. Oakland, author notes, *Understand the Times International,* http://www.understandthetimes.org/faithundone.shtml.

141. "Emerging Church Confusion: What Does It Really Mean?" *Berean Call* (Jan. 14, 2008) http://www.thebereancall.org/node/6363.

142. Franklin, *Goodbye America, Goodbye Britain,* 11.

143. We recommend that you get free downloads of verse-by-verse, through-the-Bible teaching by J. Vernon McGee, Chuck Smith, or Ron Matsen. There may be others who have also covered the entire Bible, but these are three great teachers we know of, and their teachings are available free on the Internet.

144. "Murdoch Pastor Gets Heat for Mogul's Porn Channels," *WorldNetDaily* (May 10, 2007) http://www.wnd.com/news/article.asp?ARTICLE_ID=55616.

145. "A Global Peace Plan," *Let Us Reason Ministries* (2009) http://www.letusreason.org/Popteac26.htm.

146. Rick Warren's peace plan was openly posted on his site until the end of 2004, when it was changed. Here is the new address where it is posted: http://www.saddlebackfamily.com/peace/Services/110203_high.asx.

147. "A Global Peace Plan."

148. "Archbishop Becomes Druid," *BBC News* (Aug. 5, 2002) http://news.bbc.co.uk/1/hi/wales/2172918.stm.

149. Jan Markell, "An Open Letter to Pastor Rick Warren," *Free Press* (July 7, 2009) http://thefreepressonline.co.uk/news/1/1649.htm.

Chapter Eleven
Armies of Apocalypse Arise
By Phillip Goodman

150. Josephus, *Antiquities of the Jews*, VI-I.

151. Rene Grousset, *The Empire of the Steppes* (New Brunswick, NJ: Rutgers University, 1970) 7.

152. John Lawrence, *A History of Russia*, 7th ed. (New York: Meridian-Penguin, 1993) 18–28.

153. *The New Columbia Encyclopedia* (New York and London: Columbia University Press, 1975) 2377.

154. Mark Hitchcock, *After the Empire Bible Prophecy in Light of the Fall of the Soviet Union* (Carol Stream, IL: Tyndale, 1994) 37.

155. Ibid., 59.

156. Ibid., 62.

157. Ibid., 64.

158. Ibid., 72.

159. "Securely—Betach," (0983) *Strong's Hebrew Dictionary*.

160. John F. Walvoord, *Israel in Prophecy* (Grand Rapids, MI: Zondervan, 1962) 107.

161. G. and L. Klaperman, *Story of the Jewish People* (New York: Behrman House, 1958) 229.

162. Joan Peters, *From Time Immemorial* (Chicago: JKAP, 1984) 80, emphasis added.

163. Klaperman, 241, emphasis added.

164. Ibid. The quote by Netanyahu was given in an interview with Katie Couric on the *CBS Evening News,* July 7, 2010.

165. Max I. Dimont, *Jews, God and History* (New York: Penguin/Mentor, 1962) 418, emphasis added.

166. Tovah Lazaroff, "Netanyahu: We Want Peace, But Not at the Price of Security,"*Jerusalem Post* (April 19, 2010), http://www.jpost.com/Home/Article.aspx?id=173471.

167. Ibid.

Chapter Twelve
The Temple Mount Tempest
By Todd Baker

168. This fact was powerfully reinforced to the writer when attending an archaeology seminar some years ago in the city of Jerusalem. The Israeli archaeologist showed the group in attendance an aerial photograph of Jerusalem trisected by the three valleys of the city, with the Temple Mount slightly north and right of center and lying between the Kidron and Tyropoeon valleys. He pointed out that these three valleys (the Kidron, Tyropoeon, and Hinnom) naturally form the Hebrew letter *shin* in the landscape of the city. The *shin*, written as ש, was clearly evident in the topography and represents the Hebrew name for God, *Shaddai*—which denotes God as the Almighty God or *El Shaddai*. It was this name and characteristic by which God revealed Himself to the patriarchs (Exod. 6:2–3). So when God promises that His name shall be placed in Jerusalem and in the Temple, it has been physically confirmed on the very landscape! The letter *shin* is also found on the mezuzah traditionally placed on the doorposts of Jewish homes to signify the presence of Almighty God in that place (Deut. 6:9).

169. *Tisha B'Av* is an annual observance day of mourning and fasting in Judaism that laments the destruction of both temples in Jerusalem. This day usually falls in early August and has now come to include the mourning of other major tragedies that have befallen the Jewish people throughout history.

170. Flavius Josephus, *Wars of the Jews,* VI.5.1–2.

171. Josephus, V–VII.

172. The phrase "times of the Gentiles" is used only one time in the Bible—Luke 21:24—and is prophetic of the mistreatment of the dispersed Jews by the Gentile nations coupled with the wresting of Jerusalem and the Temple Mount from Israeli hands by the

Gentile armies and rulers of the world. Permanent Jewish control of Jerusalem and the Temple will finally be established when Jesus the Messiah returns and is enthroned on an supernaturally elevated Mount Zion. There, the laws of the Millennial Kingdom will be issued—with the reigning Messiah sitting in the glorious Temple of Ezekiel (40–47), the center of His worldwide government (Psa. 2:6-9; Isa. 2:1–4).

173. Arnold G. Fruchtenbaum, *Footsteps of the Messiah*, rev. ed. (Tustin, CA: Ariel Ministries, 2003) 21.

174. Randall Price, *Temple and Bible Prophecy* (Eugene, OR: Harvest House, 1999/ 2005) 258.

175. Michael J. Wilkins, "Matthew," *NIV Application Commentary* (Grand Rapids: Zondervan, 2003) 159.

176. Edward J. Young, *Prophecy of Daniel* (Grand Rapids: Eerdmans, 1949) 218; Harry Bultema, *Commentary on Daniel* (Grand Rapids: Grace, 2002) 289.

177. Throughout history, Satan has attempted this through certain individuals. In 167 BC, Antiochus Epiphanes invaded Jerusalem and defiled the Temple. He then proceeded to erect a statue of Zeus with his face on it in the Holy of Holies, demanding the Jews worship him as "God manifest." First-century Roman emperor, Caligula, attempted to place a statue of himself in the Temple of Jerusalem in AD 40 so that the Jews of Judea would give him proper homage. They revolted, and Caligula rescinded the order on the advice from his governor in Syria. One of the fundamental truths of Bible prophecy is that future events always cast their shadows, in a smaller measure, in past events of history. The future abomination of desolation with the worship of the Antichrist as god in the rebuilt Temple of Jerusalem is no different in this respect.

178. Robert Morey, *Islamic Invasion* (Eugene, OR: Harvest House, 1992) 35–47, 211–218.

179. "The Archaeological Destruction of the Temple Mount by the

Muslim Wakf," *Israel's War Against Terror*, http://www.israel-wat. com/c1_eng.htm.

180. *Honest Reporting Communiqué* (Oct. 26, 2009) http://www. honestreporting.co.uk/articles/critiques/new/Temple_Mount_ Troubles.asp. This Web site provides good exposé on how flawed and biased the media coverage is for the Palestinian violence against Jews visiting and praying at their Temple Mount and the Western Wall below it.

181. Yaakov Kleiman, *DNA & Tradition: The Genetic Link to the Ancient Hebrews* (Devorah: New York, 2004) 17–24.

182. "Preparing for Service in the Rebuilt Temple," *Arutz Sheva* (Oct. 11, 2009) http://www.israelnationalnews.com/News/news. aspx/133801.

183. "Survey: 64 % Want Temple Rebuilt," *Ynetnews* (July 30, 2009) http://www.ynetnews.com/articles/0,7340,L-3754367,00.html.

Chapter Thirteen
Grasping for Global Governance
By Daymond Duck

184. Jamie Brendan, *Churchill Speaks, 1897–1963; Collected Speeches in Peace and War*, speech given on May 14, 1947. Quoted in "Soft-Selling World Government," *Endtime* (Sept./Oct. 2004) 25, emphasis added.

185. Rayelan Allan Russbacher, "The Art of Global Politics by Gunther K. Russbacher," http://www.whale.to/b/rm7.html, emphasis added.

186. George Herbert Walker Bush, "Toward a New World Order" (Sept. 11, 1990) http://www.sweetliberty.org/issues/war/bushsr. htm, emphasis added.

187. Samantha Smith, "Gorbachev Forum Highlights World Government," *Hope for the World Update* (Fall 1995) 2. Quoted in Gary Kah, *Hope for the World*, http://www.garykah.org/ articles8.html, emphasis added.

188. Phyllis Schlafly, "What Will Clinton's Legacy Be?" (Jan. 14, 1998) 1, http://www.eagleforum.org/column/1998/jan98-01-14.html, emphasis added.

189. Jim Davenport, "U.S. Should Kick UN Out, Says Buchanan," *Seattle Times* (Sept. 19, 2000) emphasis added.

190. "A Dangerous Trend," *Lamplighter* (May–June 2005) 10.

191. Irvin Baxter, "UN: Caretaker or Antichrist?" *Endtime* (Nov./Dec. 2006) 12.

192. J. R. Church, "One World Government," *Prophecy in the News* (June 2007) 8, emphasis added.

193. "H. Kissinger on a New International Order," http://www.youtube.com/watch?v=1LeDmsPspgI.

194. Greg McMurdie, "New World Order," *Believe All Things*, http://www.believeallthings.com/1317world-order, emphasis added.

195. Barack Obama, "A World that Stands as One," speech, Berlin, Germany (July 24, 2008) "Important Speeches and Remarks of Barack Obama," http://www.reobama.com/SpeechesJuly2408.htm.

196. "Ron Paul talks openly about the New World Order," *Break the Matrix*, http://www.breakthematrix.com/world/Ron-Paul-talks-openly-about-the-New-World-Order, emphasis added.

197. U.S. Department of the Treasury, *Prepared Statement by Treasury Secretary Tim Geithner at the G-20 Finance Ministers and Central Bank Governors Meeting*, http://www.treas.gov/press/releases/tg56.htm, emphasis added.

198. Darris McNeely, "Pope Benedict Calls for 'True World Authority'" *World News & Prophecy*, http:www.wnponline.org/newsletter/2009wnp07102009-pope-benedict-true-world-authority, emphasis added.

199. Dick Morris, "G-20 Summit: Obama Subjects U.S. Economic Policy to Global Consensus," *Red County* (Sept. 30, 2009) http://www.redcounty.com/g-20-summit-obama-subjects-us-economic-policy-global-consensus.

200. "A History of the New World Order," part 2, *Michael Journal* (Jan.–Feb. 2003) 4, http://www.michaeljournal.org/nwo2.htm.

201. "Students Train in 'Model Parliament' for New North American Union," *Americans for Legal Immigration* (Sept. 29, 2009) 2, http://www.alipac.us/article1536.html.

202. Accuracy in Media, "AIM Report: The Coming North American Parliament—March B" (Mar. 22, 2007) 1, http://www.aim.org/aim-report/aim-report-the-coming-north-american-parliament-march-b/.

203. Jay Sekulow, "U.S. Sovereignty at Risk with Obama?" (Apr. 6, 2009) 1, http://blog.beliefnet.com/lynnvesekulow/2009/04/us-sovereignty-at-risk-with-ob.html.

204. Barbara Ferguson, "Federal Agency Warns of Right-Wing Radicals," *Arab News* (Apr. 16, 2009) 1, http://www.arabnews.com/?page=4&section=0&article=121589&d=16&m=4&y=2009.

205. Jerome R. Corsi, "Obama 'Clones' Bush in Killing Sovereignty, *WorldNetDaily* (Sept. 13, 2009) 2, http://www.wnd.com/index.php?pageId=109347.

206. Lou Dobbs, "Amnesty Bill," *CNN,* http://d.yimg.com/kq/groups/17260182/1610997888/name/ftc-vi26.wmv.

Chapter Fourteen
Economic Engineering for New World Order
By Wilfred J. Hahn

207. Quoted from www.GlobalResearch.ca. Source: "Backbone of Complex Networks of Corporations: The Flow of Control," J. B. Glattfelder and S. Battiston, chair of systems design, ETH Zurich, Kreuzplatz 5, 8032 Zurich, Switzerland.

208. Simon Johnson, "Shooting the Banks," *The New Republic* (Feb. 24, 2010) http://www.tnr.com/print/article/politics/shooting-banks.

209. UN Conference on Trade and Development, "World Investment Report 2009," Annex Table A.I12, New York (2009).

210. This statistic has been compiled from sources including the Bank of International Settlements (www.bis.org) and *Wikipedia.*

211. Carmen Reinhart (University of Maryland), Kenneth Rogoff (Harvard University and NBR), "Growth in the Time of Debt" (Dec. 31, 2009).

Chapter Fifteen
God's Groaning Creation
By Al Gist

212. Gary Stearman, "Earthquakes! Are They Increasing?" *Prophecy in the News* (Apr. 2010) 3.

213. Ibid., 37.

214. "Magnitude 7.2—Baja California, Mexico," *USGS Earthquake Hazards Program* (5/24/10) http://earthquake.usgs.gov/earthquakes/eqinthenews/2010/ci14607652/ci14607652.php.

215. "Global Earthquake Search" *USGS Earthquake Hazards Program,* http://earthquake.usgs.gov/earthquakes/eqarchives/epic/epic_global.php.

216. Stearman, 37.

217. "List of Epidemics," *Wikipedia,* http://en.wikipedia.org/wiki/List_of_epidemics.

218. During World War I, more people were hospitalized for this epidemic than for wounds. Estimates of the dead range from 20 to 100 million worldwide.

219. "A Collaborative Learning Space for Science," *Scitable,* http://www.nature.com/scitable/topicpage?antibiotic-Resistance-Mutation-Rates-and-MRSA-28360.

220. "History of MRSA Infection," *eMRSAfacts,* http://www.emrsafacts.com/index.php/history-of-mrsa-infection.

221. Margie Mason and Martha Mendoza, "Infectious Diseases Mutating at Alarming Rate," *Miami Herald* (Jan. 10, 2010) http://www.miamiherald.com/2010/01/10/1418580/infectious-diseases-mutating-at.html.

222. "Famine," *Wikipedia,* http://en.wikipedia.org/w/index.php?tit le=Famine&oldid=364866045. http://en.wikipedia.org/wiki/ Famine#2007.E2.80.932008_world_food_price_crisis.

223. "Stem Rust," *Wikipedia,* http://en.wikipedia.org/wiki/Ug99.

224. V. M. Thomas, D. G. Choi, D. Luo, A. Okwo, and J. H. Wang, "Relation of Biofuel to Bioelectricity and Agriculture: Food Security, Fuel Security, and Reducing Greenhouse Emissions," *Chemical Engineering Research and Design,* 87(9) (2009)1140–1146.

225. Larry Elliott and Heather Stewart, "Poor Go Hungry While Rich Fill Their Tanks," *Guardian* (April 11, 2008) http://www. guardian.co.uk/business/2008/apr/11/worldbank.fooddrinks1.

226. "The World Hunger Problem: Facts, Figures, and Statistics," *Oracle Thinkquest Education Foundation,* http://library.thinkquest. org/C002291/high/present/stats.htm.

227. "Global Hunger," *Bread for the World,* http://www.bread. org/hunger/global/.

228. "Greenhouse Gas Emissions," *US Environmental Protection Agency,* http://www.epa.gov/climatechange/emissions/index. html#proj.

Chapter Sixteen
Israel's End-Times Zechariah Effect
By Jim Fletcher

229. Charles Krauthammer, "Nuclear Posturing, Obama Style," *The Oklahoman* (Apr. 9, 2010).

230. Christopher Barder, *Oslo's Gift of "Peace": The Destruction of Israel's Security,* (Israel: Ariel Center for Policy Research, 2001) 204.

231. Nechemia Coopersmith and Shraga Simmons, eds., *Israel: Life in the Shadow of Terror* (Aish.com, 2003) 338–339.

232. Arieh Stav, ed., *Ballistic Missiles: The Threat & Response,* (Israel: Ariel Center for Policy Research, 1999) 130.

233. Ibid., 232.

234. Ibid., 336.

235. Ibid., 213.

236. "PM Praises Christian 'Moral Clarity,'" *Word from Jerusalem* (Winter 2009) 6.

Chapter Eighteen
Big Brother Is Watching
By Alan Franklin

237. *Southport.gb.com Online News* (Feb. 12, 2010) http://www. southportvisitor.co.uk/. For similar stories from all over Britain just use a search engine to call up "bugs in wheelie bins."

238. Alan and Pat Franklin, *Goodbye America, Goodbye Britain* (Bethany, OK: Bible Belt, 2006) 7.

239. Associated Press, "Mind-Reading Systems Could Change Air Security," *Fox News* (Jan. 10, 2010) http://www.foxnews.com/ scitech/2010/01/08/mind-reading-systems-change-air-security/.

240. Kaya Burgess, "Every Step You Take, We'll Be Watching You," *Times* (Mar. 7, 2009) http://www.timesonline.co.uk/tol/news/uk/ crime/article5859932.ece.

241. Sources include *BBC News* Web site (May 1, 2007).

242. Environment News Service, "Forest Service Buys Eyes in the Sky for Surveillance" (Apr. 3, 2008) http://www.ens-newswire.com/ ens/apr2008/2008-04-03-091.asp.

243. Kelli Arena and Carol Cratty, "FBI Wants Palm Prints, Eye Scans, Tattoo Mapping," CNN (Feb. 4, 2008) http://www.cnn. com/2008/TECH/02/04/fbi.biometrics/index.html?iref=allsearch.

244. Ibid.

245. Melanie Phillips, *Daily Mail* (Nov. 25, 2002) 10.

246. Arena and Cratty.

247. Alan Franklin, *EU: Final World Empire,* 2nd ed. (Fleet, Hampshire, England: Banner, 2004) 185.

248. Charlie Sorrel, "Britain To Put CCTV Cameras Inside Private Homes," *Wired* (Aug. 3, 2009) http://www.wired.com/

gadgetlab/2009/08/britain-to-put-cctv-cameras-inside-private-homes/#ixzz0fLOaA2Gx.

249. Bruno Waterfield, "EU Security Proposals Are 'Dangerously Authoritarian,'" *Daily Telegraph* (Dec. 6, 2009).

250. Ibid.

251. Steve Connor, *The Independent* (Dec. 22, 2005) http://www.independent.co.uk/news/uk/home-news/britain-will-be-first-country-to-monitor-every-car-journey-520398.html.

252. Ibid.

253. David Millward, "Trips Abroad to Be Logged," *Daily Telegraph* (Mar.14, 2009) 1.

254. Bernard Connolly, author of *Rotten Heart of Europe,* in a letter to the *Daily Telegraph* (Mar. 9, 2001).

255. Ibid.

Conclusion
In the Twinkling
By Terry James

256. "Henceforth there is laid up for me a crown of righteousness which the Lord, the righteous judge, shall give me at that day; and not to me only, but to all them also that love His appearing" (2 Tim. 4:8).

257. Thomas Ice, "The Rapture in 2 Thessalonians 2:3," *Rapture Ready,* http://www.raptureready.com/featured/ice/TheRapturein2Thessalonians2_3.html.